To my match, Mindy

More praise for *Mixed Matches*

"Dr. Crohn has made a positive contribution towards a greater understanding of this particularly difficult aspect of the race question. His perspective shows the way for those who embrace the idea of community that transcends traditional boundaries. This is the way to the future."

> —Carlos Fernandez
> Coordinator, Law and Civil Rights and Past President
> AMEA: Association of Multi-Ethnic Americans

"In a wonderfully engaging style, Joel Crohn makes us laugh and then cry over the misunderstandings that develop in cross-cultural relationships—and then provides useful guidelines for couples to work out their relationships—with each other, with their families, and with their children. This book is a magnificent addition to the literature for our increasingly culturally diverse society."

> —Monica McGoldrick, M.S.W.
> Director of the Family Institute of New Jersey
> Author of *You Can Go Home Again*

"What a marvelous book! Sensitive, sensible, sympathetic. Neither foolishly romantic nor grimly pessimistic. It is a realistic assessment of the problems and possibilities in intermarriages."

> —Father Andrew M. Greeley
> Bestselling novelist
> Professor of Social Science
> at the University of Chicago

"Timely and insightful. Dr. Crohn has written an intelligent and practical book. *Mixed Matches* adds new clarity and understanding to the complicated and volatile issues of racial and cultural differences in a manner both reasoned and free of polemic."

> —Price Cobbs, M.D.
> Coauthor of *Black Rage*

"Its description of family and identity processes, and its helpful exercises, will make *Mixed Matches* invaluable for laymen and professionals alike."

> —Egon Mayer, Ph.D.
> Director of Jewish Outreach Institute
> Professor of Sociology at
> City University of New York

"A highly readable and informative look at marriages that defy tradition. The struggles, spirit, and triumphs of the couples and families in *Mixed Matches* provide us with an intimate scale model of conflict and cooperation between cultural, racial, and religious groups that we all face as we approach the next century. The book will be required reading for my graduate students and a gift for friends and colleagues."

—Peter Chang, Ph.D.
California School of Professional Psychology
Project Director of Curriculum Reform
in Professional Psychology

"*Mixed Matches* should be required reading for couples of mixed ethnic, religious, or racial backgrounds who are contemplating marriage, as well as for mixed couples who are already married. Dr. Crohn provides new insights to old conflicts and offers practical solutions, guiding the reader to a better understanding of his or her own specific situation. This book also shows us the first steps towards understanding ethnic, racial, and religious conflict at a global level. *Mixed Matches* is essential reading for every individual living in a multi-cultural society."

—Wise E. Allen, Ph.D.
Vice Chancellor, Peralta Community Colleges
Oakland, California
Former chairperson
Committee on Diversity
Community College League of California

"A great book! It addresses difficult family issues head-on and offers practical suggestions that will help create successful relationships."

—Mian M. Ashraf, M.D.
President
The Islamic Center of New England

"A painstaking analysis of a complex and difficult subject that will not go away. Dr. Crohn counsels his readers with compassionate wisdom."

—Rabbi Herold Schulweis
Valley Beth Sholom (Encino, CA)
Author of *For Those Who Can't Believe*

MIXED MATCHES

HOW TO CREATE SUCCESSFUL INTERRACIAL, INTERETHNIC, AND INTERFAITH RELATIONSHIPS

Joel Crohn, Ph.D.

FAWCETT COLUMBINE

NEW YORK

A Fawcett Columbine Book
Published by Ballantine Books

Names and identifying characteristics of interviewees in *Mixed Matches* have been changed except where last names are used.

Grateful acknowledgment is made to the following for permission to reprint previously published material:

San Francisco Examiner: Letters to the Editor, *Image* Magazine, March 8, 1992. Copyright © 1993 *San Francisco Examiner*.

William Morrow & Co., Inc., and Ellen Levine Literary Agency on behalf of Judy Petsonk: Adaptation of an exercise from *The Intermarriage Handbook* by Judy Petsonk and Jim Remsem. Copyright © 1988 by Judy Petsonk and Jim Remsem. Adapted by permission of William Morrow & Co., Inc., and Ellen Levine Literary Agency.

Library of Congress Catalog Card Number: 94-94570

ISBN: 0-449-90961-1

Cover design by Kristine Mills
Cover illustration by Brad Teare
Text design by Mary A. Wirth

Manufactured in the United States of America

First Edition: February 1995

10   9   8   7   6

CONTENTS

ACKNOWLEDGMENTS

In spite of the many solitary hours spent writing, this book truly was a collaborative project. Without the emotional support and intellectual contributions of more people than I can name here, it never would have been completed. Special thanks to:

Irving M. Levine and Joe Giordano of the Institute on Pluralism and Group Identity at the American Jewish Committee, who sponsored and guided my original research on intermarriage. Judy Klein, for her friendship over the years and for her pioneering research on ethnic identity and self-esteem that laid the groundwork for this book. Jim Levine, an agent and a friend, who consistently went above and beyond the call of duty in guiding me through the process of writing this book. Ginny Faber, senior editor at Ballantine, and Phebe Kirkham, assistant editor, who gave generously of their time and talent in making this a better book. All of the interviewees, for their openness and generosity in sharing their experiences.

Egon Mayer, for his encouragement and for his seminal work on intermarriage that helped develop the intellectual foundation for this book. Evelyn Lee, my colleague and friend, whose tireless work with immigrants and refugees from so many different cultures has been an inspiration. Carlos Fernandez, for his tireless work in developing a multicultural consciousness that excludes no one, and Edwin Darden, for his insights about biracial families and society. Monica McGoldrick, a pioneer in bringing cultural consciousness to the world of psychotherapy. Esther Perel, who shared freely her creative insights about theater, therapy, and life. Fred Rosenbaum and Rosanne Levitt, who provided opportunities for me to test my ideas, and Rabbi Yossi Liebowitz for his wise humor. And all of the people who assisted me in the process of setting up interviews, especially Nancy and Roosevelt Brown, Rabbi Michael Barenbaum, and Lydia Kukoff.

Tova L. Zeff, for her support, friendship, and editorial acumen. Alan Rinzler, whose help in conceptualizing the book was crucial in the early stages. Paula Stanfield and Neely Carpenter, for their timely and important assistance with the chapter on the children of intermarriage. Phebe Kirkham and Beth Bortz at Ballantine, who were always there to help. Nathan Rosen and Christine Zalecki, whose database searches helped fill in the blanks.

My good friends and colleagues who listened and offered wise counsel and encouragement: Roberta Seifert, Stephen Goldbart, Estelle Frankel, Diane Ehrensaft, Michael Cedars, Dale Larson, Wise and Joan Allen, Jerry Schwartz, Jack Schiemann, Peg Shalen, and Donna Moran.

Firdevs Demet Buyukdere, Marina Keulstra, and Caroline Guardino, friends-in-deed. Bev Silverberg, whose good magic creates opportunities out of crises.

Rita Werner, my mother-in-law, whose love of language and attention to the small details made a big difference, and Bert Werner, my father-in-law, whose ability to drive a motor home like a sports car saved the day. My mother, Marcy Crohn, whose support and love has always been truly unconditional, and my father, Frank Crohn, who died while I was writing this book. I feel his presence more and more all the time. My sister, Carol Ornelas, and my brother, Bruce Crohn, who were also there for me at important moments. My oldest son Rafi, whose enthusiasm about this project helped to partially compensate for the sacrifice of time with him, and our younger children, Shira and Jonathan, who sacrificed without their consent to make this book possible.

And last, but certainly not least, my wife Mindy Werner-Crohn, who gave birth to our third child as I began writing. More than anyone else, she has helped me to understand that creating a successful marriage requires constructive conflict as well as caring and compassion.

MIXED MATCHES

INTRODUCTION

Aquiet revolution is sweeping the world as millions defy ancient taboos to form intimate relationships with partners from other cultural, religious, and racial backgrounds. Like all couples, they work to understand each other and to build stable and satisfying relationships. But if misunderstandings between men and women, as Deborah Tannen described in her book *You Just Don't Understand*, are the result of unacknowledged differences between the "culture" of men and the "culture" of women, then intermarried couples have a double dose of differences to deal with—gender and culture.

Culture is like a lens that shapes and colors how we interpret actions and feelings. Even subtle cultural contrasts between two people can lead each to see the same event in very different ways. Partners who are unaware of the effects of their distinctive cultural lenses may have difficulty understanding how differently they go about defining that most illusive of words—*normal*. One may be shocked by what the other takes for granted because of culturally influenced value differences about gender roles and contrasting styles of expressing emotion.

Love never remains a secluded island for long, and the outside world inevitably has a powerful impact on the private inner world of love. Even in the most secular and cosmopolitan of relationships, ancient religious and cultural loyalties and prejudices can surprise lovers with their intensity. Negative family reactions can short-circuit passion, and racism and social intolerance can strain the best of relationships. And the birth of children exposes whatever religious or cultural loyalties have been minimized for the sake of new love. The process of helping children define their identities inevitably reveals the unacknowledged power of the parents' different pasts.

The following situations are typical of the kinds of culturally influenced problems that can result from these differences:

- *A young man from Greece engaged to an American white Protestant woman*: From his cultural perspective he is a "modern man" who believes in equality of the sexes; from her viewpoint he is a chauvinist who expects her always to defer to him. When they try to talk about their differences, he feels that his tone is "a little intense, but very respectful." She labels his behavior during those talks as "verbally abusive yelling."
- *An English man married to a Mexican-American woman*: Even though he likes his in-laws, he is troubled by her wish to see them much more frequently, since he feels that they already visit her parents far more than "normal."
- *A Jewish-American woman married to an Italian-American man*: She feels her husband is too strict with their children, while he sees her as tolerating behavior his parents would never have put up with. And even though she had almost broken off their engagement because he wasn't Jewish, when he converted to Judaism five years later, she was upset that he had become "too carried away with religion." She describes herself as a "cultural Jew" and is uncomfortable with him taking their children to synagogue regularly.
- *A Trinidadian black student living with an American black*: He grew up in Trinidad and is excited by the freedom

and opportunities of his adopted land, the United States. She was raised in a Detroit ghetto, is very angry with the racism she sees everywhere, and is irritated by what she feels is his naive optimism.

- *A young Irish-Catholic woman dating a Mormon student*: Since neither of them is religiously active, she feels he is using their different religious backgrounds as an excuse not to get married. He struggles to sort out the depth of his own religious beliefs from all the pressures his parents are putting on him to end the relationship because she is not a Mormon.

- *A woman from a Scandinavian-American background married to a Japanese-American man*: She has a master's degree in Asian studies and wants to teach their children about their father's cultural traditions and history. His parents had been interned in a WW II detention camp in California, and he is determined to forget the painful past his family always refused to talk about.

Mixed Matches describes methods I have developed for helping couples understand and resolve these kinds of culturally based conflicts. It grew out of my personal experiences and out of my professional interest as a psychotherapist in working with and interviewing hundreds of cross-cultural couples and families over the past decade. The vignettes in the book will allow you to learn about how other couples and families have found ways to build bridges across their differences. Their stories will enable you to develop a vocabulary to identify and discuss your own culturally based contrasts. And the exercises throughout the book will give you tools that will help you deal with your conflicts and creatively use your differences to enrich your relationship.

Background

In 1981 I began a four-year research project on the psychology of Jewish-gentile marriage for the American Jewish Committee that resulted in a monograph and a video documentary, *The Myth of the Melting Pot Marriage*. Because I was interested in how cultural as well as religious differences affected intermarried couples, I studied Jews married to Caucasians of northern European descent (which I will hereafter refer to as WASPs, even though they are not all strictly "Anglo-Saxons") and Jews married to Italians.

Culture shapes the rhythm and intensity of family life. I wanted to understand the differences in the ways WASPs and Italians went about trying to bridge the gaps in their cultural styles with their Jewish partners. I was also very interested in how intermarried couples reconciled emotionally charged loyalties to different ethnic identities and religious traditions.

What I discovered was that *how* partners in a mixed match negotiated their cultural and religious differences was as important as *what* the differences were. Whether they were discussing which holidays to celebrate, how to instill a sense of identity in their children, which religion to practice, or how often to visit their parents, partners brought their characteristic cultural styles to the process of negotiation.

These differences became most obvious in situations involving conflict. Typical of the WASP interviewees was one woman's explanation of her use of silence as a way of expressing her anger with her husband. "It's always best, if possible, to go around conflict. There's nothing to be gained by stirring things up." In contrast, the Italian-American partners tended to feel it was only natural to use a loud voice, broad gestures, and exaggeration to make a point in an argument. And many of the Jewish partners focused on their own emotional pain in situations involving conflict. As anthropologist Marc Zborowski pointed out, the emotional self-control of Anglo-Americans, the dramatic style of Italians, and the focus on suffering by Jews can persist generations after families have left the homelands where these kinds of coping styles have evolved.

The couples I interviewed often got stuck in their relationships because they had difficulty separating the *content* of their differences about religious and cultural identity from the *process* of discussing them. I found that couples were more able to make creative and constructive decisions when I could help them learn to recognize and separate out the differences in their interactional styles from the actual religious and cultural decisions they were trying to make.

As I began to give talks about my research, the reactions of both professional and lay audiences helped me realize that my work had a far more universal appeal than I had initially realized. Therapists who worked with a variety of interethnic and interracial families said that their clients had problems that were strikingly similar to those of the interfaith couples I had studied. Students and laypeople who themselves were in African-American/WASP, Asian-Irish, German-Italian, and many other kinds of mixed matches identified strongly with the Jewish-gentile couples in my documentary. In our discussions they talked about the frustration they had experienced when they had consulted with therapists who had reduced all of their conflicts to psychological categories and personality problems. They felt relieved that someone was addressing the cultural and identity issues that they had struggled with alone for so long.

I soon began to receive increasing numbers of referrals of a wide range of mixed matches to my psychotherapy practice. As different as the couples might appear to an outsider, inside the consulting room I found that these interracial, interethnic, and interreligious couples shared many common concerns about conflicts between love and tradition. By acting as a kind of simultaneous translator I developed methods that allowed partners in mixed matches to recognize and bridge the different "cultural languages" they brought to their relationships. Partners who had been stuck, recycling the same conflicts over and over again, were now able to understand each other far better. They could approach each other more compassionately when they realized that their conflicts had grown out of misunderstandings and not out of cruelty or indifference.

A Radically Changing World

As a therapist I usually meet with mixed matches when they're in the midst of a crisis of definition. As unimportant as their ancestors' legacies may have seemed when they fell in love, life passages can shatter a couple's denial of their differences. An upcoming marriage, the death of a loved one, or the birth of a child reminds them of their different heritages. Love is then forced to come to terms with tradition.

Whether the mixed match consists of a Chinese and a black, a Jew and a WASP, an Iranian and an Irishman, or a Greek and a Norwegian-American, both partners feel that the other has violated some implicit agreement about how they define the identity of their family. Like so many mini-nations involved in border disputes, they find that old treaties no longer work. These are the times when my office feels like an outpost of the United Nations.

On the surface it seems these conflicts are simply the result of competing religious or cultural loyalties. But what these crises often reveal is the uncertainty each partner feels about his or her own sense of identity. And the roots of each person's confusion often lie *not* in personal neurosis, but in the vast historical upheavals that have taken place during the twentieth century. As millions of people from every corner of the earth have been uprooted by war, revolution, or simply the search for a better life, old definitions of who is "us" and who is "them" are undergoing dramatic transformations. People from cultures all over the world are now our neighbors, friends, and coworkers. And increasingly they are our husbands and our wives. None of us is an expert at dealing with the dizzying pace of change, and at some level we are all in a state of culture shock.

Consider for a moment the magnitude of the changes. Humans have become in this century so much more effective at creating, preserving, and destroying life. Genetic engineering, antibiotics, nuclear weapons, and space travel are technologies that have transformed our view of the universe. And one hundred years ago who could have anticipated the rise and fall of Communism, massive migrations of millions between nations and across oceans, the "death of God" and the surge of religious fundamentalism, and how these changes would alter the entire face of the earth.

History has always involved dramatic shifts, but the accelerating rate of change has never approached that of today's world. Throughout most of history, change was measured in generations, and the distant horizon was more likely to be the next town than an alien land halfway around the world. The practice of religion was inseparable from the life of a community. Because they were so intertwined, it wasn't necessary or even possible to separate family loyalty, cultural identity, and religious belief. Each reinforced the other, and all were integral in giving each person a clear sense of belonging and identity. The family was part of a community that was rooted in a culture that was tied to a religion.

While people living in more stable, traditional cultures might face many hardships, they were sustained by a clear knowledge of who they were, where they belonged, and what they believed in. A Catholic peasant from a village in southern Italy, a Muslim living in a small city in Pakistan, a Buddhist craftsman in a Vietnamese town, an Irish-Catholic living in South Boston in 1960, a black Texas Baptist living on a farm in the 1950s, or a Jew in an Eastern European shtetl in 1930 all had integrated and cohesive social, cultural, and religious lives. The "identity crisis," that sense of disconnectedness so common to modern, urban people, was one issue they did not have to deal with. Everyone in a community understood the link between themselves and their ancestors and between their religious faith and their actions. Yesterday and today were as inseparably bound as heaven and earth.

Today the bonds connecting the three cornerstones that have always formed the foundation of identity—family, culture, and religion—have been weakened by the pace of change and the new world disorder. As a result we are constantly confronted with crises of definition and find ourselves asking questions that most of our great-grandparents could not even have imagined. *What is the nature of my allegiance to my family, my tribe, my nation, and my God? Are they of different intensities? Could they come into conflict with one another?* Our religious and cultural identities are no longer just accidents of birth. Today we must pick from among shattered remnants of the past to create answers to the question Who am I?

One reflection of these social changes is contained in the most recent edition of the American Psychiatric Association's *Diagnostic and Statistical Manual of Mental Disorders*, the bible of the psychotherapy profession, which is revised about every ten years. For the first time it includes a section on "Religious or Spiritual Problems" under a listing of "Other Conditions That May Be a Focus of Clinical Attention." It defines these problems as including "distressing experiences that involve loss or questioning of faith, problems associated with conversion to a new faith, or questioning of other spiritual values."

Intermarriage and the Transformation of Identity

Cultural transformations that once seemed dramatic have now become routine. Among white ethnics the steady advance of assimilation has marched forward. In his book *The Rise of the Unmeltable Ethnics*, Michael Novak celebrated the durability of ethnic identity among European whites. But more than twenty years have passed since *Unmeltable* was written, and time has shown that white ethnics are quite meltable. While many people still assume that a great deal of intragroup solidarity exists, especially among people who trace their ancestry to southern and Eastern Europe, the connections that hold each white ethnic group together have become more tenuous with each passing year.

By the mid-sixties, sociologist Richard Alba found that two-thirds of third-generation Poles were marrying out. By the 1970s the proportion of intermarriage of those of Greek ancestry had reached nearly 70 percent in New York, the largest Greek Orthodox archdiocese in the United States. And the famous "Little Italy" neighborhoods in major American cities, symbols of Italian solidarity, are quickly becoming ethnic museums. To be sure, the older generation remains solidly Italian in origin and outlook. In 1979, 90 percent of those between fifty-five and sixty-four who reported Italian ancestry were "pure" Italians, according to the *Current Population Survey*. But for the younger generation the melting pot had truly been boiling away. That same 1979 survey reported that among children under fourteen who claimed Italian backgrounds, only 20 percent were of unmixed Italian ancestry.

Many considered Jews, because of their religious as well as ethnic differences, the most unmeltable white ethnic group of all. In 1922, when the president of Harvard instituted a quota to limit the admission of Jews to Harvard in order to, as he explained it, protect them from a rising tide of anti-Semitism, fewer than 5 percent of Jews were choosing partners outside of the group. His action was the genteel face on the popular expressions of anti-Semitism of the day. Others at Harvard were more direct: "Jews are an unassimilable race, as dangerous to a college as indigestible food to man ... they do not mix." The author of those lines would be shocked to find out that today over 50 percent of all Jewish marriages that take place are intermarriages and that the current president of Harvard University is himself the product of a very much assimilated and digested Jewish-gentile marriage. Now instead of outsiders worrying about the Jews' ability to fit in, insiders in the Jewish community worry about being able to maintain their community and faith.

A peculiarly American tendency to switch religions further complicates the frequency and types of interfaith marriage. With 25 to 30 percent of Americans switching denominations or religions in their lives, it's possible to start out a marriage not being intermarried and to later have the same marriage transform into a religious intermarriage. And while sociologist and priest Andrew Greeley has argued that intermarriage rates among Catholics have not increased significantly in the past forty years, he points out that some cultural groups within the church are much more likely to leave the faith than others. His research has found that the Catholic church in America has lost almost one million Hispanics to various Protestant denominations during the past fifteen years.

Throughout most of American history religious uniformity in marriage was considered desirable for the sake of family harmony. But religious intermarriages of many varieties have been on the increase in American society in the past two decades. In 1957 6 percent of Jews, 12 percent of Catholics, and 17 percent of Baptists were married to a member of a different religious denomination. A 1968 study revealed that the high rates of religious homogeneity in these marriages could be partially accounted for by conversion: In about 60 percent of the Protestant marriages and 11 percent of the Catholic marriages, one spouse had converted to the denomination of his or her partner.

The move toward religious intermarriage where neither partner converts is best revealed by recent statistics on interfaith households. While Baptist intermarriage has not increased, 21 percent of Catholics and 32 percent of Jews now live in interfaith households. Among other religious groups, 5 percent of Hindus, 25 percent of Lutherans, 30 percent of Mormons, 32 percent of Episcopalians, 40 percent of Muslims, and 58 percent of Buddhists live in interfaith households. Overall about 33 million American adults live in households with someone of another religious faith.

It's not only ethnic and religious intermarriage rates and birth patterns that have so radically changed. Few could have envisioned how quickly changing attitudes, behavior, and immigration patterns could literally transform the faces of America. Before 1960 about 80 percent of immigrants coming to America were from European countries. Today the numbers are reversed. Of the over one million legal immigrants a year entering the United States, over 80 percent of them are non-European. The greatest numbers are from Latin American, Caribbean, and Asian nations. And without even waiting to assimilate, many of these immigrants are choosing to marry partners from other groups.

While the legacy of slavery and racism makes black-white marriage the most stigmatized, controversial, and least frequent kind of mixed match, census numbers demonstrate that even among blacks and whites, significant changes are occurring. The number of black-white married couples has tripled over the past two decades from 65,000 in 1970 to 231,000 in 1991, and over that same period of time the number of births to black-white couples had quintupled.

There are now more than a million Hispanic/non-Hispanic marriages in the United States, more than double the number in 1970. And large numbers of marriages that are considered Hispanic-Hispanic are often cross-cultural marriages, bringing together partners from different nations all categorized as "Hispanic" but with significantly different cultures, such as Cuba, Mexico, Argentina, and Puerto Rico. For every 100 births to native-American couples, there are 140 births to mixed native-American/white couples. And to the surprise of many inside and outside Asian-American communities, the great wall that had separated Asians from others is quickly being worn down by lovers who stream across it. The most recent statistics show that over 40 percent of all children born to an Asian or Pacific Islander parent also have a white parent.

The choices of the younger generation of Japanese-Americans is a particularly interesting footnote to history. Intermarriage had been very rare among Japanese-Americans before World War II, and only about 3 percent intermarried. Tradition, ethnic pride, and racism meant that very few would cross over to the other side. Then, in a traumatic period of their history, the West Coast parents of today's generation of Japanese-Americans were interned as potential enemies of the state during World War II, even though most were American citizens. But in a remarkable turnabout, almost 60 percent of the children born in recent years to Japanese-Americans also have a white parent.

While these demographic changes may be most dramatic in the United States, similar changes are occurring around the world. As Europe has worked toward a common currency, it has also, to the delight of some and the dismay of others, moved toward a common gene pool as well. One striking statistic is the fact that over 25 percent of nonwhite immigrants and their children who have moved to Great Britain from Caribbean countries, Guyana, India, Pakistan, Hong Kong, and Malaysia are intermarrying, primarily to white native Britons. Among all the immigrant groups, West Indian and African males were the most likely to marry white British females.

Even in southeastern Europe, where interreligious warfare has now destroyed what used to be Yugoslavia, love had conquered ancient prejudices before the fighting began, and marriages between Muslims and Christians were not uncommon. The prewar population in Bosnia was 44 percent Muslim, 31 percent Serb, and 16 percent Croatian. Up to one-third of all marriages were interreligious or interethnic, and in Sarajevo, one-half. As many as four million people in the former Yugoslavia are the offspring of mixed marriages.

A Personal Note

Like all obsessions, my fascination with cultural differences has its roots in my own history. While the other kids in my neighborhood were playing together at the recreation center, I would spend much of my spare time downtown at the "shop," my father's small mannequin factory. All of the workers at the shop were African-American except for the Italian foreman and the German secretary. In the outside world the boundaries between cultures were very clear, and crossing the invisible lines that separated them was unthinkable, especially in Chicago. But in the shop this mélange functioned as a team and supported my own family as well as thirty-five others. To me the mix of black, Italian, and German dialects, the blaring soul music, and the screaming band saws used to make the armless and legless dummies all seemed a natural part of life.

The shop was my introduction to a world of differences, but my early home life was securely rooted in one culture. Until I was six, we lived in a lower-class Jewish ghetto. My aunts, uncles, cousins, and grandparents were our neighbors in the large old building we shared. It was as if a *shtetl*, one of the small Jewish villages in Russia where my grandparents were born, had been airlifted and plopped down in the middle of a large American city.

Our family's first move was out of the cramped tenement apartment to a neighborhood of row houses. Our next move, when I was twelve, was to the promised land—suburbia. Both moves brought us closer to the comfortable WASP havens north of the city, and in each we were increasingly separate from family and neighbors. The melting pot was doing its job. We were becoming more and more assimilated into a homogenized mainstream culture. Every step in the process of getting ahead, though, was paid for with weakened ties to family, tradition, and group identity.

In 1967 I joined VISTA and moved into a Puerto Rican ghetto in downtown Chicago as a community organizer. Chako, the leader of a gang who also worked for VISTA, was my guide to the world of the streets. My parents were disturbed and confused by my decision to abandon the safety of the suburbs. None of us realized that the Puerto Ricans' sense of extended family, neighborhood, and feeling of shared group fate would make me feel a strange sense of déjà vu, as if I were reliving my own family's history.

On my occasional weekend drives home to visit my family, I would cruise down the suburban streets lined with trimmed lawns, big new cars, and houses frozen in air-conditioned sterility. It was a long way from the frenetic and steaming tenements I lived in downtown. My journey downtown was a pilgrimage, a recapitulation of my own collective past. My grandparents had immigrated a half century earlier to this same spot that was now a Puerto Rican ghetto.

At the time I had no sense of the connection between what I was doing and my own cultural baggage. I was caught up in the spirit of the sixties, doing my part to make the world a better place. I can now see that in rejecting what my family had labeled as progress, I was searching for the sense of community I had lost in my family's journey from ghetto to gilded suburb. In a convoluted way I was affirming my immigrant, communal, and lower-class roots.

This unconscious quest led me back to the same neighborhood my grandparents and parents had worked so hard to escape from. Macho had replaced matzoh, but here I was, literally, on the same street where my mother, growing up in poverty, had shared a bed with her two sisters. I had rejected the antiseptic homogeneity of the suburbs and romanticized the mean streets of the city. Chako couldn't see the connection between my past and my decision to return to Halsted Street, and at the time neither could I. Like a Chicago chameleon, I kept trying to adapt to the wildly varied ethnic landscape I crawled across.

These early years laid the foundation for my interest in cross-cultural relationships. Throughout my twenties and early thirties I acted out this fascination in my personal as well as my professional life. I had three relationships with women from different cultural backgrounds over the course of a decade. After college I worked for four years with a wide range of people. I was a community organizer with poor farmers in North Carolina. Then I taught elementary school in a black ghetto in Saint Louis and in a poor white rural area in Oregon before deciding to go to graduate school in psychology.

After completing my doctorate in 1976 I began to travel and look everywhere for what I still couldn't find inside. Like Diogenes carrying his lantern looking for the honest man, I carried mine to foreign lands looking for the meaning of belonging and identity.

In 1979 I went to Bali, a culture I had idealized. One night I found myself in a small village, the only outsider participating in the preparations for a burial ceremony that was to take place the next day. The Balinese were friendly and warm. But suddenly I recognized what should have been obvious—that I would always remain an outsider and would never be a part of this or any of the other cohesive cultural communities I so admired. I was a voyeur of others' group belonging, and I had lost my own.

The next night I had a dream. A long line of dark-clothed Eastern European immigrants, all holding hands, stretched from an old ship at a New York dock to a high chain-link fence. On the other side of the fence another line, this one of modern Americans, extended toward the tall, gleaming buildings in the distance. I stood at the fence, one hand connected to the string of immigrants, the other hand to the people of today. Each group pulled me toward it. I felt torn in two.

For me that dream was an epiphany, one of those moments that reveal hidden truths and change the course of a life. Questions that I had never been able to confront now became a preoccupation. What did it mean to be a minority-group member? Could people from different cultures come together in work or love and still retain their distinctiveness? Where did I fit in?

When I returned from that trip, I began to explore these questions by focusing my teaching, research, and clinical work as a psychologist on cross-cultural issues as they are played out in their most intimate forum—marriage. I wanted to learn more about how people reconciled their different cultural, ethnic, and religious pasts in a rapidly changing world.

When I married a Jewish woman in 1982, I wondered if I would lose interest in intermarriage. But if anything, my passion for the subject only intensified. Perhaps it was because in marrying her I found that I was still entering into a kind of intermarriage. She and her family were so much more actively involved in the Jewish community than mine that I felt myself to be the outsider. Although our common roots made some things easier, we discovered that intramarriage did not free us from differences over tradition. Especially after we had three children, we learned that an ongoing process of negotiation was necessary to forge a unified and meaningful cultural and spiritual path.

All of us, whether we are intermarried or not, are caught between our need for continuity with tradition and the necessity of adapting to a rapidly changing world. Each of us takes our own odyssey to search for a place and a community we can call our own. And all of us need to learn how to understand, negotiate, and creatively use our differences in an increasingly multicultural world.

A NOTE ON CULTURAL GENERALIZATIONS

One of the special challenges in writing about intermarriage is to find ways to deal with the sensitive issue of describing differences between cultural groups. In order to do so, I need to make generalizations that are just that—generalizations. Generalizations about cultural groups can be powerful tools. But tools have no morality. They can be used constructively or destructively.

Generalizations about cultural groups, when applied in a rigid manner or to further biased stereotypes about a group, are destructive. All forms of racism, anti-Semitism, homophobia, and other forms of group hatred are dependent upon the use of rigid, inflexible, distorted, or untrue generalizations. But, as Monica Mc-Goldrick, editor of the landmark book *Ethnicity and Family Therapy*, has pointed out, it is a mistake to pretend that the words "all people are created equal" means that "all people are the same." It denies the richness and diversity of different cultural groups, and of their particular strengths and problem areas.

In this book I will sometimes need to use broad strokes to convey important ideas about cultural differences and how they affect the relationships of mixed matches. I recognize the pain and problems that stereotyping can lead to. At times I may err by overgeneralizing, but without the freedom to talk about group differences, I cannot say what I need to say. Feel free to disagree with my generalizations, and certainly they may not fit for you.

Structure of the Book

The chapters of the book focus on the following themes:

Chapter 1, "Special Challenges," helps couples identify the important culturally and religiously based issues that are part of being in a mixed match.

Chapter 2, "Why Do We Make a Mixed Match?" focuses on the range of motivations that lie behind the choice of an intimate partner from a background different from your own. It will help you better understand the strengths and weaknesses of the foundation your relationship is built upon.

Chapter 3, "Decoding Cultural Conflict," creates a framework for understanding the effects of different cultural codes. It will help you find ways of dealing with contrasting values about the meaning of time, family relationships, male-female roles, and emotional expressiveness.

Chapter 4, "Many Voices Within: Clarifying Cultural and Religious Identity," will help you clarify your own sense of cultural and religious identity.

Chapter 5, "Creating a Family Identity," shows how couples can use life-cycle events as opportunities to clarify and negotiate their different cultural and religious loyalties and find solutions to questions of identity that are right for them.

Chapter 6, "Dealing with Parents, Family, Friends, and Foes," explores issues involving your parents and extended families and the reactions of others to your relationship.

Chapter 7, "Split at the Root: The Children of Mixed Matches," looks at the ways children of mixed matches have worked and struggled to deal with the contrasts in their religious and cultural heritages.

Chapter 8, "Helping Children Develop a Solid Identity," discusses positive ways to help children deal with developmental and social issues.

The Epilogue, "Beyond Categories," looks at the possibility of building bridges in a world divided up into categories.

The Resources section lists organizations, support groups, a Bill of Rights for racially mixed people, and books for young people.

Mixed Matches will help couples and families cope with the complex issues of combining two different traditions in one family.

Using the experiences of others and self-help exercises, it provides tools to help negotiate cultural contrasts, deal with extended families, overcome social barriers, and raise children with a clear sense of identity. Our differences are the source of learning and creativity in all of our important relationships, and learning to recognize, appreciate, and use these differences are the keys to enriching family life.

CHAPTER 1

Special Challenges

I was the first Turkish woman in my family to go abroad to graduate school. After I returned to Turkey from my studies in the United States, Melkon and I married in Istanbul, the city where we both grew up. Melkon was part of the small Armenian community remaining in Turkey. I come from a very nationalistic and influential Turkish family.

My mother said that my marriage would never work because of our different religions: Melkon is an Orthodox Christian and I am a Muslim. My father didn't talk to us for two years because he blames all Armenians for lying and claiming that the Turks killed millions of Armenians before and during World War I. Melkon's parents refused to come to our wedding because they have never forgiven the Turks for what they did. And some of my friends who are educated and westernized thought I was a little crazy for marrying him because he was so traditional in his view of women.

Now we have two children and I work in the marketing department of a large corporation. When I get home from work, my main concerns are having some time with Melkon and taking care of the kids. It's not always easy, because he never washed a dish in his life before we got married. When I complain that he doesn't help enough, he says he is the most liberated man he knows. I'm sad to say, he is probably telling the truth. When he semi-jokes that I was ruined by my two years in the West, I used to feel guilty, but lately I've started to get angry. When I was in Europe and the States, I met men who didn't think they were heroes for pitching in with the housework.

So I'm not so worried about what God thinks about our relationship or about righting history or pleasing my friends. I'm just concerned with getting the kids fed and to bed. My father may be upset about events that took place eighty years ago, but I am worried about tonight's battleground. I have my own territory to defend.

M ixed matches *are* more complicated relationships than those between people from similar backgrounds. As much as we would like to believe that "people are just people" or that "love conquers all," every layer of difference introduced into a relationship adds more complexity and new challenges. Differences in cultural and family styles may be fascinating, but they are also alien. Those traits that initially seem so attractive can ultimately lie at the roots of the most difficult problems. Confusing love with compatibility, cross-cultural couples often discover that the excitement of cultural contrasts can turn into the pain of cultural clashes.

More than stylistic differences complicate the lives of cross-cultural couples. The absence of shared rituals and traditions can add to the already substantial stress of modern marriage. Intermarriage is the ultimate challenge to cultural continuity, and partners from different backgrounds can feel torn by the conflicting demands of love and tradition. Mixed matches have to decide how to define a family faith, celebrate holidays, carry on cultural traditions, and deal with the reactions of family and friends to their relationship. They also have to decide how to go about instilling a sense of identity in their children. Unfortunately sometimes they have to find ways to deal with the prejudices of others. To make things even more complicated, these decisions have to be made by partners who must negotiate even while finding ways to bridge different cultural communication styles and different ideas about gender roles.

These special challenges don't mean that mixed matches are doomed to unhappiness. Millions of families around the world can testify to the possibility of finding satisfying answers to the questions raised by cross-cultural relationships. But as in all complex and worthwhile enterprises, the most successful people tend to be those who are willing to face the issues at hand and work on them. Couples who develop the skills to deal with the personal, interpersonal, and social issues that are part of being in a mixed match are the most likely to find ways to use their differences to build strong and rewarding relationships.

There are five primary tasks that people in mixed matches can take on to create successful relationships. Although I explore these issues and outline exercises to help you meet these challenges in specific chapters, I'll describe each of them now because they represent themes that are interwoven throughout the book:

- Face the issues
- Clarify your different cultural codes
- Sort out confusion about your identity
- Be aware of the social context
- Find your own path and help your children find theirs

Face the Issues

I told Reg that my grandparents were too old to travel to the wedding. I didn't want him to know that they're not coming because they don't approve of our marriage. Now doesn't feel like the right time to talk about their prejudices about blacks. We have the wedding planned, I'm really anxious about everything, and I can't handle any more stress. During our honeymoon we'll have plenty of time to talk.

IRISH-AMERICAN WOMAN WHO IS MARRYING
AN AFRICAN-AMERICAN MAN IN THREE WEEKS EXPLAINING WHY
SHE TOLD A "WHITE LIE" TO EXPLAIN WHY HER GRANDPARENTS
WEREN'T COMING TO THEIR WEDDING

All of us struggle at times with what seems to be a universal human temptation to avoid dealing with tough issues in intimate relationships. We approach them with about as much enthusiasm as we do going to the doctor to get a vaccination. Even though we are aware that confronting our differences might inoculate us against future conflict, we make excuses to justify our procrastination. Our motives are not bad. We value our relationships and fear that in trying to deal directly with our differences, we might set off an unmanageable conflict.

Occasionally it does make sense to wait for "a better time" to deal with disturbing issues. But if some couples err by talking about their concerns too soon, far more find their relationships in difficulty because of patterns of avoidance they have developed. Couples who avoid dealing with too many of life's inevitable difficulties may discover too late that a cancer of silence has spread throughout every part of their relationship.

The "perfect couple" who suddenly and mysteriously split up are often people who got too good at avoiding tough issues. Their relationship may have looked ideal to outsiders, and sometimes they may have even fooled themselves into believing that they were fortunate to have such a harmonious marriage. More often they were all too aware of their silent resentments and regrets. By the time they tried to face their problems, it was too late. Their marriage had been hollowed out by a habitual retreat from conflict, and there simply wasn't enough life left in their relationship to tolerate the stressful process of attempting to revive it.

Avoidance can grow out of the best of intentions but lead to the worst of results. People who really care about each other can end up destroying their relationships because they fear dealing with problems that are obvious to both of them. That's the really sad part of the process. Facing the issues may be difficult and frightening, but it's far less risky than avoiding them.

One young couple, Lydia and Chris, found that crisis was the price of their avoidance of dealing with their different religious backgrounds. Lydia was from a German-Swedish-American background and had been raised in a conservative Lutheran household. Her father had been a deacon in the church all of her life. Chris, whose family was Polish-American, had been an altar boy in the Catholic church where his parents had taken the family every Sunday since he could remember.

A month after the birth of their first child, Lydia's mother talked her into taking him to their church without Chris's consent and having him baptized as a Lutheran. When Chris found out, he was silently enraged. The next day Chris and his parents took Sean to be baptized in their Catholic church. The chaos that followed these events catapulted them and their extended families into a period of painful conflict.

When I asked them if they had ever discussed these issues before Sean was born, Lydia answered, "I thought we had worked it all out." But when I asked her what that meant, she told me, "Actually when we were on our honeymoon, I said that I wanted to raise our children as good Christians, and Chris said okay, and *that was that*. I really thought that constituted a clear agreement that I could raise them as Lutherans. I relaxed a lot after that talk, and we never mentioned anything about it again until Sean was born."

Lydia and Chris are both attorneys who were in their mid-thirties when they got married. They are intelligent and successful people who pride themselves on being thorough and competent. They have spent their lives helping other people craft workable agreements. But when it came to one of the most important contracts in their own lives, they tried to settle the emotionally complex issue of the religious upbringing of their children with just a few sentences. They never would have been so negligent with a client.

Lydia and Chris's avoidance was motivated by the ordinary anxiety that most couples feel when making difficult, complicated, and potentially divisive decisions. There are a number of additional reasons why people in mixed matches sometimes sidestep dealing with their differences even more than other couples. First of all, mixed matches are often *very romantic relationships*. The novelty of being with someone *not* like the boy or girl next door adds an element of excitement. Novelty is one of the spices of life, and its power can distract people from focusing on the ordinary problems that are part of every relationship.

When a relationship includes an element of *forbidden* love, the attraction can become even more powerful. Choosing a partner over the opposition of family, friends, or religious traditions can lead to an idealization of the relationship, at least initially. Each partner silently reflects that "If I have chosen her (or him) in spite of these obstacles, I must *really* be in love."

While lack of family acceptance can destabilize a cross-cultural relationship, it can also have the opposite effect. Cut off from the usual sources of support, the couple who feel exiled are figuratively pushed into each other's arms. Resenting the judgments of others, they focus their anger on their families and may fail to experience normal ambivalence about their new relationship. Like a nation threatened by enemies from without, they close ranks and temporarily forget their own differences.

Few couples want to disrupt the delicious experience of new love with disturbing thoughts of *possible* future problems. And who can blame them? Falling in love is one of the most sought-after experiences in life, a magical emotional and sexual state of being. Frequently part of falling in love includes the belief that we have found our true and unique soul mate. And if our beloved is from a background unlike our own, it may even reinforce the feeling of specialness, of having found our missing half. After all, how else can we explain these intense feelings?

There is only one problem with being head-over-heels in love. No matter how high up we start, we always come down. Time is the gravity of love. The intoxicating and delusional state of *new* love—that sense of finding the perfect other—never lasts.

The real test of a relationship comes when the bubble bursts. Whether it's dealing with family rejection, planning a wedding, coping with a child's birth, making religious choices, or deciding who is supposed to wash the dishes, differences eventually emerge. New love ends, and couples are able to begin forging deep and solid relationships by acknowledging and dealing with their differences. Don't be so attached to your fantasy relationship that you miss the opportunity to build a real one that will last.

Clarify Your Different Cultural Codes

Culture shapes every aspect of how we view the world and what we consider "normal" and "abnormal." It molds our attitudes toward time, family, sex, and monogamy. Cultural rules govern how we expect anger and affection to be expressed, the ways that children are supposed to be disciplined and rewarded, how we greet strangers and friends, and the roles of men and women. Behavior that I consider neighborly you may define as seductive; what you intend to be friendly disagreement I may be just as sure is a threat; when you say you visit your parents "often," you may mean twice a year, but for me "seldom" might mean twice a week. If we are not able to identify the existence and the nature of these differences in each other's cultural codes, we will have problems dealing with stressful situations.

Partners in a mixed match raised in different countries can have very different cultural definitions of "normal." Just imagine the potential value conflicts in an intermarriage between a Japanese man from a culture where men average 11 minutes of housework a day to an American woman where men average 108 minutes. Their expectations of what is "normal" are not likely to mesh easily.

Even when both partners in a mixed match are born in the same country, speak the same language, and are from the same class background, they may find themselves tripping over cultural differences in the meanings of words, behaviors, and values. Regional, ethnic, racial, and religious differences may lead two native-born partners from different subcultures to interpret the same action in very different ways. Differences in accents between one part of a country and another are usually obvious; contrasts in cultural codes often are not.

Consider, for example, a recent dispute between Erik, a Norwegian-American man, and Serena, an Argentinian-American woman. Both of them were the grandchildren of immigrants to the United States. Both were well educated. They had met in graduate school and shared many common interests. They cared deeply about each other, and it never occurred to them during the first year of their relationship that their different cultural conditioning might lead them to react very differently in stressful moments.

A seemingly minor incident revealed the different cultural lenses through which they each viewed the world. They were cooking dinner together one night at Erik's apartment. Serena's hands were wet and slippery, and she accidentally broke one of Erik's favorite bowls that had been handed down to him by his grandparents. Serena apologized profusely, and Erik told her not to worry about it. But in the hours that followed, he retreated into a silence Serena found unbearable.

Finally she blew up. "I know you're upset, but you just don't say anything. I feel guilty enough about breaking the bowl, but your silence is really driving me crazy." Erik responded to her outburst with more silence, to which Serena responded with even more anger. The incident sparked the first major fight they ever had, highlighting differences that they had only been subliminally aware of.

When they finally began to discuss what had happened, they began to see the contrast in the ways their families had dealt with conflict. Erik said that he felt being quiet was the way to keep the peace. He had *never* seen any direct expression of anger between his parents. For him silence was the normal way to communicate feeling upset.

In Serena's much more expressive family, one of the ways that people demonstrated their sense of connection was through direct, and sometimes loud and angry, outbursts. If you were angry and *didn't* show it, it meant you didn't care. And since people cared about one another deeply in her family, recurrent anger was a normal and expected part of family life. She sensed Erik's irritation about the broken bowl, but to her his silence meant that he must not really care about their relationship. Her way of trying to reconnect was to demonstrate even more intense emotion to show how much she loved Erik.

It wasn't just that they had grown up in different families that led Serena and Erik to very different conclusions about what constituted normal and expected behavior; it was the differences in the entire social worlds they had experienced as children. Erik had grown up in a predominantly Scandinavian-Lutheran neighborhood in Minneapolis. Serena had grown up in a neighborhood in a Miami suburb populated primarily by families from all over Latin America. The values and behavior inside their home were echoed and reinforced by their friends and in other social exchanges they experienced and observed. Until they went to college, each of them had had little opportunity or need to question their families' definitions of normalcy.

Unfortunately the contrasts in the cultural rules we bring to our relationships are usually invisible until they have been violated. We internalize the norms of our subculture as children and grow up taking them for granted. Therefore, when I get angry with your behavior, my first assumption is that you as an *individual* are behaving in an offensive manner, not that we are operating by two different sets of cultural rules. One of the most important tasks for partners in mixed matches is to learn to understand and deal with the differences in the cultural codes they bring to their relationships.

Sort Out Confusion About Your Own Identity

Whether we admit it or not, most of us carry a mixed bag of contradictory feelings about our cultural, racial, or religious identities. In a rapidly changing, culturally diverse society, it's hard for anyone to maintain a clear and consistent sense of group identity.

Our desire to melt into the melting pot is always at war with our wish to be a member of a distinct group. It's hard to have it both ways. Most of us at some time find ourselves struggling with inner confusion about where we fit culturally.

People who have experienced racism or religious persecution often feel that their group identification is an unwelcome burden. Those who have not suffered directly from discrimination in their own lives, but know of the victimization of their parents or grandparents, may wear their cultural label with ambivalence and anxiety. They may try to minimize or even obliterate their identity as a member of their group.

Even people from groups that have no memory of oppression may be ambivalent about their cultural identity. Their discomfort derives not from real or perceived external danger but from an internal sense of incompatibility with their group. They may feel that their identity is "boring," or they may feel that their group's primary values do not fit well with their own.

But humans are profoundly social animals. We need to feel connected to a group. The group defines who is friend and who is enemy and provides a system of social support. Its norms help sort out priorities in a complex world.

So it should come as little surprise that so many people are strongly ambivalent about their connection to the identity inherited from their ancestors. The fact that membership in the group, be it African-American, Jewish, Asian-American, Mexican-American, or even New England Yankee, can be a source of support and emotional nurturance *or* can target us for the hostility of others means that we often experience group identity as a mixed blessing. And when either partner in a mixed match has conflicted feelings about his or her *own* racial, religious, or cultural identity, it can create confusion, conflict, and pain in a relationship.

Many of the people I interviewed spoke of the conflicting messages their parents had given them about their own cultural identities. Alex, a Japanese-American man, described how the contradictions of his family's cultural life as he grew up led to a painful incident in his relationship with Ashley:

> My parents gave me a lot of mixed messages about being Japanese-American. All of their friends were Japanese, but we lived in a neighborhood that was almost entirely Caucasian. They told me that it was important that I always remember that I was Japanese, but they didn't keep up any of the traditions at home. When we would visit my grandparents, I would watch my father go in and bow at the altar where they kept my great-grandfather's ashes in an urn, but they never included me in any ritual. I always pretended I hadn't seen him bow and felt vaguely embarrassed, as if I was witnessing something I shouldn't.
>
> When I started dating Ashley, who is from a WASP background, I acted like being Japanese was of no real significance to me. We never talked about our different backgrounds. But when my mother became ill and died last year, I was shocked by my own feelings—I suddenly started to feel very Japanese for the first time in my life. I couldn't believe that I felt guilty about bringing Ashley to the funeral because she was white. I made up excuses to explain why I wanted to go to the funeral alone, and Ashley got very upset and asked me if I was ashamed of being with her.

Historically, identity as a member of a group was a matter of destiny, not decision. But as barriers have fallen, especially in the last twenty-five years, group identification has increasingly become a choice. We now face the complicated task of *creating* our own sense of identity. Like painters standing before a palette of colors, we can choose the shades and shapes of our identities. This can be both an exhilarating and a confusing task.

This book will help you resolve your own personal cultural confusion. It will help you acknowledge and come to terms with the painful parts of your cultural identity. It will show you how you may have internalized society's negative judgments about your group. And it will help you reclaim and affirm the positive and nourishing parts of your identity. By sorting out the complex feelings about your own group identity, you will be better able to compromise with your partner and find creative ways to synthesize your pasts.

Be Aware of the Social Context of Your Relationship

Romeo and Juliet's love was doomed not by their personalities but by their families' hatred of one another. No matter how much two people share, they exist in a social world. Many of the challenges they face are shaped by the stage on which they act out the drama of their love. Societal attitudes about your particular kind of racial, cultural, or religious intermarriage will have a major impact on how well your relationship is accepted by family, friends, and strangers. And because the social context is continually evolving, being attuned to its changes will help you understand and deal with the reactions of others.

We can be thankful that we do not live in the time and place in which Mildred and Richard Loving began their relationship. In July 1958, soon after returning home to Central Point, Virginia, from their honeymoon, Richard, a white bricklayer, and Mildred, a young black woman, were arrested in the middle of the night by the county sheriff for violating the state law against interracial marriage. They were tried and found guilty of the crime of being married to each other. Judge Leon M. Bazile, who presided over the case, angrily told them, "Almighty God created the races white, black, yellow, Malay, and red, and He placed them on separate continents and but for the interference with His arrangement there would be no cause for such marriages."

Sentenced to a year in jail, they were only set free by the judge on the condition that they not return to Virginia for the next twenty-five years. In 1967, after nine years of trials and appeals, the United States Supreme Court finally used their case to strike down all laws forbidding interracial marriage.

The Lovings didn't have to examine the subtle nuances of their relationship to know that being an interracial couple had greatly complicated their life together. Even though they were not political people, nor had they married as a way to defy social norms, their relationship had to endure the persecution and unwanted scrutiny of others.

Racism, anti-Semitism, and other forms of intolerance still exist in many places. While the public marches of thousands of Ku Klux Klan members through the streets of Washington, D.C., that took place in the 1930s are no longer part of the social landscape, individuals and organizations still exist whose hatred is focused on the race or creed of others different from themselves. Hate crimes directed at interracial couples still occur every year in the United States. And even though intermarriage is far more accepted today around the world, a two-hour plane ride across Europe—or a half-hour car ride across New York City—can take you from an area where no one would ever bother to notice you and your partner's different backgrounds to a place where your existence as a mixed match would place you in physical danger.

Not all opposition to intermarriage results from simple bigotry, and it can sometimes be an inaccurate oversimplification to label it as such. There are many truly religious people, for example, who welcome interracial marriage, but not interreligious marriage. They are not concerned about the mixing of races, but are dedicated to maintaining the integrity of their religious beliefs.

Other people who are generally tolerant and who maintain good relationships with people from a variety of backgrounds may draw the line at intermarriage. While not hating those who are different, they worry that intermarriage will erode cultural traditions they value and break down the solidity of their extended families. They may be concerned that intermarriage will undermine a sense of racial cohesiveness that is crucial to group solidarity. Or they are concerned that if their children intermarry, they will lose face and status in the eyes of their neighbors.

But whether out of racism, prejudice, ignorance, or the desire to protect religious or cultural continuity, mixed matches often find themselves confronted with intense negative reactions to their relationship. This additional stress is another reason that mixed matches need to learn to be especially skillful in handling difficulties within their relationships and dealing with their differences.

NEW TOLERANCE AND OLD PREJUDICE
One of the difficulties in being attuned to the social context of your relationship is the rapidity with which it changes. In spite of the continued existence of different forms of opposition to intermarriage, the walls separating different groups of people have come down in many places in the world. We live in an era of incredible transformations, and relationships that were unheard of and unthinkable in one time and place have become common and taken for granted in another.

More than anywhere else, the United States is in the midst of a massive cultural and social metamorphosis in its attitudes toward intermarriage. Twenty-five years after the *Loving* decision, the United States Supreme Court, rather than hearing cases on the legality of interracial marriage, now includes Justice Thomas, a black man married to a white woman. And while America is far from an intergroup utopia, interfaith relationships between Jews and gentiles that were once shocking and interracial relationships between Asians and whites, and blacks and whites, that were illegal, have become relatively commonplace.

Throughout the history of the United States the definitions of *insider* and *outsider* have repeatedly and dramatically changed. National background, religion, and ethnicity, as well as race, have all at different times been the focus of negative reactions to mixed matches. If you were of German background, for example, you probably would have had some problems if you had tried to marry Benjamin Franklin's daughter. Franklin feared that Germans would destroy America with their alien culture and language.

Some segment of every ethnic group that came to America found ways to express their dislike of those that followed, even when they themselves had been exposed to discrimination and rejection. Of course these attitudes affected those who chose to marry outside of their group in spite of widespread prejudices.

In various forms Franklin's distaste for German immigrants has been replicated in widespread hostility directed at succeeding waves of newcomers by those who came before them. The Irish, Italians, Poles, Jews, Greeks, Chinese, Japanese, Mexicans, and every other group of immigrants has at one time or another been characterized as dirty, menacing, disloyal, anarchistic, unassimilable, inferior, unneeded, and unwanted. And of course none of them would ever master proper English.

This rejection of newcomers has extended even to members of what others would consider "their own kind." Emma Lazarus, the German-Jewish-American author of the famous words of welcome inscribed on the Statue of Liberty, "Give me your huddled masses," lobbied against extending that invitation to Eastern European Jews. Expressing an anxiety that was common among the established German-Jewish community, she feared that this great unwashed and far less civilized horde would tarnish the good name of her community. Free northern blacks were embarrassed by and tried to keep separate from the waves of newly freed slaves from the South after the Civil War. And even with strong cultural connections and emotional loyalties to their kin across the border, a large percentage of Mexican-Americans favor restrictions on immigration into the United States, including that from Latin America. But in spite of the resistance to each wave of immigration and of the very real racial, cultural, and religious divisions that still exist, the United States has been the most inclusive of nations.

Find Your Own Path and Help Your Children Find Theirs

There are many questions that people in mixed matches have about their relationships and the cultural and religious decisions they must make.

- Shall we practice two religions or one?
- Is it better for biracial children to have an identity rooted in one race?
- What should we tell our parents?
- What are the divorce statistics for our kind of match?
- What kind of neighborhood is best to live in?

- How should we deal with racism?
- Should children be allowed to make their own decision on how to identify?

My goal in this book is to encourage a process of self-exploration, open communication, and negotiation that will enable you to find creative solutions to the challenges you confront. Many of the couples you meet in this book found answers that worked for them. Some of their solutions may fit for you, but others will not. Your situation may be different in obvious or subtle ways. What is important is to do the hard work to reach decisions that are right for your relationship.

The biggest challenge most cross-cultural couples face is in raising children. Finding creative ways to explain an often bewildering world to the next generation and helping your children develop a clear sense of identity are complex tasks. While it's important to offer your children guidance and structure in their lives, it's also crucial to remember that your children are trying to find ways to adapt to a world that is radically different than it was a generation ago. Just as your path was different from your parents', it's likely that your children's will be somewhat different from your own. More than most people, parents and children in cross-cultural families understand what we must all deal with—the tension between our need for continuity and the necessity of adapting to change.

A Lifelong Process

Many people are burdened with idealized Hollywood images of what a "successful" relationship is supposed to be like. So many films end with the happy couple, having overcome great difficulties, figuratively or literally riding off into the rose-colored sunset. We know with great certainty that *they* will live happily ever after. And of course we feel that we should be able to as well.

But we discover that our relationships can never successfully compete with these perfect two-dimensional celluloid images. As three-dimensional flesh-and-blood humans, we all have weaknesses as well as strengths, and flaws as well as beauty. And unlike the stars on the screen who never age, we do.

As three-dimensional humans, however, we have some big advantages over the perfect images. We can learn and grow in our relationships over the course of a lifetime. They can't. We are real. They aren't.

The following chapters will help guide you in finding ways to meet the challenges of creating meaningful and satisfying family relationships. While the examples and exercises in *Mixed Matches* focus primarily on cross-cultural couples and families, in this era of change all relationships can be strengthened when people find ways to bridge the barriers that separate them. Make learning about and dealing with differences part of a lifelong process.

CHAPTER 2

Why Do We Make a Mixed Match?

He sincerely believed that by marrying this good woman, the product both of a tough lower-class upbringing and of a rich communal culture very unlike his own, he was breaking with an establishment past, a liberal-conservative tradition that had always hung him up. Already he felt almost self-righteous about his new life because it was going to be Down to Earth, Humble, Unpretentious, *Real*. . . .

To Bloom's private horror, he discovered almost immediately that far from being proud of, or even content with, her Chicano heritage, Linda almost hysterically wanted out of her poverty-stifled past. . . .

And their dilemma was instantly this: he desired what he thought she had been, whereas she desired what she thought he had been. Immediately both of them felt cheated and they began to resent each other, although they kept their mouths shut, praying for some kind of miracle to come along and straighten things out or at least fashion a workable compromise.

JOHN NICHOLS, *THE MILAGRO BEANFIELD WAR*

Search for Completion

In one of his meditations on love in *The Symposium*, Plato, the Greek philosopher, wrote about the myth that in the beginning we were never alone because we were each whole unto our-selves. Our ancestors were not humans as we know them but were beings that incorporated both male and female. Then the cataclysm occurred. The gods split each into two and created man and woman. Ever since, we have been condemned to wander the world, searching for our lost halves to complete ourselves.

Many psychologists have used this story as a metaphor to de-scribe the hunger for fusion with another person and the preoccu-pation with the idea of a single unique soulmate. In its extreme form the obsessive quest for the nonexistent perfect other be-comes destructive. One potential mate after another is rejected when a relationship reveals, as it always does, a flaw. Too late the seeker discovers that no one can rescue him from his own empti-ness and his inability to commit to another flawed human being.

But in a less extreme and healthier way some form of this search is crucial to our development. Each of us is incomplete, and we all can grow from intimacy with another who has traits and abilities that complement our own. In *My Fair Lady*, the story of Eliza Doolittle and Henry Higgins shows how two people can help each other become more whole. Even as Eliza learned from Henry how to become a lady and, more importantly, to be-lieve in herself, he learned from her how to open a cold heart. The appeal of the story lies in its affirmation of the possibility of tran-scending our limitations through the struggle of creating an intimate relationship.

No one would say that Eliza and Henry started out as soul mates. Theirs was a difficult and improbable relationship. Rather than love at first sight, they were a very odd couple whose love grew out of conflict, confrontation, doubt, and difficulty. Seen as a myth, *My Fair Lady* is a far more optimistic one than Plato's. It offers the hope that love results not from the unlikely luck of finding *the* right one but from working hard to create a real love with another imperfect being.

When I first started asking people what had drawn them to their cross-cultural partners, I expected most to explain their attraction to their partners in "Platonic" terms—to say things like "We just met and fell in love and he seemed like a soul mate in spite of our different backgrounds." But years of talking with people in mixed matches has led me to believe that many of them were very aware of their attraction to others from distinctly different cultures *before* they met their partners.

Some had very specific cultural preferences, while others were attracted to a group of cultures. But they rarely felt that their choice of a cross-cultural spouse was an accident. For a variety of reasons, people from other cultures seemed to offer something missing in their own. Choosing a partner from another culture can represent a search for completion and wholeness.

There are, however, no simple answers to the question of why people defy tradition and marry outside of their own cultural or religious group. Up until the last few years the great majority of research on intermarriage focused on the psychopathology of those who choose to intermarry. Researchers assumed that those who broke with tradition were clearly disturbed in some way, or at least were misfits, outsiders, or rebels who defied convention as a way of acting out their inner conflicts. Characteristic of the earlier research on intermarriage was "Psychopathology in Mixed Marriages," an article published in 1967 by Samuel Lehrman, a psychiatrist who attributed the motives for choosing outside of one's group to include "exaggerated narcissism, including the phallic significance of the marriage bond ... exhibitionism ... and choices that defend against castration anxiety."

"Exchange" theory, another model of intergroup attraction, has often been used to reinforce the long-held stereotype of the finan-cially successful minority-group man who "buys" a higher-status white Protestant, preferably blond wife. This stereotype was often invoked by those who couldn't imagine relationships between minority-group members and white Protestants as being moti-vated by more prosaic forces—such as love.

In its most materialistic and cynical form, exchange theory has also been used to explain the behavior of a WASP who is seen as somehow deficient and who is willing to exchange the value of her superior social or racial status for improved economic status. The fact that many unusually successful people from stigmatized groups such as Jews and blacks married out before intermarriage was common reinforced the view that love had far less to do with these matches than money and status.

While accurate statistics do not exist, there are numerous exam-ples of the elite of many minority groups marrying out before inter-marriage was common. Black leaders and entertainers such as James Farmer, Pearl Bailey, and Harry Belafonte were in some ways immune to the powerful barriers against interracial marriage. Irving Berlin, the Russian-Jewish immigrant son of a cantor who wrote "White Christmas" and "God Bless America," married a Christian, as did George Burns, Groucho Marx, and many other Jewish entertain-ers during an era when religious intermarriage was rare. Differences in earning power and privilege meant that many of those marrying out ahead of their time were men. Women had fewer choices.

Doubtless the desire for wealth and the wish to be accepted by "higher" levels of society have been powerful motivations in choos-ing partners among members of all groups in society. The American saga has continually used marriage and intermarriage as the lubri-cant of social mobility. In ways both subtle and obvious, modern American society is permeated by a cultural and racial caste system.

But it is an increasingly fluid one. The speed with which various groups become "mainstream" varies, but history has demonstrated that yesterday's outsider can become today's royalty.

Few people now think of Irish-Americans as minorities, but the marriages of John F. Kennedy to Jacqueline Bouvier or Grace Kelley to Prince Rainier marked the culmination of decades of bitter struggle by Irish Catholics like the Kennedys and the Kelleys to achieve an acceptance they long found lacking in their adopted country. Signs that read NO IRISH NEED APPLY are now museum pieces rather than the painful daily reality for Irish-Americans of 120 years ago.

But while some people use intermarriage to improve their social or economic standing, the motives that lead *most* people who choose a partner from another cultural group are far more complex and less materialistic. Demographic studies have shown that the majority of black-white intermarriages, for example, involve partners both of whom are more educated than the average members of their respective groups. In a study of intermarriage in England between native-born whites and nonwhite immigrants, the intermarrying immigrants had significantly higher levels of education than those who did not intermarry. The whites they married also tended to have slightly higher-than-average levels of education. This suggests that in most of today's mixed matches, an exchange of wealth for social acceptability is not a crucial motivating factor for either partner. Rather it's higher levels of education and income that lead to exposure to different kinds of people and ideas, including the idea of love outside of one's group.

Quite recently some ethnic and religious leaders have argued that, far from being a sign of deviance, intermarriage is an indication of enlightenment and the path to a better world. From their perspective those who intermarry are at the forefront of the breakdown of inter-group barriers, models for a future world where people will no longer divide themselves by antiquated and dangerous cultural identities. Through their choice the cross-cultural couple validates the universality of the human condition. Their relationships will lead to a creative and life-enhancing genetic, cultural, and spiritual cross-fertilization. One religious group, the Baha'i, a universalistic religion founded in the late nineteenth century by Baha' a' llah, an Iranian, actually encourages racial and cultural intermarriage to further these goals.

In reality intermarriage is neither an automatic indicator of emotional problems *nor* the cure to the world's problems. As exposure to people of different cultural, religious, and racial groups becomes more common, and as the barriers that traditionally separated these groups have lowered, more people in mixed matches choose their partners the way anyone else does, drawn together by their own unique combination of hopes and fears, problems and possibilities. Many of these couples feel that their differences are just one part of their relationship, not its reason for being. They see their cultural contrasts as enriching their relationships or simply as the source of another level of complexity and challenge.

Range of Motives

There is seldom a *single* motive that lies behind two people's choice of each other across cultural and religious barriers. But it's worth considering if any of the following four motives are part of what attracted you to your partner. Use the case studies and the exercises at the end of this chapter to learn more about your relationship.

- The power of positive stereotypes
- A struggle with identity

- Separation from family
- Balancing individual and communal styles

THE POWER OF POSITIVE STEREOTYPES

Positive images of men or women in some cultural groups sometimes lead to the creation of mixed matches. Some examples follow:

- "Black men are studs."
- "Jewish and Asian men are good providers and loyal husbands."
- "Asian women are compliant and sexy."

While these alluring images, some based on partial truths, others on wishful fantasy, are part of what motivates some marriages, they often do not fit with the reality of peoples' actual experiences. While some black men may enjoy and manipulate the images of sexuality attached to them, many feel oppressed by this stereotype. Not every black man wants to take advantage of or try to live up to the myth of superpotency. One African-American man I interviewed spoke somewhat bitterly about being rejected for not fitting into others' stereotypes:

I met this really interesting woman at a party who happened to be white. We talked for a long time and she seemed as interested in me as I was in her. When I told her that I was a computer programmer, she acted a little surprised and slightly disappointed, but we kept on talking. Then the music started playing and she asked me to dance. I told her that I wasn't a very good dancer because I couldn't keep the beat. That's when she made up some excuse about having to leave the party. I never saw her again.

It just brought up a lot of bad feelings. I had been rejected by some of the black kids I had gone to high school with because I studied so much. They used to tell me I was acting so white. And now I felt rejected once again for not being black enough, except this time by a white. I wish people could just see me as an individual.

Jewish and Asian men talked about feeling oppressed by expectations that they be superachievers. One man, a Chinese artist, complained that none of his teachers took his love of art seriously. They all assumed that he was a math or science major. An attractive Irish-American woman he met at a party seemed suddenly distant and disappointed when she discovered that his love was murals, not mathematics.

Many Asian-American women I interviewed felt burdened with images of what one Chinese woman I spoke with called the "Suzy Wong syndrome." She went on to say, "Men expect us Asian-American women to be passive and sexually receptive. We're supposed to fulfill every man's fantasies and validate any questions they might have about their masculinity. I don't want to sign on for that."

Even when people more or less fit into a positive stereotype of their group, they can feel constricted and limited by it. Not every sexual and attractive black man and Asian woman wants to spend their whole life living up to a youthful persona they developed. High-achieving Jewish and Asian men don't want to be always seen as production machines. Even the most positive and exciting stereotypes, when rigidly applied, become burdensome and limiting over time. As exciting as new love is, it is superficial. It glosses over differences, focuses on partial positive truths, and doesn't want to be disturbed with contradictions.

A STRUGGLE WITH IDENTITY

When a strong preference for partners from outside of one's group is combined with an intense dislike of the opposite-sex members of one's own cultural or racial group, it may be a manifestation of what psychologist and ethnotherapist Judith Weinstein Klein labeled *ambivalent identification*. Ambivalent indentifiers accept their own cultural label but uniformly reject members of the opposite sex of their own cultural group. They project the dominant culture's negative stereotypes about their cultural group onto the opposite-sex members of their own group. By placing the negative stereotypes onto the opposite sex, the minority-group member is unconsciously saying, *The negative stereotypes about us (blacks, Jews, Asians, Hispanics, etc.) are true—but they are only true of the opposite-sex members of my group. I don't like them for the same reasons you don't. But my half of the group is okay. Accept us.* When asked, "Why don't you go out with people from your own group?" the following answers are typical of these ambivalent identifiers:

> "All of my best friends are Chinese women like myself, but Chinese men are too nerdy and repressed."

> "I get along fine with other Jewish men, but Jewish women are too pushy and controlling."

> "I have no problem being a black man, but black women just try and yank the steering wheel of life out of your hands. I just won't put up with it."

This kind of struggle with identity can result from the tendency alternately to hate one's persecutors and to identify with them. The abysmal self-esteem of abused children demonstrates one of its most sadly common forms. Abused children can try to make sense of and survive in a crazy world by taking on the views of the powerful and cruel adults they are dependent upon. The larger social version of this phenomenon, which has been called identification with the aggressor, has been described in a variety of groups whose members are dependent on those who are prejudiced against them. Some Jews in concentration camps began to identify with their Nazi tormentors' degraded view of their Jewish prisoners, just as there are blacks whose self-hatred results from the internalized attitudes of white racists. Hate infects not only those who persecute others but can spread even to its victims.

Our images of what is beautiful and good are always measured against the attributes of those who are most powerful. A white man I spoke with who taught at a predominantly black elementary school told me how the children would come up to his desk and stroke the hair on his arms while telling him what "good" hair he had. It was just this sort of association of Caucasian characteristics with beauty and superiority that Malcolm X attacked as a form of self-hate when he urged his followers not to destroy their hair in an attempt to look more like whites. One could be both black and beautiful. While these ideas, first developed by the black-power movement, have had some success in helping blacks, Asians, Jews, and other minority-group members feel better about their natural appearance as well as their behavior, many still feel burdened by what they consider their physical and psychological inability to conform to white Protestant norms.

Throughout the world we have seen people who have come to adapt western European and American images of beauty and power as their own, feeling that evidence of their connection to their racial or cultural group somehow diminishes them. They have spent great amounts of time, energy, and money to change the contour of their faces, the color of their skin, the sound of their names, and the rhythms of their speech. Blacks still spend millions of dollars a year straightening their hair, Jews continue to get nose jobs, and surgery to shape eyes to look more Caucasian is a growth industry in Japan and even in Communist China. And for some, marriage to an outsider represents the ultimate strategy in trying to erase the stigma of a minority identity.

Paradoxically in these days of gender and cultural turnabouts, it's not just minorities who question their sense of identity. Even as some minority-group members have struggled to minimize or erase their distinct identities, many white Protestants have begun to wish they had one. Some WASPs experience themselves as "cultural orphans" and long for a sense of tribal connectedness. They may de-sexualize potential WASP partners and only be attracted to members of certain distinctly defined minority groups. Renee, a woman who had been raised as a Methodist in a midwestern city, described this phenomenon: "Yeah, most of my other women friends are white like me. And come to think of it, most of them are from WASP backgrounds. But I always seem drawn to Mediterranean or Hispanic men. I never get turned on by WASP guys because they just seem like white bread."

Robert Christopher points out in *Crashing the Gates: The De-WASPing of America's Power Elite* that no group has a weaker sense of itself than today's WASP. It's ironic that the white American Protestants, whose cultural images are powerful, pervasive, highly visible, and attractive to so many others, now look into the mirror and see no reflection. As diverse ethnic and racial groups, led by blacks in the sixties, have begun to assert their distinctiveness, it has become increasingly difficult to know what being a "real American" means. White Protestants, especially those of the middle class, began to have difficulty identifying with a concept as large and diffuse as "American." While persecuted minorities sometimes feel burdened with too strong an identity outside the "norm"—too much *somethingness*, WASPs can feel deprived by what seems to them to be their *nothingness*. Both the identity-hunger of the WASP and the self-hate of the minority-group member can lead to the same result—the desexualization of the opposite-sex members of one's group.

SEPARATION FROM FAMILY

Some family theorists have focused on how intermarriage is motivated by attempts to separate emotionally from dysfunctional families of origin. Edwin Friedman, the rabbi-therapist, in an article entitled "The Myth of the Shiksa," claimed that in the great majority of the Jewish-gentile couples he worked with, Jewish partners were motivated to marry out in an attempt to separate and individuate from Jewish parents they saw as intrusive and controlling. He went on to say that almost all either were first children who felt an undue amount of parental pressure by virtue of being the eldest or were the children "most triangulated" in their parents' marriage, acting as emotional go-betweens for unhappy spouses. In either case, Friedman argued, the children who are stuck in propping up their parents' marriages use intermarriage as a way to escape. He makes an important point. Some people, by choosing a partner from another race or religion unacceptable to their parents, use their relationships as a way to distance themselves, emotionally or literally, from complicated and painful family situations.

BALANCING INDIVIDUAL AND COMMUNAL STYLES

One of the most commonly cited reasons for attraction across religious-ethnic-racial lines is the fascination between people from individualistic and collectivistic cultures. Individualistic cultures

stress autonomy, self-realization, and personal initiative and decision making. Collectivistic cultures, on the other hand, stress loyalty
to the group and place a high value on the interconnectedness of
family, community, and society. Many Americans of northern and
western European descent, who were raised with individualistic cultural values, found themselves drawn to partners from more collective, communal cultures. They felt attracted to what seemed to be
the warmth and caring of their partners' more interdependent personal and family styles. Conversely many of the people from Latin
American, southern and eastern European, African-American, and
Asian backgrounds were drawn to the sense of autonomy and freedom that their cross-cultural partners seemed to embody.

When Alexis de Tocqueville studied American culture over 150
years ago, he coined the word *individualism* to describe the
dominant American ethos. He noted that the freedom from rigid
customs and overly strong family ties as well as an emphasis on
individual liberties and self-sufficiency created a flexibility that allowed Americans to explore and innovate. But he also saw that
the price of all this freedom was the isolation of the individual. In
the book *Habits of the Heart*, sociologist Robert Bellah and his
colleagues retraced de Tocqueville's path. Like de Tocqueville,
they found embedded within the strengths of American culture
the seeds of its biggest problems—the erosion of the traditional an-
chors of cultural identity, community, religion, and extended family.
They observed that it was increasingly difficult to know what held
people together in an incredibly mobile and rootless society. Increasingly it has become each person for himself or herself.

The northern European and white American Protestant culture
that has traditionally been at the center of what until now has
been known as American culture represents the most individualistic end of the continuum. It is strangely appropriate that only in

the English language is the word for the self, *I*, represented by a single capitalized letter, proud, tall, and unsupported on either side. People in these societies tend to expect love and intimacy between two individuals to be built on a foundation of self-disclosure, warmth, and mutual dependence. But for many the romantic expectations of individualistic cultures are often difficult to fulfill. The individualistic ideology of self-fulfillment that leads to expectations of romantic love also creates a psychology that makes it difficult for many to put another's interests ahead of their own— even that of their beloved. Egon Mayer, in his book *Love and Tradition*, observed that the idea of romantic love has existed for millennia, but that the reality of romantic love has been rare. Throughout history few societies have been either enriched or burdened with modern Western images of romantic love.

This concept of the separate, bounded, autonomous self that many Americans take for granted would be considered bizarre, if not downright evil, in many other more collective societies. In agrarian and less industrialized cultures it is clear to everyone that the fate of the individual and the fate of the group are inseparable. Even the technological achievements and modernity of Asian countries such as Japan have not transformed them into individualistic societies. While "love marriages" are more common in Japan than in the past, 50 percent of all marriages were arranged by families as recently as 1980. Unlike individualistic cultures, which place a high value on romantic love as a basis for marriage, collective cultures stress the nurturance that the family group, the social group, and the work group has to offer.

The Japanese construct of *amae*, which stresses a kind of passive dependence on others' benevolence, provides a good example of the emphasis on interdependence that characterizes Asian psychology. Japanese are shocked when they discover that such an important concept as *amae* lacks an equivalent word or concept in English.

Ida, a young woman from the Indonesian island of Bali, met Louis on the first day of his vacation to her island home. She was a woman who had tasted enough of Western culture to want to free herself from what increasingly felt like a constricted and limited life. She was educated, spoke excellent English, and had a great deal of contact with Western tourists. Without her family's permission she impulsively ran off to the United States with Louis at the end of his three-week vacation. But after a month in California she began to suffer from an intolerable symptom. She was certain that her head was literally swelling, growing larger day by day. The pain was unbearable, and she was convinced that her family had placed a curse on her for leaving and that if she did not return immediately, her head would explode and she would die. She frantically made her trip back to Bali and survived. But clearly, to act as such an independent agent in Balinese culture was truly to have "a swollen head."

Most Americans, at least those who ascribe to the Anglo-Protestant set of values, would be extremely uncomfortable with the Balinese definition of self. As members of the most individualistic culture on earth, to Americans the only commonly shared ideology is that everyone is unique. Each individual is therefore ultimately and individually responsible for his or her own destiny. Success and failure are private affairs.

Balinese culture is as intensely communal as American Anglo culture is individualistic. What traditional cultures such as Bali lack in personal freedom and autonomy, they replace with security and certainty. In those parts of Bali that have not been overrun with tourists, life is as it has always been—completely contained within the village and its traditions. The music, myths, and rituals of daily life have been repeated and reinforced over hundreds of years. The separate roles of men and women are perfectly clear. One's caste is determined by birth. Trades are passed from generation to generation. There are no words in Balinese that would translate into what we call "existential alienation."

In this age of mass migrations and easy travel across great distances, people from cultures that have had little to do with one another throughout history are suddenly thrown into close contact. Cultural assumptions that had been secure and stable for countless generations are suddenly challenged and sometimes uprooted. People living in communal cultures who are exposed to the freedom of the West suddenly find themselves feeling limited by traditions that had always seemed unquestionable. And Westerners who have had the opportunity to experience the unity and support that more communal cultures offer suddenly find their self-sufficiency and individualism very lonely. It's no wonder that people from opposite sides of the earth could feel so attracted to one another. Idealization is the other side of the coin of prejudice, and it is just as easy to project our wishes as well as our fears onto people and cultures unlike our own.

Gian and Shelly

Part of what attracted Gian and Shelly to each other was the very different emotional climates of their families and their very different feelings about group identity. Gian came from an intensely emotional and interdependent Italian-American family. The sense of boundaries between individuals was vague, the expectations of loyalty to the family were intense, and the pressure to remain close to the family—emotionally and physically—was ever-present. Shelly, on the other hand, came from a particularly disengaged

WASP family where autonomy and self-reliance were the most highly prized values. But these culturally bound differences, which were initially so attractive, later became the focus of conflict.

Gian summed up their differences by telling about his reaction to seeing *Annie Hall* recently at a theater that was showing a retrospective of Woody Allen's films:

> Shelly and I sat, mesmerized, through two consecutive showings of *Annie Hall* without leaving our seats, almost, it seemed, without even blinking. We felt as if Woody Allen had been a Peeping Tom looking through the window of our life. It wasn't really Alvy Singer (Woody Allen) and Annie Hall (Diane Keaton) in the film; it was us.
>
> There on the silver screen was Shelly's New England WASP, *Daughters of the American Revolution* family dinner table. They were so controlled, it was almost unbearable for me to watch. No one ever interrupted anyone else. They carefully picked at the tiny portions of food on their large plates. There was a slight pause between each word. Nothing of any emotional significance was discussed. The gravitational field that held the family together seemed weak, as if any moment everyone might begin to float away from the table and out the windows.
>
> The screen splits in two, and there was Woody Allen's family. They were just like mine when I was growing up. Everyone was crowded around the table, which was overflowing with food. People bumped elbows as they ate, talked, and interrupted each other. A woman talked about someone's coronary. A husband ate from his wife's plate as she cut his food and yelled at her brother at the same time. If it weren't for the table and the flesh that separated the family members, it seemed like they would all merge together to form a single six-headed being. I knew exactly what it felt like to be at that table.

Gian was as strongly drawn to Shelly's Yankee independence and self-sufficiency as she was to his Italian desire for contact. Gian was in effect offering Shelly a more intense, interactive emotional life and a more involved family style. Shelly was offering Gian a more contained emotional style with more respect for psychological boundaries and separateness from family. If they were to succeed as a couple, they would have to learn from each other and at least partially synthesize their differences. A conversation between them clearly revealed their mutual attraction:

> GIAN: I've been mellowized out here on the West Coast. I like how civilized Shelly's family is. When I go home to Brooklyn to visit my family, I just want to turn the volume down. I want to tell everybody to just relax a little bit. Not everything is *that* important.
>
> SHELLY: I'm attracted to their intensity. I would much rather have people yell and throw things than just turn off. In my family when people got mad, they didn't speak to one another or see one another—sometimes for five years at a stretch. To me that kind of silence is much more painful, much harder to take.

Yet just two years later, after Gian and Shelly had moved in with each other, these appealing differences became the source of conflict between them. Like many couples who have problems, they blamed each other. Gian was convinced that Shelly's admirable autonomy had somehow evolved into a form of emotional withholding. If he sometimes seemed needy, it was only because she was so withdrawn. She was just as certain that he had perversely transformed his warmth into an unpleasant intrusiveness. If she was distant, it was only to protect herself from his demands. What neither of them could understand was how the differences that had drawn them together seemed to have mutated into the forces that pushed them apart.

Gian had been raised to expect a demonstrative style of emotional support that Shelly, with her reserve, was not able to duplicate. While he sometimes resented what seemed like his parents' and siblings' intrusiveness, he also felt comforted by their frequent phone calls, their advice, their encouragement, and even by their quickness to argue with him. For better *and* for worse, he knew he was never really alone.

Gian began to realize that Shelly could be feeling supportive toward him even when she was silent. And Shelly tried to help Gian understand that the pleasure she got out of spending an evening alone in the library each week was not a way of rejecting him. Even though he could understand these differences intellectually, it was difficult to accept them emotionally. He recognized that a settled, committed relationship was far more complex and difficult than their early courtship.

To create a successful relationship with Gian, Shelly had to learn to express herself more directly and forcefully, especially around Gian's family and Italian friends. When she wasn't able to, she felt like an outsider. Yet even as she worked to turn up her own emotional volume, she had to accept that she and Gian would also always be different.

After a year of living together they began to recognize that Shelly could never fully match Gian's intensity and that Gian could never be as self-contained as Shelly. They could learn from each other, but they would never be the same. It was one thing to be attracted by each other's differences but quite another to learn to live with them.

In their struggles to understand each other, Gian and Shelly were negotiating more than getting their emotional needs met;

they were conducting a second conversation about cultural identity itself. Both were grappling with questions about their own sense of belonging. Gian was as ambivalent about the "somethingness" that was his Italian legacy as Shelly was about her "nothingness."

Gian had many negative associations attached to his blue-collar Italian background. He had grown up in a mixed Italian and Irish neighborhood. But the Catholic school he attended was run by Irish nuns, who, he felt, came down harder on the Italian kids. He hated their strictness and deeply resented having his hands hit with a ruler when the nuns said that he had misbehaved.

Even more confusing was his parents' attitude about being Italian. It was always clear to him that they preferred being around other Italians and—most of all—around other members of the family. But before he was born, his parents had changed their name from Guardino to Gardner. His father, the youngest of five brothers of immigrant parents from Salerno, was the most educated and successful. His marriage to Gian's mother, whose northern Piedmontese grandparents had immigrated to the United States a generation before his paternal grandparents, cemented his family's view of him as disloyal and elitist.

When Gian was in fourth grade, his family moved to a mostly WASP suburb. In spite of his dislike of the nuns, he missed his old neighborhood friends and seeing his grandparents as often as he had before the move. But the message of his upwardly mobile family was unmistakable: Play down being Italian. You are now an American. Be just like everyone else. Gian knew without asking that "everyone else" meant the WASPs they lived among.

Gian's marriage to Shelly, who wasn't even sure which northern European countries her ancestors had immigrated from, mirrored his father's marriage to a higher-status northern Italian. He had completed the process of assimilation. As an adult he spoke of his Italian heritage with a combination of vague nostalgia and dismissiveness: "Oh, yeah, sure I'm Italian. It's no big deal really. I like to see my parents and celebrate the holidays with them. But Shelly and I are not really different from anyone else."

Shelly, though, was interested in borrowing some of the identity that Gian and his family were so ambivalent about. When she spoke of her initial attraction to Gian, it became clear that part of her attraction was to his Italian heritage: "When I got involved with Gian, I felt that for the first time in my life I was becoming part of something bigger than just myself. I started taking evening courses in Italian language and literature. When we got married, I organized our honeymoon in Italy. But Gian always seemed a little reluctant. Sometimes I think I'm more interested in being part of Italian culture than he is."

Gian and Shelly's relationship revealed a paradox that is part of the relationships of many mixed matches: The cultural style and even the sense of identity that one partner finds attractive in the other may be precisely what the other partner rejects. The contrasts that are initially the most attractive can become the focus of a couple's most difficult conflicts as well as point the way toward their greatest potential for growth.

Ellie and Art

Many of the basic assumptions of the Taiwanese and American cultures that Ellie and Art grew up in were mirror images of each other. In collective and communal cultures such as the Chinese, the roles of men and women are clearly but rigidly differentiated. In modern American culture men and women from many different backgrounds interact, and sex roles are increasingly blurred.

While Chinese tend to be most comfortable with hierarchical social structures that emphasize clear lines of power, Americans
constantly rail against rules and authority.

The bonds of loyalty and obligation in Chinese culture are
tremendously strong and extend back through the generations. In
contrast, mobile middle-class Anglo-Americans expect and accept
that one generation may be geographically and emotionally isolated from the next. In Chinese culture, marriage exists in the context of extended family and long-term interfamily relationships.
Americans expect to make new sets of friends several times in
their lives and are expert at saying good-bye to friends and family
and building new, if sometimes superficial, relationships.

Ellie and Art's relationship brought together all of these differences between East and West. Art was thirty-seven years old and
was born and raised in an Irish Catholic family in Winnetka, a
prosperous suburb north of Chicago. Ellie was also thirty-seven,
but until 1987, when she moved with Art to the United States, had
spent all of her life in her native Taiwan. Ellie and Art had been
married for six years and had two young children—a boy, Max,
five, and a girl, Sara, three. Art described how they met:

> The company I work for, which is involved in software develop-
> ment, had assigned me to their office in Taipei. I had prepared
> for the position by studying Mandarin intensively in the States
> for six months, but I still couldn't speak that well when I arrived.
> I ended up spending a lot of time smiling, nodding, and saying,
> "Ni Hao," which was a common greeting I knew.
>
> I met Ellie at a business luncheon the second week I was in
> Taiwan. She worked in marketing for one of the companies my
> firm did business with. She spoke about as much English as I
> spoke Mandarin, but she was very patient and intelligent, and I

had my first really satisfying human contact since I had arrived in Taiwan with her over lunch that day.

We quickly realized that there was some form of chemistry, of electricity passing between us. *Yuan fen* is a Chinese concept, not of fate but of a kind of resonance. We were consciously trying to resist this force that seemed to be pulling us together. Language, nationality, and religion separated us. But in spite of our best intentions and what seemed to be the impossible nature of our relationship, it wasn't long before we started spending more time together. We could communicate and understand each other even though neither of us was really fluent in the other's language. We felt like we had known each other for a long time.

Three months later Ellie asked me to have dinner at her parents' house. They assumed that we were just business associates and had no idea that we had become romantically interested in each other. It was the first time I had been invited to dinner in a Chinese home. They had these two little, irritating yapping dogs running all around the house. And her sister spoke in a high-pitched, sweet nasal voice which is very popular and cultivated by Chinese women. It's not a natural voice, and for me it was a shock. I immediately got worried. I knew we were very attracted to each other, but would meeting her family be a disaster?

Ellie's mother welcomed me as an honored guest by serving a real delicacy—duck's feet. Of course I was expected to eat them. When her mother wasn't running in and out of the kitchen to serve us, she stood next to me to see how I was enjoying this rare treat. She kept asking me to "please eat more." As you might imagine, ducks' feet taste much like they look—like warm rubber, like old tires. Suddenly I was looking furtively about for those obnoxious dogs each time she left the room. Maybe I could get them to eat the ducks' feet. But they didn't seem any more interested in them than I was. I ended up sneaking them into my pockets. I just couldn't bring myself to swallow them, no matter how hard I tried.

Ellie went on to explain some of the reasons she was receptive to romance with an outsider:

I was thinking about what Art said about my sister's voice. It brings up a sore point. My mother would often criticize my voice. She thought that it was too low and that I should develop some kind of sweeter voice. She thought it was not feminine or ladylike enough. And I also often got the message that I was too loud and aggressive. My family saw me as a tomboy.

And I was the darkest one in the family. That wasn't good. My mother was always telling me to carry an umbrella to keep the sun off of me. Neighbor women and my aunts would feel free to walk up to me and say, "Oh, you're such a pretty girl, but you're so dark." And to make matters even worse, my family thought I was too "friendly" with strangers in a way that implied I might be sexual. I never felt like a typical Chinese.

I think the other thing that made me receptive to an outsider is that I had real mixed feelings about some of the values of my culture. Especially late in high school, the academic pressure is unbearable because there are only a limited number of openings in the university. I knew several students who committed suicide by throwing themselves off of the education building during their senior year in high school. Even though I was accepted to college and was academically successful, I hated the conformity that was demanded of us and the way that the pressure destroyed spontaneity. It made me very curious about the outside world.

I was also angry about some aspects of the role of women in Chinese society. I call it the cult of virginity. If you are not a virgin, forget it. Some girls have surgical reconstruction if they are not virgins or if their hymens have been broken some other way. And when a woman is raped, she is the one who is shamed and considered unworthy of marriage. Many of the more obvious abuses of women are part of the past; women no longer have their feet bound. But men still expect a lot of male prerogatives.

An intelligent and adventurous woman, Ellie was part of the first generation of Taiwanese women to have meaningful contact with people and ideas from outside of Chinese culture. But the effects of social progress are often paradoxical. Even though she had more freedom than her mother and women of past generations, exposure to the possibilities of the outside world made Ellie feel more confined by the limits of her own.

Ellie's decision to marry Art was not a simple one. It involved some losses. She explained her feelings in a firm voice tinged with a little sadness:

> Don't get me wrong. There are many things about being Chinese that I value very highly, including the respect for learning, tradition, and family. In spite of my reservations about some aspects of my culture, being Chinese is still very important to me. I know that my roots lie in the Chinese culture that nurtured me and that I never want to lose my connection to it. Even though I have married and live in the Caucasian world, a big part of me remains with my parents and grandparents. We plan to spend this summer in Taiwan with the children, and it's important to me that they know about their Chinese heritage.

When Art speaks about the beginning of his relationship with Ellie, he also attributes much of his attraction to *yuan fen*, the experience of a harmony that transcends cultural barriers. And although his personality and his life in the United States were very different from Ellie's, he also longed for possibilities that did not seem readily available in the world he was born into. But his path to intermarriage was precisely the opposite of Ellie's. She was looking for a world that was more accepting of a bright and forceful woman; he was looking for someone who appreciated his more contemplative nature.

> In high school I was always identified as the quiet and intellectual type. Coming of age in the early seventies, I tried to be "with it" like my older brother and sister, but I never really felt comfortable with the kinds of radical experimentation that so many people were involved with at the time.

Ellie's description of the lack of privacy and personal boundaries she had experienced in Chinese culture contrasted sharply with Art's portrayal of his family's subdued emotional climate and of the lack of connection to others in the upper-middle-class suburban American environment he grew up in.

> If I had to characterize my family life, I would say it was pretty quiet. We lived in the suburbs and it never felt like a real community. It was like every home was a world unto itself. We didn't know what our neighbors were up to and they didn't really know what we were doing. All the rest of my extended family lived out-of-state, so my mother, my father, my brother, my sister, and myself were it.
>
> My mother was a housewife who was involved in volunteer work and my father was a physician. He was gone a lot, and when he was around, he wasn't too available. My mother would

worry that I was too involved in my own little world and tried to encourage me to go out more and become more involved with life, but I was more comfortable with my books and my studies. I guess you'd have to say that I came from a pretty emotionally austere family.

I started dating late, around nineteen, and I found myself attracted to women who came from backgrounds that were more intense than my own. I was involved with an Italian woman for several years, but that didn't work out. She was an emotionally tumultuous person, and I just didn't feel I could handle her intensity. But I knew I didn't want to live a life that was as emotionally isolated as the one I had been raised in. And I did kind of associate that emotional sterility with people who had been raised like I had been, in a white upper-middle-class environment.

Sharing a feeling of being different from the norms of their own cultures, therefore, did not make Ellie and Art similar to each other. If Ellie felt suffocated by the intense and rigid expectations of Chinese family and culture, Art suffered from the void created by the lack of definition in his own. If Ellie sought a more flexible role as a woman through her marriage to an outsider, Art was looking for a more clearly defined role.

In important ways their personal and cultural differences seemed to enable both Ellie and Art to offer each other much of what they each needed. From her Chinese perspective, Ellie saw herself as too extroverted and aggressive. She found in Art an acceptance that she had never before experienced. Even though Ellie was not "feminine" enough for her family, she was the most traditionally feminine woman Art had ever known. And while Art had always worried that he was not assertive enough, Ellie's appreciation of his sensitivity and intelligence helped him to feel good about himself. They both felt that their differences, rather than being obstacles to their relationship, had enriched each of their lives in important ways.

EXERCISE: Family Inventories

The attraction between you and your partner is partially a function of your positive and negative feelings about your own culture and family of origin as well as those of your partner. You can use the following exercise to better understand why you and your partner chose each other. It will help you clarify some of the sources of attraction in your relationship, and it will lay the foundation for later chapters, which focus on dealing with misunderstandings and difficulties.

You and your partner should do this exercise separately. Later you will share what you have written.

Make two identical charts (see below) and label one "My Family" and the other "My Partner's Family."

MY FAMILY		
	POSITIVES	NEGATIVES
Sex Roles		
Family Involvement		
Emotional Expression		
Cultural Identity		
Religion		

MY PARTNER'S FAMILY		
	POSITIVES	NEGATIVES
Sex Roles		
Family Involvement		
Emotional Expression		
Cultural Identity		
Religion		

Sex Roles: The division of roles of men and women in
your (your partner's) family regarding work, power,
money, housework, and child rearing.

Family Involvement: Sense of concern, mutual
involvement, and support in your (your partner's) family.

Emotional Expression: The intensity and nature of
emotional expression in your (your partner's) family.

Cultural Identity: The manner and intensity with which
your (your partner's) family expresses its cultural
identity.

Religion: The way your (your partner's) family expresses
its religious beliefs.

Use each sheet and write down some adjectives or a sentence or
two that describe your feelings and perceptions about your family
and your partner's family in relation to each of these dimensions.
Don't worry about creating a balanced perspective. The goal of
this exercise is to get in touch with your emotional responses to
these issues and to increase your self-understanding.

Don't be "politically correct," be emotionally honest. And don't be concerned if your "positives" and "negatives" seem to cancel each other out. We often have contradictory feelings that seem incompatible. We may not like it, but ambivalence is central to the human condition. By learning to acknowledge our mixed feelings, we are much better able to deal with them. Denying them gives them too much power over us.

The following charts were completed by a woman from a Mexican-American background who was married to an Irish-Catholic man:

MY MEXICAN-AMERICAN FAMILY		
	POSITIVES	NEGATIVES
Sex Roles	No ambiguity. Women knew their roles and men knew theirs.	Rigid expectations. No chance for women to experiment.
Family Involvement	Knew my family would always be there for me. No doubt about the strength of our connection.	Felt suffocated at times. Felt guilty if I tried to be independent.
Emotional Expression	I liked how warm and expressive everyone was.	Sometimes felt embarrassed by how boisterous my family was in public.
Cultural Identity	Felt proud of my traditions.	Felt ashamed that people looked down on us because we were Mexican. I used to trade my tortillas for white bread with a friend before school.
Religion	Loved pageantry of Church as I was growing up.	Turned off by rigid morality of Church as I got older.

MY PARTNER'S IRISH-AMERICAN FAMILY		
	POSITIVES	NEGATIVES
Sex Roles	Seems like women have a little more freedom.	Men seem less involved in family life.
Family Involvement	Everyone was free to do their own thing.	No one seemed very connected to one another.
Emotional Expression	They are more "polite" in public than my family was.	Family seems very cool compared with mine, except when they got boisterous after drinking at parties.
Cultural Identity	Being Irish-American makes it easy to fit in. Seems just white to me.	Being Irish doesn't really seem that important to them.
Religion	They don't take the Church as seriously. Makes it easier not to get caught up in all the rules.	Their version of being Catholic seemed much more austere. Not much color or celebration.

When you have finished your inventories, set aside an hour with your partner and share your responses with each other. Remember that as simple as this exercise is, it taps into deep feelings about family and culture. It's difficult enough to acknowledge negative feelings about your own culture, and hearing your partner's reservations about your heritage may be very unsettling. Be especially sensitive to your partner's reaction when you talk about your feelings about his or her heritage.

This exercise can provide you with important information about the roots of both the attraction between you and of some of the misunderstandings in your relationship. Acknowledging these feelings will help point the way to how your relationship can help you grow and develop as two individuals and as a couple. Like Eliza Doolittle and Henry Higgins, you have much to learn from each other.

CHAPTER 3

Decoding Cultural Conflict

We were having a very heated discussion this weekend about whether to buy the house we were looking at. To me it felt like an argument. I said to Bob that we shouldn't buy the house if we were arguing, and he said, "Who's arguing? We're having a discussion. We're not arguing."

It's taken me two years to begin to realize that for Bob a raised voice doesn't mean an argument. After we visited his family in Chicago last year, I could really see where he learned that way of expressing himself. I've learned that his family and my family really do have different cultural codes, and it takes some of the pressure off. Even though I still get a little tense when he gets too animated, I'm now able to take a deep breath and say to myself, "It's going to be okay." I don't have to back down, nor do I have to fight for my life.

KAREN, WHOSE GRANDPARENTS IMMIGRATED TO THE UNITED STATES FROM NORWAY, TALKING ABOUT HER RELATIONSHIP WITH HER HUSBAND, BOB, WHO WAS BORN IN PUERTO RICO, BUT WAS RAISED IN CHICAGO FROM THE TIME HE WAS TWO YEARS OLD

While the novelty of contrasting backgrounds can be exciting, misunderstandings resulting from different cultural codes can lead to conflict.

In relationships with people we know *less* well, we may be more likely to make some allowances for personal and cultural differences. While we may not always like those differences, at least we are not too surprised by them. But in intimate relationships feelings of closeness and connection can disguise the fact that our partner is viewing the world through a very different set of cultural lenses. When we don't recognize just how different those lenses are, we set ourselves up to painfully misunderstand our partners' intentions and the meaning of their behavior. We may misinterpret behavior that is *intended* to convey respectful emotional restraint as rejection, or passionate excitement as a threat of violence.

A World of Differences

Just as children cannot identify the complex rules of grammar and syntax that they learn and successfully use long before they study them in school, we usually cannot clearly describe the rules of our culture. But these complex and largely invisible cultural codes permeate every aspect of our beliefs and behavior and are primal in their power. They are programmed into us from birth by our mother's touch, the smells and sounds of our home, and the entire social world we were raised in. They have a profound influence on our attitudes about money and work, what kind of behavior we consider to be on time or late, eating habits, child rearing and discipline, flirting and sex, small talk and big talk, why and how we get angry, or how we apologize.

Jorge and Marla's relationship clearly illustrates the effect that even subtle cultural differences can have on a relationship, years after people leave the direct influence of their birth cultures. Jorge and Marla lived in Tucson, Arizona, and were both twenty-eight years old when they met. Jorge was born and raised in an upper-middle-class family in Monterey, Mexico. When he was eighteen, he moved to Los Angeles to live with his aunt so that he could study structural engineering at UCLA. Marla, who worked as an architect, had been raised by her middle-class Irish-WASP family in Los Angeles.

Six months before meeting Marla, Jorge had gone through a painful breakup with his previous girlfriend. His old girlfriend had accused him of being too intense, too demanding, too dependent, and too preoccupied with sex. He was determined that his next relationship would be with a woman who would not be frightened by his emotional intensity or his sexuality.

Before meeting Jorge, Marla had been involved in an unsatisfying three-year relationship with a WASP man whose upbringing had been similar to her own. They had met at the architectural firm where they both worked. In that relationship Marla had felt stuck in the role of the pursuer. She complained that she always felt like a beggar with him, pleading for time, conversation, and sex, all of which he doled out sparingly. She made a resolution that in the future she would avoid men who worked in technical professions and that any man she got involved with would not be another distancer.

Marla immediately felt drawn to Jorge's warmth when they met at a mutual friend's party. He seemed so different from her former boyfriend. She distinctly remembered how close he stood to her during their first conversation. She felt that his body language clearly communicated his interest in her, and she responded to what she perceived as his advance by looking directly into his eyes and lightly touching his arm. He didn't fit her negative stereotype of a "technical type," so she immediately forgave him for being an engineer. They danced alone in a quiet room for an hour before leaving the party together.

Jorge's memory of that initial meeting was quite different. He remembered feeling reserved and keeping his distance for the first fifteen minutes they talked. Even though he thought Marla was very attractive, he didn't want to take any chances. He was still recovering from the rejection he felt in his last relationship. He clearly recalled Marla's touch as the first sign that she might be interested in him and that it would be safe to relax a little. *At last*, he remembered thinking to himself, *a woman who is not afraid to be warm.*

In a sense their relationship began because of an interlocking set of misunderstandings. Both of them were convinced that the other had been the first to invite closer contact. Neither of them felt that they had been ready to risk reaching out to someone who did not reach out to them first. Months later they teased each other about who had made the "first move." But in those early days of their relationship neither of them actually cared very much about who really made the first move, because they fell passionately in love.

A year later they moved in together and, a short time after, got engaged. On the way to mail the invitations for their wedding, they got into a big fight. Marla was very upset about how seductively Jorge had behaved with another woman at a party the night before. Jorge was hurt by Marla's lack of trust, because he knew that he had been simply behaving in a friendly but nonsexual manner. He became very angry, grabbed the box of invitations, threw them in the back of his car, and said that it was clear that they weren't ready to get married.

Their fight was set off by unacknowledged contrasts in their cultural codes. Just as they had each seen the other as making the "first move" when they met, they were now just as convinced that the other had initiated the current conflict. Since they were in love, they had incorrectly assumed that they understood the meaning of each other's behavior. They didn't.

Psychiatrist Carlos Sluzki observed, in "The Latin Lover Revisited," that all cultures have rules that define the meaning of placing one's body at close, intermediate, or distant positions relative to another person. These rules are crucial in the ways we define and negotiate our relationships. We use our bodies like the subtitles in a foreign movie. They tell us what's really going on.

We reserve the distant zone to communicate respect *or* dislike, the intermediate zone to convey an emotionally neutral social interaction, and the close zone to broadcast threat *or* sexual interest. In almost all cultures, standing in the close zone and smiling at someone of the opposite sex has connotations of intimacy or sexuality.

The definition of these zones is programmed into us by our observations of social interaction beginning in infancy. How and when our parents touch us, watching our family interact with kin, friends, and strangers, and the responses of schoolmates to our awkward experiments in touch all provide us with an intuitive and visceral sense of the appropriate use of our bodies. No one ever has to spell it out, but we all end up knowing the exact definition of each of the zones within a centimeter or two. But, as Sluzki points out, the distances are "relative rather than absolute." Latin American zones happen to specify shorter distances than Anglo-American zones. In each of the three zones Latin Americans tend to position themselves closer to those they interact with than Anglo-Americans do. These differences create the potential for misinterpretations; distances the Latin defines as neutral the Anglo may interpret as threatening or sexual, while distances the Anglo defines as being in the close zone may be seen as neutral by the Latin.

When Marla saw Jorge speaking to the other woman, she saw him standing in what was, from her Irish/Anglo-American perspective, the zone that connoted sexual interest. But for Jorge the distance was, from his Mexican cultural framework, the middle, neutral zone reserved for social and nonsexual conversations. He was using the same set of cultural rules that had guided his behavior the first time he and Marla met. Both Marla's initial positive reaction to Jorge and her negative reaction to his behavior with the woman at the party resulted from the same culturally based misinterpretation of his actions.

Social scientists have long observed that a combination of nonverbal and subverbal forms of communication—body language, silences, interruptions, and the tone, intensity, and tempo of our words—convey more information than the actual content of what we say. Words themselves are like the notes of a musical score written down on paper. They are brought alive only by how they are performed. The way we use and interpret nonverbal cues determines the emotional significance we give to our own words and to those of others. And every aspect of how we use and interpret words is governed by our cultural conditioning.

The unconscious rules that governed Jorge's behavior and Marla's emotional reactions to it were part of primal cultural codes that were as invisible as air but as specific as if they were written in stone. These rules are very resistant to change, because they are mostly unconscious and learned early in life. Neither their love for each other nor Jorge's successful adaptation to American culture could erase the differences in their cultural conditioning.

Six Cultural Dimensions

It would be an impossible task to list all of the specific differences that define the myriad variations that exist between different cultures. It took a thick book by social anthropologist Desmond Morris and his colleagues just to outline how the meanings of twenty different hand gestures varied throughout Europe. But partners in mixed matches need a framework to describe and understand their differences. It's useful to think about the contrasts between cultures in terms of six broad organizing dimensions:

- Time
- The nature of the universe
- Cohesiveness of the family
- Emotional expressiveness
- Interpersonal relations
- Gender roles

Every culture has a mix of attitudes about each of these dimensions with a most-valued, secondary, and least-valued form. The specific priorities a culture assigns to each of these dimensions influence the way its members interpret all of the inevitable ambiguities of the human condition. In any given setting these cultural value preferences serve as a personal compass that points people toward their culture's definition of correct behavior, shaping inner experience as well as outer behavior. The sets of cultural rules that partners in mixed matches bring to their relationships may be comfortably similar in one or more of these dimensions, and disturbingly different in others. As you read through the descriptions of each of the six dimensions, reflect on which values are most and least important in your family and culture.

	FUTURE	PRESENT	PAST
TIME	Always plan ahead for tomorrow.	The enjoyment of today is most important.	Remember and honor family and cultural history.

"Time is money," "Every second counts," and "The early bird catches the worm" are maxims that define Western culture. It is very clear to the future-oriented Western European and Anglo-American that time is measured in very small increments and that the future is determined by what we do now. In future-oriented societies time is measured in minutes, seconds, and increasingly in nanoseconds. The obsession with time is not a celebration of the moment. Rather it represents an attempt to shape and control the future, which is its focus. To the extent that a culture is future-oriented, it stresses production, accomplishment, and accumulation of wealth.

For traditional societies, whose values and roots go back to the land and agriculture, time is more likely to be measured in seasons, not seconds. The peasant and the farmer know that they cannot control the future or the weather. When today is all that one can do anything with, life is focused on the present. When work is done, the person in the present-oriented culture knows that the free moments are to be used for rest and pleasure. Tomorrow's day of labor will be here soon enough. Southern Italy and rural Mexico are examples of cultures where today is most important.

In certain past-oriented Asian cultures the most important unit of time is generations. One's actions are constantly influenced by the memory and values of those who have come before. Family shrines in the home are constant reminders of the importance of ancestors, tradition, and the past.

No culture is purely present-, past-, or future-oriented. But cultures vary in the importance they place on each of these temporal frames of reference. Different cultural time frames may be part of what people find attractive about one another as well as a source of conflict. These different values about time may mean that partners in a mixed match have very different definitions of what constitutes being late, how important achievement and production are, and even when to eat or sleep.

	GOOD	INDIFFERENT	EVIL
THE NATURE OF THE UNIVERSE	Life and people are inherently good. There is a force that makes things turn out for the best.	Life is neither inherently good nor evil. We are responsible for trying to make it good.	You must never put your guard down. Human life is difficult, and people can't be trusted to be good.

Does life have some intrinsic orderliness? Or do we live in a random and ultimately meaningless universe out of which we ourselves have to create any pleasure, satisfaction, or meaning? Are people naturally evil or good? Are children amoral creatures who have to be taught to distinguish between right and wrong?

It's not just theologians and philosophers who struggle with these ultimate questions about the nature of the universe. We all do. In intimate relationships each partner's existential perspective affects how he or she approaches the business of life. The ways that people create answers to these questions are shaped not only by their religious heritages but by the history of their cultural group. Even the worldview of assimilated and secular grandchildren of immigrants is deeply affected by the historical experience of their ancestors. The history of slavery for African-Americans, the Holocaust for Jews, the struggles for survival of Southeast Asian refugees, the Civil War for southerners, Hiroshima for the Japanese, and the genocide of the Armenians early in the twentieth century are existential shocks that reverberate through the generations.

It's not just trauma that shapes peoples' worldviews. Even though they often have difficulty seeing the shape of their experience, sixth-generation New England Yankees whose families have been secure in America for two hundred years are just as affected by the experience of their ancestors as anyone else. The hyper-individualism and stoicism of the WASP are just as much products of their historical experience as is the anxiety of Jews and the anger of blacks. Whether ignored or worshiped, the effects of cultural history are powerful and pervasive.

Ulysses and Connie have lived side by side for fifteen years, sharing everything but their views of the universe. Connie's universe was basically safe and benevolent; Ulysses' was not. Contrasts in their cultural backgrounds and life experiences made it inevitable that they would see life very differently.

He was Greek-American, and she half jokingly called herself a "generic American." They said they had a "few differences" in their attitudes about their two children, and went on to joke about how their backgrounds affected the way they parented.

> CONNIE: My family does not worry. When I was thirteen, my father gave me ten flying lessons for a present.
>
> ULYSSES: I was lucky [at that age] to be able to cross the street myself.

But as they continued talking, it became increasingly clear that what they had lightly touched on had much deeper personal and cultural significance to them. Child rearing revealed the interaction of individual and cultural history.

Ulysses' parents had immigrated to the United States from Greece after World War II. A number of Ulysses' relatives had been killed during the war, and the tough, blue-collar neighborhood in Newark, New Jersey, where they settled further rein-forced his parents' feelings that the world was a dangerous place. When Ulysses was four, his six-year-old cousin, who lived down the street, was killed in a car accident. The accident added per-sonal tragedy to the family's cultural anxiety.

Connie, whose Methodist family had been in the United States "longer than we can trace back," had grown up not far away in the very comfortable upper-middle-class town of Montclair, New Jer-sey. In that safe and protected community Connie's parents en-couraged her to go out and freely explore the world. To them the world seemed as safe and secure as it seemed dangerous to Ulysses' parents.

Ulysses and Connie didn't really come face-to-face with the way their different pasts affected them as a family until their oldest child, Andy, turned five. Their conflict occurred during a discus-sion about how old Andy had to be before he could walk down the street to his friend Patrick's house. Connie felt it was important to encourage Andy's independence. Ulysses thought that letting a five-year-old walk a block alone was a totally unacceptable risk. When Connie pointed out what a safe neighborhood and quiet street they lived on, Ulysses picked up a newspaper that had a front-page story about the kidnapping of a child in suburban Long Island.

Ulysses' Greek family's protectiveness was just as "normal" for them as it was for Connie's WASP family to grant the freedom to explore the world at a young age. Their reactions to the idea of Andy walking down the street provided a clear example of the contrasts in their cultural and personal frames of reference.

Their differences over child rearing led them into discussions about their pasts. Their grasp of each other's histories had always been more intellectual than emotional. They had treated the dif-

ferences in their backgrounds as the material for jokes, using humor to distance themselves from the very different emotional realities of their pasts. But the debate about Andy brought their
different histories into focus.

	ENMESHED	MIXED	DISENGAGED
COHESIVENESS OF THE FAMILY	To be separate from family is to be missing an essential part of yourself.	The needs of the family and of the individual need to be balanced.	The individual and his or her needs are more important than those of the family.

A culture's values regarding family connections, interdependence,
and loyalty shape the nature of parents' and children's relationships,
the frequency of interaction between members of the nuclear family
as well as the extended family, and the process of separation and in-
dividuation that children go through as they develop.

Leaving home provides dramatic illustrations of cultural contrasts
in the cohesiveness of families from different cultural groups. For
example James, an Irish-American married to Teresa, an Italian-
American, discovered just how different their values were as their
oldest child, Jay, was getting ready to apply to college. Teresa felt
very strongly that Jay should live at home, at least for his first two
years of college. James was equally adamant that Jay have the freedom to make his own decisions about where to go to school. In spite
of their common Catholic backgrounds, their notions of how much
independence should be granted their children were very different.
Stimulated by the conflict over Jay, they began to talk about their
own experiences of leaving home for the first time. Their conversa-

tion revealed that, relative to each other, James's Irish home was as disengaged as Teresa's Italian family was enmeshed.

James described a scene of emotional disconnectedness as he told his story of leaving home to go into the army:

> I got the Selective Service Bureau to draft me in September. I knew about it several months before I was to go in. I told my mother in mid-August, "Oh, by the way, I'm going into the army in two weeks." I guess I should have told her a little sooner, but it didn't seem like that big a deal.

The contrast between James's story and Teresa's provided a vivid illustration of the kinds of cultural differences that can deeply affect the relationships of mixed matches. Teresa had lived with her parents all through college. After graduating she felt that she needed to "learn how to be more independent." She decided to move from her family's home in Columbus, Ohio, to a world that seemed far away and alien—California. But leaving wasn't so easy. Over twenty years after she left, her memory of the final good-bye scene with her mother was still vivid!

> I remember my mother is downstairs pressing my blouses in the basement, and she starts crying. She's pressing this green blouse, I'll never forget it, and I know that my friend Mickey is on her way to pick me up. And she starts crying, "Why you gotta do this, Teresa, why do you have to go?" And I swear to God, my arms were coming up. I could feel them moving, and I was just going to throw them up and say, "Okay, I'm not going," and just then the horn blew outside. I got my bag, kissed my mom, grabbed my blouse, and I left. I felt like I was eloping.

When asked how often they now had contact with their extended families, they answered in culturally characteristic ways. James said that he had "a lot" of contact with his family and was very close with them. Teresa, on the other hand, answered rather sadly that she often missed her family and was only "seldom" able to get together with them because they lived so far away. She said that if it wasn't for the expense of flying to visit them, she would want to see them much more often. But when I asked James what he meant by "a lot" and Teresa what she meant by "seldom," it became apparent that the meaning of their words only made sense when placed in a cultural context.

> JAMES: What I mean by saying that I have a lot of contact with my family is that I call them every month or so and visit them at least twice a year—usually at Christmas and Easter. I've always considered my family close. But if I was expected to see them much more often than I do, I'd feel a little smothered.

Just how different was James's cultural frame of reference became clear when Teresa talked about how "seldom" she had contact with her family. While James almost felt smothered by twice-a-year visits, five times a year wasn't enough for Teresa.

> TERESA: I miss my family a lot. I talk to my mother and father every Sunday for about a half hour. We only get to visit them about five times a year, and I feel really bad for myself, our children, and my parents that we don't get to see each other more often.

	HIGH INTENSITY	MIXED	HIGH FORMALITY
EMOTIONAL EXPRESSIVENESS	Feelings are meant to be expressed.	It's only okay to show how you feel in particular situations.	Emotional self-control is most important.

Cultures that stress a high level of emotional intensity are those that value emotional engagement more than calmness and order. High-formality cultures, on the other hand, are more rule-bound and structured, especially when it comes to social interaction. While we may associate high intensity with tight, enmeshed families, emotional expressiveness and family cohesiveness are independent characteristics. Both Spanish and Japanese cultures foster enmeshed-style families. Both value keeping child and parent tightly emotionally bound. But the rules governing the expression of emotion in the two cultures are vastly different.

My interviews with a Spanish/Japanese-American couple demonstrated how different styles of expressing emotion can be, even when both partners share common class and educational backgrounds. Sam, a second-generation Spanish-American, and Adrian, a Japanese-American, had been married for twenty years.

Neither of their families had been very religious, and they had never actively practiced any religion during their marriage. They had both gone to the same college, where they met studying journalism, and eventually went on to build a small public relations business together. They also shared common memories of growing up in families where there had been a lot of disagreements and anger. In fact when they first met, they had felt that conflict in their families was part of what they had in common. But as their relationship progressed, they learned that what they each meant by the word *conflict* was very different.

When asked what conflict was like in his family, Sam reported,

> Oh, my aunts and uncles and cousins would come over on Sunday afternoons and all the adults would get into these heated political debates and people would get all excited and shout at one another. It was actually kind of exciting and fun.

The contrast with Adrian's description of what she called conflict was stunning:

> Well, my mother and father and brother and myself would each sit on a different side of the large dining-room table. And if someone was angry, we would sit in silence. When it was really bad, the whole meal could pass without a word. There were these kinds of angry, tense glances at each other, but that was as far as it went.

Even though Sam and Adrian were bright, articulate people who were aware of the cultural contrasts they brought to their marriage, the different meanings of silence continue to affect them on an emotional level to this day.

> ADRIAN: When Sam is quiet, even though I know in my head that nothing is really wrong, I still have this uneasy feeling in my gut that if he doesn't say anything, it means that he must be angry. For me, growing up, the silent treatment was the worst punishment I got.
>
> SAM: In my family it was hardly ever quiet. And if someone didn't like something you did, you heard about it fast and loud. I really savor silence now—for me it means I feel really relaxed and content.

	HIERARCHICAL	COOPERATIVE	INDIVIDUALISTIC
INTERPERSONAL RELATIONS	Respecting authority and tradition are most important.	The needs of the group are more important than the needs of any one person.	Each person is ultimately responsible for self.

The relational style of a culture describes how it organizes social relationships. The three basic styles are hierarchical, cooperative (or collective), and individualistic.

People in hierarchical societies, such as Japan's, tend to use status, age, power, or caste as the primary organizers of social life. In individualistic societies, such as the United States, individual rights are protected, and the responsibility for success and failure falls upon the individual. The fluidity of American society requires constant interaction with new people. Minimizing differences in authority and creating a quick sense of familiarity with strangers are essential in lubricating the social gears of a culture where the only constant is change. Most Europeans and Asians, for example, would be shocked by the expectation of Americans that their leaders behave like "just ordinary folks." England can support kings and queens and Japan emperors and empresses, but American mythology, and sometimes reality, focuses on how common people can transcend the limitations of birth.

Collective cultures put the interests and welfare of the group before the importance of authority or the rights of the individual. Collective cultures are typically agriculturally based societies or ethnic groups who are minorities in a hostile environment. For these people the survival of the group is dependent on close cooperation. In spite of their dramatic differences, the Mexican peasant, the southern Italian farmer, and the prewar Eastern European

Jew knew that the survival of the individual and the survival of the group were inseparable. The solitary Rambo hero so worshiped in American culture was inconceivable to those whose fate was totally interdependent with others.

Alicia and Boris's sometimes-conflicting values about interpersonal relationships grew out of the very different cultural milieus in which they were raised. They met six years ago when Alicia, a Caucasian-American woman from a liberal Protestant background, was on a tour of Russia. A Russian college teacher, she was traveling with a group of her colleagues. She and Boris met at a reception for the Leningrad Symphony, where Boris was a cellist, and had a whirlwind romance during the three remaining weeks of Alicia's trip. They wrote each other romantic letters every day for six months after Alicia returned to the United States. Then they decided to marry. After a lengthy and difficult process in which Boris lost his job for trying to emigrate, he was finally able to join Alicia in America, "the land of milk and honey where all the streets are paved with gold." Well, not exactly.

Actually their first year together in America was very difficult. Even though life in Russia had been oppressive, Boris had enjoyed the prestige and status of his position with the symphony. In the United States he had to take what he considered menial work— giving music lessons to children who seemed spoiled and ungrateful for all that they had. It bothered him that Alicia made more money than he did. And he found English a difficult and illogical language. Boris was, in two words, immensely frustrated.

Maybe the whole idea of marrying Alicia and coming to America had been a mistake. Maybe he should have remained with the life he had known. To make matters worse, Boris had been suffering from lower-back pain since the first week he had been in the States. He had tried to ignore it for several months, but finally, with great reluctance, he decided to go to a doctor. He was wary and anxious about the prospect of getting involved with what he viewed as the frightening world of high-tech American medicine.

Alicia went to the doctor with Boris to make sure that his imperfect English wouldn't lead to any misunderstandings. As they walked out of the clinic after the appointment, Boris was visibly upset. "I can't believe it," he complained to her in Russian. "I go to get help for this terrible back pain, and all the nurses and the doctor think it is funny. I'm sick of America and all these grinning heads. Why is everybody always smiling?"

Alicia was totally caught off guard. She replied, "They didn't think your problem was funny. They were just being friendly." Boris erupted in anger. The fight that ensued lasted hours.

What had happened in the clinic? Both Alicia and Boris had been in the examining room together. Alicia had found the doctor warm and respectful. In fact she was surprised when he had taken a few extra minutes to ask some personal questions and had even used some humor to try to relax Boris. When the doctor gave Boris a range of treatment options, Alicia considered it as the best of modern medicine, which puts the physician and patient in the role of collaborators. She remembered her childhood, when doctors always acted like gods, and was happy that progressive medicine now defined the patient-physician relationship as a partnership.

But Boris had found that same behavior disrespectful, callous, and incomprehensible. Boris was used to somber and serious Russian doctors. They never smiled. When the American doctor introduced himself by his first name, Boris was disturbed. When the doctor and Alicia spoke in a friendly and casual way, he felt jealous and angry. And when the doctor tried to engage him in deciding which treatment to choose, it became obvious to Boris that his concerns were not being taken seriously. The doctor's job was to diagnose and prescribe a treatment, not to act as if he was a friend or a colleague. Why go to a doctor and pay a fortune if he knew no more than you did?

What the doctor didn't know and even Alicia, after years of studying Russian, was not clearly aware of were important differences in American and Russian cultures. History shapes interpersonal relations. In societies such as Russia's, where people have a strong sense of place, where families have been rooted for generations, and where outsiders have more often been foes than friends, it is only natural that smiles be reserved for intimates. The legacy of Western European invasions from Napoleon to Hitler, as well as the oppressive state security system under both the czars and the Communists, did not create an environment where quick and easy trust of others was wise. One should always be cautious and reserved with strangers, especially those in positions of authority.

Cultures evolve like living organisms to help humans deal with the challenges that confront them. Clearly the cultural norms that shaped Boris's experience in Russia helped him cope with a life that was very different from the American suburban Protestant world that Alicia was raised in. Even though they were very interested in each other and each other's worlds, they needed to develop tools to grasp the nature of their different attitudes about interpersonal relationships.

	OVERLAPPING	PARTIAL OVERLAP	DIFFERENTIATED
GENDER ROLES	Men and women are equal. Each person should be able to be what he or she wishes irrespective of gender.	There should be some overlap in the roles of men and women, but it's also important to acknowledge differences between the sexes.	The worlds of men and women are totally different. It is important to keep them separate.

Of all the contrasts that affect mixed matches, perhaps none has greater impact than differences in cultural rules that define men's and women's roles. Most people within a particular culture and class share a common notion of what constitutes "normal" male and female behavior. In fact, each of the other five cultural dimensions we have just looked at have gender variations within a culture. No matter how future-oriented a culture is, for example, women almost always have the primary responsibility for the here-and-now business of raising children. And whether or not a culture values high intensity or high formality in the expression of emotion, the rules governing *how* emotion is expressed have distinctively male and female forms.

Cultures also vary greatly on how much overlap is tolerated in the division of gender roles. While Western European nations, the United States, and Canada are far from gender-neutral societies, they accept and even legislate more overlapping of male and female roles in the public and personal realms of life than do most other cultures. Rigid differentiation of men's and women's roles, which seems increasingly alien to Westerners, is more the norm than the exception in cultures throughout the rest of the world.

Complicating the definition of gender roles for couples are the historically unprecedented changes that have taken place in the past generation in almost all cultures, even those known for their rigid divisions between male and female. Although men remain dominant in many areas of life, the fact that women have emerged as political leaders in countries as diverse as England, Pakistan, Israel, and India is one indication of how widespread the changes are. And perhaps more men have changed diapers throughout the world in the past fifteen years than in the preceding one hundred and fifty. Men and women in mixed matches must grapple with the contrasts in their cultural conditioning about gender as well as adjust to all of these historic changes in order to successfully negotiate the division of life's tasks.

Sacha and Ellen—Common Roots, Different Lives

People's cultural differences seldom fall into one neat category. Culture and our life experiences can create differences around a whole range of issues. Sacha and Ellen's relationship revealed important value differences in three important cultural dimensions: their perception of *gender roles*, their values concerning the *cohesiveness of the family*, and their sense of the *nature of the universe*.

People who didn't know them well never thought of Sacha and Ellen as a mixed match. They were both attractive, olive-skinned, athletic, Mediterranean-looking people. They had been married for five years and had two young children. They were both Armenian and were both brought up in the Orthodox Church. But that is where their similarities ended. Ellen was raised in the United States and Sacha in the minority Armenian community of Iran. Their common ethnicity and religious background helped them to feel familiar and close, but their experiences growing up in two very different cultures meant that many of their values did not fit together easily.

In miles and milieu Ellen had grown up a long way from Tehran in an affluent and safe suburban neighborhood outside Philadelphia. The daily political anxiety of Sacha's life in Iran was not part of her experience. But the memory of oppression was. Her grandmother lived in a quiet, dark room on the ground floor of their house and carried memories that everyone knew of but never spoke about. She had lost her parents and almost all of her family in the Turkish slaughter of the Armenians when she was a little girl. She survived only because of relatives who rescued her and walked her to safety across the Syrian desert.

When Ellen was five, she began to ask her grandmother and her parents questions about grandmother's accent and about where she came from. Her parents told her that they were Armenians and that she should be proud of their ancestry, but they forbade her to speak about the past—it would upset grandmother. Although her parents could be emotionally volatile about many other subjects, the tight anger in their faces demanded a silence about the family's history that she didn't dare break for many years.

Her father also let it be known, mainly through his dinner-table lectures, that *his* family had freed itself not only of the unnamable anxieties of the past but of the shackles of conservative Armenian culture. His daughter was free to get an education; his son would not be the most important child. His wife would be "allowed" to pursue her own interests. They were not like those they had left behind. They were modern and rational and would be free to shape their own destinies.

As Ellen went through her adolescence, she became increasingly aware of the discrepancy between what her father said and the reality of her family life. If they were proud of being Armenian, why weren't they supposed to talk about it to outsiders? And if males and females were equals, why was her brother sent to private school when she had to attend public school? Why was it that her mother was totally responsible for running the household and her father never lifted a finger? Who were they fooling? This was no partnership. Men had the power.

Ellen threw herself into her studies and was a successful student. But being different in high school was not a good thing. She quickly learned that none of her friends knew where Armenia was.

She also felt different because her skin was darker than that of most of the other girls. To make it worse, the other girls also seemed so composed when she compared herself with them. She worried that her laugh was too loud, her tears too quick to flow. She wished she was blond and calm instead of dark and intense. Strong emotions and a strong sense of cultural identity became linked together. At the time it seemed better to suppress both.

Ellen remembered an incident in a college political science class that deeply affected her and was a turning point in her feelings about her identity. The class was discussing the Middle East, and one of the students mentioned, almost casually, that Middle Eastern men could never be trusted, that they always lied. No one challenged the statement.

Ellen began to sweat and feel nauseated. She instantly found herself in a terrible bind. She could remain silently humiliated, and at least no one would know that she was one of *them*. But if she didn't speak up, she would be lending her silent assent to a statement that she felt unjustly stereotyped and stigmatized her people. She made her decision. Slowly she raised her hand, and when the teacher called on her, she spoke in a quiet, but clear voice: "I am Armenian. My father is Armenian. My grandparents on my mother's side were raised in Syria, but they were also Armenian. Many people in my grandparents' generation were murdered by others who lied about them. When you casually state that you can never trust Middle Eastern men, I instantly think of my grandfathers and my father and my uncles and my brother. They are not all perfect people, but they definitely aren't liars. I resent what you said."

The class fell into an uncomfortable silence, but Ellen felt a tremendous sense of relief. The teacher changed the subject, and no one said another word about the matter. Ellen felt, though, that for her the incident marked a crucial defining moment. She felt that if she was going to be a strong woman, she had to be able to speak out, even when it was difficult. She would not hide who or what she was. For her, psychological survival meant bearing witness to her personal and historical reality.

Sacha's life had been very different than Ellen's. He was born in 1952 in Tehran and came of age during the early 1970s before the Islamic Revolution. He and his younger brother were brought up to believe that they, along with their father, held very special rights and responsibilities as the men of the family.

The pattern of family life, with its patriarchy and strictly defined gender roles, meant that there was very little overlap between men's and women's worlds. His mother attended to the needs of the children and the home; his father to the demands of the outside world. Women were very clearly different and definitely not equal. He never once saw his mother openly disagree with his father. While his father was less harsh than many men, by Western standards he ruled with a heavy hand.

Sacha grew up in a world where fear was familiar. As a small Orthodox Christian enclave in the midst of a Muslim world, the Armenians always felt vulnerable. Sacha remembered being eight years old and feeling very upset after a Muslim boy he considered a friend told him, "You are not a real Iranian." And if the regime of the "Western-oriented" shah had attempted certain reforms, it was not burdened with Western ideals of political freedom. Sacha knew people who had disappeared and others who had been tortured. He learned that it was best to be careful about revealing personal thoughts and feelings. For him silence and survival were synonymous.

Several years before the Islamic Revolution convulsed Iranian culture, Sacha left to travel in Europe and ended up settling in the

United States. When he went back to visit his family in Tehran three years later, nothing felt the same. He had partially assimilated Western values and attitudes. He no longer found the girls he had grown up with attractive. The young Armenian women his mother introduced him to seemed too dependent, traditional, overweight, sexually repressed, and emotional. He wanted a woman who wasn't so tied to her own family, who could be a friend, a companion, and a lover.

In spite of his attraction to the world outside of Iran, though, he never became totally comfortable with the lack of strong family ties he observed in Western countries. He was also disturbed by how quickly and superficially people seemed to make and break friendships. He had become a stranger in his own land, but wasn't entirely comfortable in his new home either.

When Sacha met Ellen at a party given by some mutual friends in Wilmington, Virginia, it felt like a perfect match. She was a modern woman—educated, attractive, playful, thin, and openly sexual. He would have a partner who was Armenian like himself but who had absorbed much of the openness and freedom of the West. He would get to have his cake and eat it too.

When Ellen met Sacha, he also seemed ideal. He was Armenian and familiar in a way that she liked. The fact that he had grown up outside of America and in an Armenian community helped her feel more connected to her roots. But she also liked his worldly, cosmopolitan demeanor. She knew that she didn't want to re-create a traditional Armenian marriage, and he seemed like a perfect combination of the past and the future.

But in important ways theirs was actually a cross-cultural relationship. Their shared sense of alienation from the communities they were raised in did not mean they shared a common value system. While Sacha was far more Western in his outlook than the friends he had left behind, he was far more traditional in his values than either he or Ellen initially understood. And while Ellen longed for a connection to tradition and her cultural identity, she was far more individualistic and Americanized in her worldview than she realized.

A year after they met, they decided to move into a small house together. After they had lived there only a month, the phone rang one evening and Ellen overheard Sacha saying, "Sure, come on over right now. We're home." Ellen asked Sacha who he was talking to. He said that it was his second cousin and his wife and two children and that they were coming over to stay with them for a few days.

Ellen was in shock. Sacha's cousins, who had immigrated from Iran five years ago, lived in Denver. She had met them once and had not liked them. Sacha, she found out later, wasn't very fond of them either. Ellen pressed Sacha to explain why he had invited them. The argument that followed was shaped by their different cultural assumptions about the nature of family obligations *and* the division of power between men and women.

> SACHA: Well, they called me last week and asked me if they could come stay with us sometime and I said, "Sure." I didn't know that they were coming today.
>
> ELLEN: How could you not ask me or at least tell me what you've done? We have a small two-bedroom place and you invite a family of four to stay with us for God knows how long. You know I'm under all kinds of pressure with the project I'm doing for work and I've been using the extra room. What do you expect me to do? You don't even like them. How could you do this?
>
> SACHA: I knew you would act like this. They are my kin. I don't have a choice. What do you expect me to do, *tell them that I've become an American*?

Somehow they both managed to calm down, and Ellen reluctantly agreed to have them stay. That night as they sat around trying to make conversation, Sacha's cousin turned to Ellen and bitterly complained, "I can't believe that America is not helping the Armenians. Go tell your President Bush what a hypocrite he is. Don't you care what happens to us?"

Ellen turned to see what Sacha's response was. He looked the other way and said nothing. That was the last straw. After the cousins left the next day, Ellen told Sacha that if their relationship was going to survive, they were going to have to find new ways to talk about the old issues of family bonds as well as male and female roles.

Sacha felt he could never directly say to his relatives that they were not welcome. To do so would make him feel that he was denying a basic value and a very important part of who he was. But he also wanted things to work with Ellen. Trying to satisfy both love and tradition seemed impossible. What Sacha considered a minimal obligation to family, Ellen considered an oppressive burden that put her needs second. She interpreted his "putting his family first" as a sign that he didn't really care about her needs.

Even though Ellen intellectually understood the reasons behind their differences, it did not take away the emotional difficulty of living with them.

    I know, Sacha, that for you, responding directly to your relatives' political complaints about the American president as well as to their not-so-indirect criticism of me for being an "American" feels dangerous. You grew up in an environment where keeping your beliefs to yourself was a matter of survival and where all political talk seemed threatening. But if your physical sense of security depended on silence, my psychological well-being required that I speak out. It took me many years to learn to defy my family's conspiracy of silence.

And finally, even though Sacha believed that he was free of traditional ideas about the roles of men and women, he still felt that he was owed a certain degree of deference as a man. He found this difficult to admit to Ellen or himself, partially because he had difficulty believing it. He was much more flexible and open in his relationship with Ellen than any of the men in his family had been in their marriages. He was proud of how liberated he was and felt hurt by her anger. He began to feel that the price of the relationship was giving up his sense of being a man.

However, Ellen was not measuring Sacha's behavior against the standards of the Iranian world that Sacha had grown up in, but against the values of the suburban WASP world that she knew best. In the midst of a crisis she summed up her feelings about their relationship in two sentences: "If I act the way Sacha wants me to, I will lose the sense of an independent self I have worked so hard to create. If I am true to myself, I will be alone."

Both Sacha and Ellen were psychologically suspended between the contrasting values of two very different cultures. Even though they each had internalized both Armenian and American cultural values, they had done so in different proportions. In spite of her attraction to traditional Armenian values and culture, Ellen was more assimilated into the American value system, which stressed individualism, a more optimistic view of the universe, loosened family ties, emotional control, and, most importantly, overlapping and more equal roles for men and women.

And in spite of Sacha's attraction to Western ways and a Westernized woman, he had spent the majority of his life in an Armenian cultural milieu whose organizing principles stressed authority over individualism, saw the world and other humans as dangerous and inherently evil, established the family as the basic organizing principle of life, and defined men's and women's domains as separate and unequal.

These differences in their cultural templates led to very different interpretations of the same behavior. Sacha thought Ellen's behavior toward his family demonstrated uncaring disrespect. Ellen felt that Sacha was not taking the needs of their relationship seriously. And while from Sacha's Armenian perspective he was liberated and modern in his attitudes about male and female equality, from Ellen's more Americanized perspective he seemed too traditional and bound to male privilege.

To make matters even more complicated, they both oscillated between the values of the two cultures. Like people listening to two dissonant sound tracks on stereo headphones, each of them would first adjust the cultural dial toward the Armenian side, then toward the American. Neither channel seemed complete without the other. But together they always seemed to clash.

After they got married, when Ellen was pregnant with their first child, they began to have a series of long talks about their differences. While some couples seem to be further separated by the stress of a first pregnancy, they began to grow closer. Realizing how much higher the stakes were now that a child would be involved, they each began to make the compromises necessary to make their relationship work. When they returned to the topic of family, Sacha agreed that the next time his relatives called, he would consult with Ellen before making any plans with them. Ellen told Sacha that she would try to change her schedule to accommodate his family next time they came into town.

Even after they began to recognize their differences, they didn't always find them easy to deal with. But as they learned to label them, they became better able to exercise more control over their clashing cultural sound tracks and found new ways of harmonizing them. When they felt the pressure rising, they developed a code to defuse the tension by asking each other, "Which voice are you talking in—your American or your Armenian?"

EXERCISES: Conflict Resolution
Use the following five principles to work on identifying and resolving your culturally-based conflicts.

1. Identify Your Differences

Dealing with differences is much easier when you are aware of what they are. On a piece of paper write a list of numbers from 1 to 18. Then look at the following chart and write down either *A* or *B* after each number, depending on which of the two statements (Column A or Column B) best describes the message you got from your family. The exercise will help you to better understand your own and your partner's cultural backgrounds and clarify some of the differences in what each of you considers normal.

Set time aside to share your responses with your partner after you've both completed the exercise. Talk about the reasons behind each of your choices. Your discussion will be most productive if you assume, at least for the moment, that the differences this exercise reveals about your families are neither good nor bad. They are simply the way you perceive your family. While you may not like all of the values that these statements reflect, they are honest expressions of personal and cultural values. If you are really honest with each other, you may discover that the kinds of differences that lead to conflict in your relationship are also part of what attracted you to each other in the first place.

	COLUMN A	COLUMN B
1.	Life is short; enjoy it while you can.	Never play until your work is done.
2.	Success should not be pursued at the expense of family ties.	The best way to serve yourself as well as your family is to be very successful.
3.	Somebody has to have primary responsibility for the home and family. It's almost always better if it's the woman.	Women have a right to achieve as much as men. The division of labor should be gender-neutral and openly negotiated.
4.	Modesty is noble; boastfulness is crude.	A person has a right to be openly proud of achievements.
5.	Actions speak louder than words; talk is a waste of time.	You can best solve a problem by talking it through.
6.	Words can be used for effect. Exaggeration is just a way to make the point.	Words are never to be wasted. They should be used carefully and precisely.
7.	Marriage is between two families.	Marriage is between two people.
8.	Anger is expressed by continued fighting and debating.	Anger should be avoided or discussed rationally and calmly.
9.	Parents' authority is nondebatable.	All family rules can be negotiated by everyone.
10.	Your problem is my problem.	Don't interfere in others' affairs.
11.	Food is an expression of giving and love.	Food is for sustenance. Eat with moderation and never waste.
12.	A little clutter just makes a house look warm and lived-in.	Cleanliness is next to godliness.
13.	Drinking alcoholic beverages is a normal part of family life. Getting a little loose is a good release.	Alcohol should be used rarely and always in moderation.
14.	Intense expression of emotion at a funeral is normal and expected. A large, long social gathering after the burial is important.	A funeral is a solemn and quiet affair. Open displays of emotion should be kept to a minimum and the service should be brief.

15.	People are basically selfish and can't be trusted.	People are inherently good. If you treat them well, they will generally treat you well.
16.	Men are impulsive creatures. You can't expect them to be totally monogamous.	If either partner has sex outside of the relationship, it means the relationship is over.
17.	Men and women can never be "just friends." There is always a sexual element to any close relationship between the sexes.	Close friendship between men and women is perfectly natural and acceptable. It doesn't have to have a sexual component.
18.	Money is to be enjoyed.	Money is to be spent only when necessary. Save as much as possible for future needs.

2. Don't Assume You Understand Each Other

One of the fathers of family therapy, Salvador Minuchin, an Argentinian, made a practice of not understanding people. Even though he has an excellent command of English (he has written a number of lucid books in English), he still speaks with an accent. At a workshop of his I attended, he used a videotape of a therapy session he had conducted with an American family. He explained to the family that he had difficulty understanding some "big English words" they were using and asked them to speak more slowly and use simpler words. He used this "dumb" ploy—and it was a ploy—to encourage the family members to be clearer in their communications. If they assumed that he had trouble understanding them, they might spell out their feelings and thoughts more clearly.

If all of us were to act as if we and our partners were not fluent in a common language, we all might end up communicating more clearly and effectively. We assume too quickly, especially with those we care the most about, that we really understand the meaning of each other's words, motives, beliefs, and values. We must. Why else would we be together? Unfortunately that assumption is often not true, especially in cross-cultural relationships. Ask for clarification. Go more slowly. Be curious. It will help you stop jumping to unpleasant and sometimes incorrect conclusions.

3. Make Anger Your Ally

One of the most important gauges on the control panel of a car is the one that alerts us that our car is in danger of overheating. By giving us an early warning, it creates the opportunity to deal with a problem *before* any actual damage is done.

Anger is our overheating gauge. If we learn to use it in its early stages, before it has become too intense, it can make us aware of problems that need to be dealt with. Used properly, anger can protect our relationships from damage as effectively as the temperature gauge on the car protects the engine.

In order to use anger as a positive force in your relationship, it's important to understand and accept the cultural differences in the ways that you express it. This is one of the most important challenges for every cross-cultural couple.

4. Accept That Dealing with Cultural Differences Takes Work

All relationships are complex, but being part of a mixed match adds another level of complexity. Your differences present both dangers and opportunities. The dangers of culturally based misunderstandings are obvious. But if you are willing to do the extra work it entails, learning how to recognize and deal with your differences can enrich and deepen your relationship. These skills will help you create a family that incorporates and synthesizes the best of both cultural ways of being.

5. *Don't Assume That Understanding Equals Acceptance*

Many therapists begin their careers assuming that insight automatically leads to change. I have heard many young counselors complain about their clients that "I pointed out to them what they were doing and they seemed to understand, but they still didn't change," in a tone that implies that change is an obligation once insight is established. If only it were that easy.

Insight can be a tool. Unrecognized differences often do cause distress, and understanding differences can help to depathologize conflict. But insight is no guarantee of happiness. Some people understand their differences all too well but never find a way to bridge the gaps that separate them. Acceptance and appreciation of differences is a process that takes time, patience, goodwill, humor, and the desire to make a relationship work.

As we have seen in this chapter, different cultural codes can have a powerful impact on the relationships of cross-cultural families. Learning to identify, discuss, and negotiate differences are important steps you can take in creating a successful family life. When you approach your own relationship with the curiosity of a good anthropologist, respectfully working to understand another culture, you enrich your own.

CHAPTER 4

Many Voices Within: Clarifying Cultural and Religious Identity

In *Hunger of Memory*, [Richard] Rodriguez imagined the world as a stage on which he got to be the playwright and play all the parts. . . . "I think of myself as Irish," he tells me beginning a characteristic riff by fondly recalling his boyhood among the Irish nuns in Sacramento. "And most of the people who have been closest to me in my life have been Irish. When I read William Saroyan I discovered I was Armenian. When I read Philip Roth I discovered I was Jewish, too. Passing that white church on Fremont Street in Sacramento, hearing those hymns sung with so much optimism, I saw myself as Protestant—as someone who had moved from the Catholic 'we' to 'I,' who believes in jogging and working on machines that improve my body. . . . Increasingly I see myself as Indian, though I never thought I'd say that. I live in a gay, Chinese city, from which I take my identity. When Bill Moyers asked me on TV whether I was Hispanic or American, I told him I was Chinese.

FROM AN ARTICLE ABOUT RICHARD RODRIGUEZ
BY DAVID KIRP

Confusion of Cultural and Religious Identity

Couples in mixed matches often find negotiating the identity of their family complicated by each partner's confusion about his or her own religious and cultural identity. Although they traditionally overlap, culture and religion are not the same.

Religious faith offers a language for the soul and brings order out of the chaos of human life by creating moral codes that regulate the relationships between husbands and wives, parents and children, workers and employers, and even friends and enemies. Its rituals comfort people through times of loss, and sanctify and give meaning to the life-cycle transitions of birth, marriage, and death.

The great religions are by their very nature transnational and multicultural. Each of them points toward transcendent and universal values. All hold open the possibility that their truths can be discovered by anyone, regardless of who they are or where they came from. Each religion is nurtured in a variety of cultural settings, but none is the possession of any one culture. The spread of religions across continents and oceans demonstrates their universal appeal. Saudi Arabia no more possesses Islam than Israel, Judaism; Rome, Catholicism; or India, Buddhism. Each of these religions ultimately belongs to all of humankind.

Culture is more particular. There are black Ethiopians and Caucasian Americans who claim common identities as Jews but have little else in common besides their religion. Ireland and Italy share their Catholicism but have very different histories. While each religion includes many cultures, cultural identity is an affirmation of a distinctive sense of peoplehood. Whether mythical or literal, cultural identity honors common ancestors and is reinforced by food, festivals, folkways, language, and ritual. It is rooted in the remembrances of a common past and the expectation of a shared fate in the years to come.

No one knows better the importance of separating religious belief from cultural identity than religious converts. Frank, a young man I spoke to, was born and raised as an Italian Catholic in a large city on the East Coast. Two years ago he was introduced to Islam by a black friend and decided to convert. When I visited him at his mosque, he was very clear that he would always be an Italian, but he was equally clear that he was now a practicing Muslim and no longer a Catholic. Since his new religious community included Muslims from Lebanon, Pakistan, India, Bangladesh, Trinidad, China, and over twenty other nations, few people questioned the sincerity of his conversion because of his ethnic background. With their amazing collection of languages, cultures, and personal histories, everyone in this black, white, Arabic, and Asian community recognized that the only thing that held them all together was their common belief in Islam. While the immigrants could remember when their cultural and religious backgrounds were inseparable, their children took for granted this potpourri of cultures sheltered under the umbrella of Islam.

Rachel Cowan is also very clear about the differences between ethnicity and religion. Several years ago, when I was giving a talk on intermarriage in New York, I was introduced by Rachel, who traces her Anglo-Protestant roots to the arrival of the *Mayflower*. In the book *Mixed Blessings*, which she wrote with her husband, the late Paul Cowan, she traced her own spiritual journey that took her from 1960s secular politics to conversion to Judaism to ultimately becoming a rabbi.

When Rachel mentioned to an acquaintance that she was Jewish, the woman remarked, "It's funny, you don't look Jewish." Rachel responded with a wry "Well, isn't it funny how Jews look these days?" In fact, Rachel pointed out, she was a WASJ, a white Anglo-Saxon Jew. Her decision to convert to Judaism did not alter her ethnic background, the way she moved, the inflection of her voice, who her ancestors were, *or* how she looked.

The woman's comment may have been insensitive, but it is not surprising. The radical changes of the twentieth century have resulted in people inside and outside of a wide range of cultural and religious communities having difficulty defining exactly what belonging to their group means. And most people are not as clear about the distinctions between the cultural and religious components of their identities as Frank, the Italian Muslim, or Rachel, the Anglo Jew.

Modern life has fused and confused cultural, family, religious, and national loyalties in ways that make it difficult for many partners in mixed matches to understand and deal with the differences they bring to their relationships. When uprooted people reach back into their collective pasts in an attempt to create an identity, each person reclaims different components of identity. Instead of a balanced cultural-national-religious-family identity, some people emphasize religion, others their cultural or national roots, and some their family roots. Often they end up having difficulty distinguishing between the different meanings of the elements of their identity collage.

Many have attempted to deal with their confusion by trying to forget the past altogether in diverse and rapidly changing societies such as that of the United States. Rather than honoring tradition, each generation acts as if it has been dropped out of the sky onto an unknown landscape and must reinvent itself. Cultural amnesia is used to ease the discomfort of working together with strange people in an alien land. For some, sacrificing the past and its traditions seemed to be the price of creating a new and better future.

But even when ties to the past have been eroded or broken, the need to belong has not disappeared. Whether it's an ethnic group or a race, a church or a nation, the Republican party or the Communist party, a cult, a commune, a corporation, or a gang, almost all people search for something they can feel part of that is bigger than themselves. This is not a human weakness. It is merely evidence of what incredibly social creatures we are and how our survival has always been intertwined with that of our group.

All of the confusion and change of modern times have also led to the creation of new composite identities. One example is the development of "Asian identity" among those who had emigrated from Asian nations to the United States. Within Asia, national, linguistic, and ethnic identities remained more important than any sense of a shared Asian identity. The Chinese, for example, who remembered a wartime occupation by Japan, knew that they shared a common continent with the Japanese, but certainly never saw themselves as sharing a cultural, historical, or ethnic identity.

But millions of younger postwar-generation Japanese, Chinese, Filipino, Cambodian, Indian, Vietnamese, Korean, and Thai immigrants, who uprooted themselves from their Asian homelands, found that in the eyes of their adopted country they were all now simply Asians. Faced with discrimination and the breakdown of traditional communities, they began to put aside ancient feuds and deal with the emotional and political necessity of living in an alien environment. More concerned with the present and the future than with the past, they gave birth to a new meta-identity that made many of their grandparents shudder. They became Asians.

Of course this process of identity change does not occur overnight. Evelyn Lee, a leader in Asian mental health, once noted that it was only years after she immigrated to America from Hong

Kong that she began to have any kind of identity as an Asian. She had always been Chinese, but separated from her homeland, she slowly found herself becoming Asian as well.

All of this taking apart and putting together of identities has created a lot of uncertainty in almost everyone's mind. The confusion that these new identities has created complicates the relationships of mixed matches. When either partner in a mixed match is uncertain of the cultural and spiritual ground he stands on, it is difficult to negotiate any meaningful agreements. You have to have a good idea of where you came from and where you are now to have a clear sense of where you want to go.

Five Steps Toward Clarifying Individual Identity

I've developed a five-step process to help each person in a mixed match clarify the nature of his or her own cultural and religious identity. By following these steps, partners in mixed matches will be better prepared to find creative ways to reconcile their own cultural and religious conflicts.

Often we keep the painful parts of our cultural pasts locked up in a windowless room, hoping that they will stay there and leave us alone. We wonder if we should burden ourselves, our families, or our partners with memories that hurt. But by attempting to bury the past, we end up imbuing it with a perverse power. As we will see from people's experiences throughout this book, failing to come to terms with our history leads us to act out ancient wounds in confusing and painful ways.

These steps can take you through the emotional minefields of dealing with your own and your partner's pasts. The process can bring you face-to-face with tales of war, persecution, hardship, and immigration as well as with intense loyalties, deep personal meanings, struggles with religious faith, and connections to a long string of generations. Even though the process can be emotionally difficult, exposing the past to the light of day can lead to a great sense of relief and give you access to the positive and healing memories that get locked up along with the pain.

STEP ONE: DISCOVERING ANCESTORS' SHADOWS

"Discovering Ancestors' Shadows" is a powerful exercise that helps us clarify our feelings about our religious and cultural backgrounds. It allows us to hear the chorus of voices of family members and other important people we carry within us.

It's easy for us to remember those voices that represent people we feel loved by and whom we respect. But often the voices that affect us as much are the ones with which we are least comfortable. It's very difficult to work out a clear sense of family identity with your partner until you are able to acknowledge all of the voices you carry within. Only then can you really come to terms with your own complex identity.

Begin by taking a piece of paper and draw a circle to represent each female family member and a square to represent each male family member, including your grandparents, parents, and siblings. Leave enough room under each circle to write in two sentences.

Underneath the symbol that represents each person, write down your fantasy of what he or she would say in response to each of the following two statements:

1. *I am a* (fill in whatever combination of religious or cultural identity that seems most important to the person) *and to me that means:*
2. *I get my way in life by:*

◯ = Female   ▢ = Male

	PATERNAL		MATERNAL	
GRANDPARENTS	◯	▢	◯	▢
PARENTS		▢		◯
SIBLINGS	◯		▢	

After completing these sentences, imagine using them in a group setting like the one that I will describe. When we have used this exercise as a group psychodramatic exercise, after all of the group members have written down their sentences under the circles representing their family members, we ask a participant to volunteer to be the central character. That person stands in front of the group and chooses people from the group to play the roles of his or her family members. The sentences he or she has written become the script for a family drama.

In one group, Mechtild, a woman from Germany who was a foreign graduate student in psychology, volunteered. She quickly added that she couldn't complete the whole exercise because she never knew her paternal grandparents and didn't know what they would have said. I suggested that Mechtild use her imagination and create lines for her grandparents based on absolutely anything she knew or imagined about them. She agreed and quickly wrote down the final sentences before she began the psychodrama.

She looked carefully at each of the fifteen group members as though searching for something in their faces or body posture that reminded her of the person she was casting them to play. She selected someone to play each role. Then I asked her to coach each of them on how to deliver the sentences she had written for them with the inflection and intensity of the person they were playing. Sometimes it would take three or four tries before they could say the sentences to her satisfaction. Then I had her face her family. Standing together like a Greek chorus, each person in her newly re-created family spoke in turn directly to Mechtild.

MOTHER: To me being German means that you work hard and don't ask too many questions.
I get my way in life by being silent and hoping people will not notice me.

FATHER: To me being German means that you are proud of who you are, but that it is a private matter.
I get my way in life by saying what I want and not putting up with fools.

OLDER BROTHER: Being a German means that we must do penance for what the Nazis did and work to make the world a better place.
I get my way in life by working hard for myself and others.

YOUNGER SISTER: Being German doesn't mean anything. I identify with being a European because I speak four languages. I just happen to have been born in Germany. I am no different from anyone else.
I get my way in life by taking care of myself.

MATERNAL GRANDFATHER: Being German means being blamed for the sins of a few for which most were not responsible.
I get my way in life by doing what I am supposed to and staying out of trouble.

MATERNAL GRANDMOTHER: Being German means carrying a burden of shame.
I get my way in life by not expecting anything.

PATERNAL GRANDMOTHER: I am a Christian, and being German is
not as important as my belief in God.

I get my way in life by praying and holding my faith.

PATERNAL GRANDFATHER: To me being German meant doing my
duty as an officer in the army.

I got my way in life by following orders and doing what I was
told.

After all of the family members had spoken, I asked them to act as
a choir and to say all of their lines in unison. I asked Mechtild to
listen and to hear whose voices emerged from the group. After
they recited their lines once, she asked them to repeat them. She
reflected for a moment on her reaction to the chorus and said that
even though they weren't the loudest, she heard her brother's and
sister's voices the most clearly.

Then I asked Mechtild to respond to the group by creating her
own lines. What did being German mean to her? And how did she
get her way in life? She thought for several moments and then
spoke directly to the symbolic family she had created:

MECHTILD: To me being German is something I would rather
forget.

I get my way in life by being smart and trying to analyze everything and rise above it all.

Mechtild began to cry as she responded to her chorus. She went
on to tell the group that she had always suspected that her paternal grandfather, who had died in World War II, had been more
than just an ordinary German officer. She had found documents
that indicated that he had worked in a concentration camp in
Poland.

I suspected it because of small pieces of information that my family seemed to slowly leak out over the years. And once, when I was packing to come to the States, I came across a letter from the army sent during the war telling of his death and that he had been an officer at a "relocation center."

No one had ever come right out and admitted what he had done, and this is the first time that I have spoken of my suspicions in front of a group. In fact I have only ever spoken about it once, when I was fifteen, to my closest friend. Then I never uttered another word about it until this moment. I was in therapy for two years during graduate school, and my therapist never asked me about my family's experience during the war, and I never brought it up. I think we both acted like it was a very long time ago and not relevant to the anxiety or depression I had been experiencing.

In graduate school Mechtild had studied family therapy and was particularly interested in family secrets. Until now she had never fully understood the connection between her academic interests and her personal history. She decided to try to break down the walls of secrecy in her own family and to begin with her brother and sister.

She had always thought of her brother, who was involved in the environmental politics of the Green party, as too morally righteous and rigidly doctrinaire, and of her sister, who worked as a linguist for a cosmetics firm in Paris, as selfish and concerned only about herself. She felt that both of them saw her pursuit of a doctorate in psychology as somehow trying to prove she was intellectually superior to them.

Now she began to see that all three of them, in their own ways, shared a struggle to come to terms with being German and their family's legacy of secrecy and shame. They had all chosen a very

German path of using words, intellect, and hard work in their attempts to escape from a German past. She wrote to her brother and sister about her insights and was gratified to find out that they were far more receptive to discussing the past than she had thought.

Mechtild was dating Angelo, an American who had worked his way up from a blue-collar Irish-Italian background. He was the only member of his family who had ever gone beyond high school, and he was now teaching history at a community college. While they had talked at great length about their common interests in music, art, and health care, for the first time they began to talk about their cultural pasts. She found out that he could identify with her feelings of being a dislocated person. Like Mechtild, he found himself living and working in a world that as a child he could never have imagined being part of. As they started a process of revealing their many voices to each other, they began to realize that both of them often felt like strangers in a strange land, and they found themselves feeling closer than ever before.

We have used this psychodramatic exercise in many group settings with dramatic results. It has helped people begin to understand and accept the myriad of voices we all carry inside. Rather than making us more confused, acknowledging the chorus of voices inside each of us can help us feel less troubled by the contradictory thoughts and feelings we inevitably experience. It reveals how our own sense of group belonging can be an evolving and dynamic aspect of our lives.

STEP TWO: EXPLORING THE CULTURAL HISTORY OF YOUR
CHILDHOOD
The cultural content of the world you were born into—however rich or deprived, clear or confused—was simply a given. You did

not choose it, and you were not responsible for it. But it had and still has a profound influence on your life. The emotional impact of your early experiences affects your feelings about your identity and all of your negotiations with your partner.

But when you have been restrained by personal, family, and societal taboos from exploring your complex, rich, and sometimes painful cultural history, the past can create problems. Instead of being a source of knowledge and wisdom, the past can become like an old bitter lover who has developed an unpleasant habit of knocking on your front door at the most stressful moments in life.

The unique history of your group can have a major impact on your cultural identity. Almost every immigrant group has made steady movement toward assimilation into a mainstream American culture, even as they have transformed it in the process. Caucasian groups have tended to assimilate more rapidly, but even among them there has been wide variation in the rate of adaptation. Many racial minorities have assimilated more slowly because of cultural contrasts with the dominant Anglo culture's values and because of racism, but over the course of several generations almost every group has seen many of its members incorporated into a kind of universal American culture.

The process of assimilation for African-Americans has been significantly more difficult than that for all other groups. The legacy of slavery and the intense racism of other groups have resulted in a tragic but evident fact: African-Americans have remained on the bottom of America's socioeconomic ladder. There is a growing black middle class, many of whom have assimilated into the mainstream American culture. But their success does not erase the painful reality for the majority of blacks in the United States. More than four times as many blacks than whites live below the poverty level.

Whatever your experience has been with your group's cultural history, Step Two furthers the work you began in Step One. It helps you learn more about your cultural past and enables you to begin to sort out your feelings about your own sense of group identity. As you get more comfortable facing your past, you will become better able to share these memories and feelings with your partner in order to prepare for the future.

One way to prepare yourself to answer the following questions is to look through any family picture albums you are able to find. Look at them by yourself, and pay attention to the memories and feelings attached to each picture. Then ask other family members to share their pictures and ask them about their memories of your common cultural history. This is a relatively nonthreatening way to open conversations about the cultural roots of your family. While some people in your family may not be open to talking about the past, you may be pleasantly surprised by others who are.

Use the following questions as a way to guide your self-exploration and conversations with others. You won't always be able to keep the cultural and religious aspects of your family members' identities separate, because they are often intertwined. But in these conversations try to stay as focused as possible on the racial, ethnic, linguistic, and national parts of identity, as opposed to the religious parts.

- How did your family express their pride as well as their anxiety about their ethnic or racial roots? Remember people in your life who embodied the positive or negative aspects of being part of your cultural group.
- Do you have foreign-born relatives? What was their experience of immigration to a new land? Do you have

relatives who are bilingual or who don't speak a
language in common with you? Do you have relatives
who are of a race or culture different from your own?
What were your feelings about these family members
as you grew up?

- Did you or your family experience prejudice,
discrimination, racism, or stereotyping as a member of
your cultural group? Do you have relatives or ancestors
who were persecuted or who persecuted others? How
did your family deal with these kinds of painful events
and memories? How have you?

- What were your family's attitudes toward "outsiders,"
those who were of other ethnic, racial, and cultural
groups? Whom could you bring home for dinner?
Whom could you not?

- What was the most important thing to you about
belonging to your group as you grew up?

- Have you ever visited your family's cultural homeland?
What was that experience like for you? If you haven't
ever gone, what are your feelings about visiting it?

Study the following chart. Which definition of cultural connectedness best fits for you? For your parents? For other members of
your family?

CULTURAL CONNECTEDNESS			
MONOCULTURAL	*TRANSITIONAL*	*BICULTURAL*	*ASSIMILATED*
DIFFERENT FROM DOMINANT CULTURE	*MINORITY EMPHASIS: PRIMARY IDENTITY IS WITH NONDOMINANT CULTURE*	*MAJORITY EMPHASIS: PRIMARY IDENTITY IS WITH DOMINANT CULTURE*	
Live in a racially or ethnically homogeneous or segregated neighborhood. Use language of old country or a nonmainstream dialect in everyday life. Avoid or don't have access to social contact with members of other groups.	Speak group's language or dialect as well as the mainstream language, but more comfortable with language of the group. Live among high concentrations of people of own cultural group. Or live temporarily as a foreigner in another country for work or educational purposes.	Dominant culture's language is primary and may not be fluent in group's language or dialect. Defense of group may remain important, but many cultural traditions are ignored. Retain a "hyphenated" identity, where group culture is referenced, at least in some settings, but new culture and its norms are most important.	Born more than three generations after immigration of ancestors. Intermarriage may have already diluted identification with primary culture or racial-minority appearance. No clear understanding of or meaningful identification with old culture's language or rituals. May have some vague, nostalgic connection to cultural traditions, but little more. May downplay any aspects of identity that are different than those of the dominant culture.
EXAMPLES: Immigrants, inner-city African-Americans, Hispanic migrant workers.	Strong sense of interconnected fate with other members of the group, and most social connections are with group members.	EXAMPLES: Grandchildren of immigrants, African-Americans living and working in integrated environments.	EXAMPLES: White Protestants who have lived in the U.S. for many generations, white ethnics, and some Asians who have
PRIMARY CONCERNS: Economic survival, discrimination, protecting children from influence of dominant culture.	EXAMPLES: Children of immigrants living in ethnic neighborhoods, African-Americans who live in inner city but work in integrated jobs.	PRIMARY CONCERNS: Fitting in. Finding some way to find comfort in an increasingly vague identity. Sometimes	

	PRIMARY CONCERNS: Economic success. Education of children. Making sure children get partially, but not totally, assimilated.	overemphasis of ethnic or racial identity to solidify shaky sense of it.	culturally or through intermarriage merged into a larger identity. PRIMARY CONCERNS: Maintaining position in society. Many perceive their decreasing proportion of the population and the new assertiveness and successes of minorities as a threat to their status.

STEP THREE: RESEARCHING YOUR RELIGIOUS ROOTS ✞ ☪ ✡ ☾ 卍

When couples can't find ways to deal with their religious differences, it can lead to what Paul and Rachel Cowan called spiritual gridlock. This gridlock usually takes the form of an unspoken agreement by both partners to minimize their connection to their religious heritages out of fear of the consequences of facing their differences. *You give up whatever connection you have to your religion in exchange for me giving up mine.*

The risk of not dealing with differences is that they may later reappear in spite of efforts to suppress them, especially around life-cycle rituals. Dealing with them now may not be easy, but trying to resolve them in the midst of a crisis surrounding a wedding, birth, or death is usually even more difficult. *Now* is almost always the best time.

Some of the problems that interfaith couples experience in their attempts to reconcile their different faiths result not only from very real differences in theology but from partners who bring different degrees of religious literacy and different intensities of religious practice to their relationship. Many people end their formal religious training in early adolescence. Although they may be very sophisticated in many aspects of their lives, their vocabulary for talking about religion is often very limited. Other partners in mixed matches have strong religious backgrounds, and some are still actively involved in their religious practice. Even many who have "fallen away" from a strong religious faith remain deeply affected by the values and thought patterns of their religious pasts.

Study the following chart to identify the nature of your religious background:

PERSONAL RELIGIOUS HISTORY			
RELIGIOUSLY FLUENT	MEANINGFUL RELIGIOUS EXPERIENCES	MINIMAL	TOTALLY SECULAR OR ATHEIST
Religion and prayer were an integral and very important aspect of everyday life. Family participated in rituals and holidays and attended religious services.	Religion was a regular part of life, but other aspects of family life were equally or more important. Familiar as child with basic outlines of religion.	Family occasionally participated in religious observances, but religion was a minor part of family life.	No religious observance. Family might acknowledge the religious roots of their family but did nothing to affirm them. More likely to define roots as cultural than as religious.
Extensive formal religious training, at least through adolescence.	Regular religious training, at least through age thirteen or fourteen.	Little formal religious training.	No formal religious training.

Now spend time reflecting on the meaning of your religious heritage and beliefs and talk with family members and your partner about the evolution of your own religious and spiritual beliefs. Work on answering the following questions:

- How important are your religious beliefs to you now?
- How do you put those religious beliefs into practice?
- Are religious practice and belief more of an individual spiritual path that you can pursue by yourself, or do you see your religion as inseparable from its practice in a community of others who share the same beliefs?
- Do you contribute money to religious institutions or causes?
- What feelings are you aware of when you consider exploring your partner's religion? How would you feel about your partner exploring your religion?

STEP FOUR: FACING YOUR OWN CHOICES THROUGH THE LIFE CYCLE

For most people, cultural and religious identity evolves over the course of a lifetime. While we don't choose our families, we do become responsible for creating our own identities. It's important to look at the choices you have made and how you have changed.

Step Four, in clarifying cultural and religious confusion, involves developing a better understanding of the ways that you have shaped your own identity. Up until modern times a person's cultural and religious identity was more a matter of destiny than decision. But as social change has accelerated, we now begin in adolescence to pick and choose from different strands of our cultural and religious heritages to create our own unique sense of identity. Often this process involves trying on, discarding, and then adapting new forms of identity.

By acknowledging all of the different cultural and religious choices you have made in your life, you can avoid the trap of talking about your identity as if it was fixed and unchanging. Part of preparing to negotiate with your partner involves first being aware of how you yourself have changed over the years. When you can begin to see all the changes you have gone through in the development of your own identity, it makes it much easier for you to deal with the emotionally charged issues of forging a family identity.

The following two exercises can help you to understand how you have molded your own identity during the different stages of your life:

I. Use the following chart to write one or two sentences about your cultural identity and about your religious identity at ages five, twelve, eighteen, twenty-five, and today.

AGE	CULTURAL IDENTITY	RELIGIOUS IDENTITY
5		
12		
18		
25		
TODAY		

As an example, the following chart was filled out by a twenty-nine-year-old Vietnamese man born in Oakland, California, into an immigrant family:

AGE	CULTURAL IDENTITY	RELIGIOUS IDENTITY
5	My parents only spoke Vietnamese at home. It was my first language until I started school. I lived in "Asia Town" in Oakland, but our family only spent time with other Vietnamese, and my friends were Vietnamese, so it was clear to me that I was part of that group.	Parents were religious Buddhists. We had a family shrine, and I observed religious rituals and rules both in the home and when I was away from my parents.
12	My parents' lack of much English meant that I was out of their control in a lot of ways. They counted on me to translate, and it made me feel like I was smarter than they were. Got involved some with gang that was Vietnamese and Chinese. Made me feel more like an Asian than a Vietnamese.	At home I was still a good Buddhist boy. But outside, I began to follow the rules of the street more often than Buddhist precepts. But I still considered myself Buddhist.
18	Left the gang and got into community college. Started to identify with being a college student, but often felt like I was different from most other people. I started to feel like being an outsider was a big part of my identity.	Took a philosophy course and began to feel that all religion was "stupid." Still living with my parents and paid minimal acceptable respect to Buddhist religious practices.
25	Got married last year to a Chinese woman.	We had to design the wedding ceremony and decided to use elements of both her background in Christianity as well as mine in Buddhism.
TODAY	Now we have a child. Starting to feel like we will make him into an Asian-American child and teach him about both halves of his legacy.	My wife is comfortable with Buddhism, and recently I have started to feel like it is important that we give our four-year-old daughter some religious education. We have decided to incorporate some Buddhist practice into our life and some Christian. They don't feel incompatible to me. I am starting to feel grateful now that my parents gave me a religious background, even if I have modified it.

II. Look at how your sense of cultural, racial, and religious identity has changed over the years by answering the following questions:

- When did you feel the best and the worst about your cultural and your religious heritages?
- Have your changes been gradual or dramatic?
- If your background is culturally or religiously mixed, did you emphasize different aspects of it at different points in your life?
- Have you ever strongly identified with a religious or cultural group that you were not born into?
- Have you changed your name or looks to hide your ethnic origins?
- How has your choice of neighborhood, your religious practice, or your political affiliations strengthened or weakened your cultural connections?

STEP FIVE: CLARIFYING WHAT'S REALLY IMPORTANT

As you become more aware of the nature of your own cultural and religious identity, you need to begin to sort out what is really important to you.

Below in random order are listed various components of cultural and religious identity. Sort the list in the order of their current importance to you to further clarify what you mean when you say "I am a ____." Put the statements that most accurately reflect what is important to you toward the top of your list. Put the statements that are less true for you lower in the list. Feel free to create additional statements that fit for you.

- A. I participate in cultural festivals of my group.
- B. I practice my religion in the context of a religious institution or community.

C. I socialize with other members of my cultural group.

D. I am not interested in my religion.

E. I live in an area where there is a high concentration of people of my group.

F. I practice my religion individually.

G. I visit the homeland of my ancestors.

H. I contribute money to causes related to my race or culture.

I. I learn about the history of my culture.

J. I contribute money to religious organizations of my faith.

K. I am involved in organizations that protect the rights of my group.

L. I learn and practice a religion other than the one I was brought up with.

M. I am involved with arts and literature related to my group.

N. I study cultures or religions other than my own.

O. I am not interested in my culture.

P. I study my religion.

Now answer the following sets of questions:

A. Religion

1. Which aspects of the religious traditions you were raised in are still important to you?

2. Which aspects of your religious heritage have you rejected?

3. Which aspects of your religious beliefs and practices could you compromise with your partner on?

4. Are there any issues that you are not willing to negotiate?

5. What practices do you want to teach to your children?

B. Cultural Traditions

1. Which aspects of your national, racial, or cultural heritage are important to you?

2. Which have you rejected?

3. Which aspects of your cultural background and identity could you compromise with your partner on in creating a family?

4. Are there any issues that you are not willing to negotiate?

5. What parts of your cultural traditions do you want to pass on to your children?

C. Identity

1. How much of your identity is positive and affirmative and how much angry, defensive, and defiant?

2. In what ways would you like to change your identity?

D. Ultimate Issues

1. Imagine being an old person looking back on your life. Culturally and religiously what would you want to be able to say about what was truly important to you in your life?

E. Changes

1. What did being involved with someone from another culture or religion mean to you when you met your partner?

2. What does it mean to you now?

Melissa and Ed: Sorting Out Religious and Cultural Identity

Melissa had been raised as a Presbyterian and Ed as a Jew. As a young married couple living in Washington, D.C., neither of them had thought of themselves or of their partner as very religious before Melissa became pregnant. But the birth of their first child started a crisis of personal confusion, interpersonal conflict, and negotiation.

They knew the baby was going to be a boy, and when Ed told Melissa that he wanted to have the child circumcised, she reluctantly agreed. Even though she wasn't convinced of the medical necessity of it, she felt she could accept doing it as long as she thought of it as a potentially beneficial procedure and not as a religious act.

When Ed offhandedly suggested that as long as they were going to circumcise their baby, they might as well have a bris (a Jewish ritual circumcision), Melissa felt herself stiffen. Ed was breaking their unspoken contract: Neither of them were supposed to upset their relationship by introducing religious symbols that would remind them of their different heritages. By asking for a bris, Ed had gone too far. She began to feel that she had made a mistake by agreeing to any kind of circumcision. The week before, her doctor had given her some literature that questioned the need for routine circumcision, but Melissa had decided to throw it away because she knew it would upset Ed. But now, by bringing up the idea of using an explicitly Jewish ritual, he had upped the stakes, and she wasn't sure what she should do.

Melissa and Ed's attempts to avoid conflict by denying the symbolic power and religious significance of circumcision had backfired. By trying to secularize and medicalize an act that was an identity-defining ritual and act of faith, they had set the stage for a crisis. They had tried to buy temporary peace by pretending that they were dealing with the cool logic of medicine and not the primal power of ancient tribal loyalties. Now they were paying the price.

> MELISSA: These discussions are opening up things we shied away from. We've been trying to avoid some really deep feelings, and this whole circumcision issue has to be dealt with.
>
> ED: Most things in our relationship we work out on an equal basis, but on this issue I feel very threatened by retreating to only 50 percent. What are we going to do? Circumcise half his penis?
>
> MELISSA: I can see now that I was being more agreeable than I really felt because I hadn't really sat and looked at it and talked with you about it. I know I agreed to have him circumcised, but I'm not so sure anymore. I'm beginning to feel like we've pretended to have an equal relationship. As long as something isn't that important, you are flexible. But when it comes to something like this that you really care about, I think you expect me to be the one to give in.
>
> If things were really equal, you would have taken the time to learn things about Christianity just like I took the time to learn about Judaism. I like to be exposed to new things, but I'm afraid that I've been too compliant.

For Melissa the ancient ritual of male circumcision brought up a very modern female concern. She worried that if she yielded on the issue of circumcision, she would lose her hard-won sense of power and autonomy. She saw herself as the first woman in her family to achieve real independence and equality in a relationship with a man. She was a successful professional and, up until this crisis, had felt that her marriage was a model of how men and women could share equally in creating a life. In fact a big part of her attraction to Ed had been what she had perceived as his comfort with her strength.

Now she was troubled by the idea that all of their talk of equality had been play-acting and self-delusion. It wasn't that she minded exploring some sort of Jewish identity for her child and possibly even for herself. It was just that Ed was so adamant about not even looking at Christianity. It just didn't feel fair or equal. If she gave in on this issue, she feared she would be slipping back into a modern version of the old female trap: As the price for having a man, she would be expected to return to traditional female subservience. In some ways it would even be worse. Ed would expect her to pretend that they were equal partners, even as she quietly yielded to him on all the big issues.

Melissa thought about her mother's bitterness. She had been a very talented woman who now felt that she had foolishly sacrificed her promising career in music for her husband, who left her for another woman when Melissa was twelve. She dreaded the idea that she might repeat her mother's sad history. Her autonomy as a woman and the discussion of their child's identity had become merged in a way that made them difficult to separate or successfully negotiate.

Ed had a lot of difficulty understanding Melissa's concerns. He didn't feel that his desire to have their son circumcised demonstrated his attempt to be dominant in their relationship. He reacted defensively and angrily to Melissa's accusations that he was trying to be the boss. He felt that he and Melissa had always had an equal partnership.

Because his formal religious training had been minimal, he had difficulty finding the words to explain the importance of enacting a key ritual of a religion he seldom practiced. As their conversation continued, it became obvious that both religious and cultural loyalties as well as the equality of their relationship were important issues:

ED: I appreciate your openness to Jewishness, but I just can't reciprocate in the same way. I have strong negative reactions to a lot of Christian symbols, and you don't have the same reactions to Jewish symbols. Remember when we went to see a performance of [Handel's] *Messiah* in that church last December? I don't want to go there again and I wouldn't want to take my child there. I don't mind listening to the music on a record. I don't have any objection to the arts and music. My objection is to the faith issues.

MELISSA: Your reaction to seeing Christ draped over the cross was very eye-opening to me. The church I grew up in was Presbyterian, not Catholic. There was only a bare cross in my church. We didn't have a scene of the crucifixion. I didn't even notice it when we went into the Catholic church. I understand your sensitivity. That doesn't bother me. [angrily] But do you get that that's not even my church?

ED: When you say, "There was only a cross on the wall," to me it's like saying, "I went into this room and there was only a guillotine on the wall."

MELISSA: [angrily] That's why I want you to learn about it. A cross is not a guillotine. And a cross with a body with blood coming out of it is going to push your buttons more, I think, than a bare cross. [crying]

ED: A cross is something the Romans used to stick in the ground and nail people to, and the people in this instance that they nailed were Jews.

MELISSA: So you don't want to go in a room with a cross in it.

ED: No, it bothers me intellectually.

Their disagreement brought out very different fears in each of them, and they were hardly just intellectual. For Ed, not circumcising his son meant that he would be the first man in a long string of generations who would break the long chain of Jewish tradition that so many others had fought for. For Melissa, circumcision was a religious act that she worried would somehow make her child different from herself—that he would become more Ed's than hers. Neither of them fully understood the other's concerns.

SYMBOLS EXERCISE: Gateway to the Unconscious

The following exercise that I used with Ed and Melissa to help them work out their conflict is useful for understanding the differences you and your partner bring to your relationship. You can use any set of relevant cultural or religious symbols that have meaning for you. For Ed and Melissa I suggested that they use a Christmas tree and a Hanukkah menorah as a less-charged set of symbols than the crucifix and the ritual of circumcision to redirect their attention to basic and underlying issues.

Both holidays occur in December, share common roots in pagan Solstice rituals, and emphasize light during the darkest days of the year. But the central symbols of these two holidays, the Christmas tree and the Hanukkah menorah, have very different meanings.

Symbols that are part of religious, seasonal, and life-cycle rituals are keys to our inner worlds of fantasy and dream. This unconscious realm uses emotion-charged symbols to serve as a primal shorthand that unites our hopes and fears, our past and future. Even when we cannot identify them, we sense their power beneath the surface of our everyday consciousness. But the emotional reaction we have to any symbol is not universal. Our reactions are shaped by the particular meaning a symbol has for our family, culture, and religion. When a partner in a mixed match doesn't fully understand the specific meanings a symbol has for him and his partner, painful misunderstandings can result.

I asked them to remember the time of year around these holidays as they were growing up in terms of the following three dimensions:

1. *Family Meaning:* What are your memories of your family's reaction to the symbol?
2. *Sense of Belonging:* What did the symbol mean to you as a member of a cultural group?
3. *Religious Meaning:* What was the religious meaning of the symbol to you?

I then gave them the following grids and had them write down a brief description of their childhood memories of each of the symbols and their associated holidays. I told them not to worry about the inevitable overlap between the three categories, but just to do their best in trying to separate their reactions.

	ED	MELISSA
FAMILY MEANING		
SENSE OF BELONGING		
RELIGIOUS MEANING		

THE CHRISTMAS TREE		
	ED	MELISSA
FAMILY MEANING	*Stress* My family felt stressed during December because we were one of the few Jewish families in the neighborhood. My father would complain that Christmas was just a way to get people to buy too much stuff they couldn't afford. He tried to give us the message that Christmas was stupid so that we would be glad we were not Christian and so that we couldn't say we were jealous.	*Warmth and comfort* It was one of the few times during the year that my disconnected family got together and celebrated. We had a large family meal and we got presents. We spent a lot of time looking forward to it. The only time I ever remember my parents holding hands was in front of the Christmas tree.
SENSE OF BELONGING	*Anxiety, envy, and resentment* I felt left out of what seemed like a national holiday. Since everyone else seemed to be celebrating Christmas and it was on the TV day and night, it made me feel that being a Jew meant I was different and an outsider. I felt like my father would get angry if I told him how much I wanted a tree in our house.	*Belonging* I felt like the whole human race was connected and that we could be friendly with strangers in a way that we weren't able to the rest of the year.
RELIGIOUS MEANING	*Anger and anxiety* My father used to describe the tree as a "soft-core crucifix" and talk about how stupid the "goyim" were to believe in "fairy tales." When I got older, it became a symbol of the oppression of Jews.	*Awe* The Miracle of the Virgin Birth of Jesus was very real to me. It was the one time of year my whole family used to go to church together. I was always moved by the idea of Jesus coming to take away our sins.

THE MENORAH		
	ED	MELISSA
FAMILY MEANING	*Pleasure* Got together with grandparents and cousins, lit the menorah, and ate a lot of potato pancakes. *Stress* Father resented having to "keep up with Christmas" and would argue with my uncle about how many presents to give the children.	*None* I didn't have any Jewish friends or neighbors as a child and didn't learn what a menorah was until I was a freshman in high school and became friendly with a Jewish girl.
SENSE OF BELONGING	*Pride and defiance* Always connected Hanukkah to the story of the Macabees fighting for freedom to be Jewish.	*None*
RELIGIOUS MEANING	*Awe of miracle* Impressed as a child with the story of how one day's supply of oil for the flame lasted for eight. It made me feel that God was on our side.	*Little or none* When I asked, my father told me that Hanukkah was the Jewish Christmas. Until I got involved with Ed, I thought of a menorah as the Jewish equivalent of a Christmas tree.

After they completed the exercise on paper, I asked them to share their responses and reactions to the exercise. The exercise helped them begin to understand the incredibly different meanings they attributed to both of the symbols. Melissa began to understand better that the Christmas celebrations she had found so pleasurable as a child tapped into painful memories for Ed of feeling like an outsider.

She also began to understand that for Ed, Hanukkah was not some kind of Jewish Christmas but actually symbolized to him the idea of fighting off others' attempts to suppress Jewishness.

It was the first time that Ed had stopped long enough to really listen to what Melissa was trying to say. He began to understand how, for Melissa, the Christmas tree had tremendous significance as one of the few symbols of warmth and unity in an otherwise disconnected family. And even though he found it very alien, Ed also began to grasp the idea that Christmas had a spiritual meaning for Melissa as she was growing up.

By learning about their differences Melissa and Ed began to understand the many asymmetries they had brought to their relationship. They saw that it wasn't so simple as "my religious beliefs versus yours." Rather they were dealing with different intensities of family loyalty, identity with their cultural groups, as well as religious differences. In the process they were also able to see how dealing with any differences meant that they also were defining how they would share power and define male and female roles in their relationship. They could both now see that they had to clarify and communicate their own feelings about each of these tribal, religious, and gender issues before they could successfully negotiate their conflicts.

Understanding each other's very different feelings and experiences helped break the emotional logjam that had prevented them from making decisions. As they began to sort out what was really important to each of them, they were better able to negotiate the next steps they would take. The process didn't provide easy answers, but for the first time they felt that they could talk about their concerns without getting into a major fight. And they were able to reach some decisions about a number of important points:

- They worked out an agreement that Melissa would be able to return to work sooner after the baby was born than they had originally planned and that Ed would take more responsibility for arranging and providing child care. This helped Melissa feel better about her worries that their relationship had only been pseudo-egalitarian.

- Melissa agreed to have their child circumcised, but not to have a bris. She got Ed to agree not to use their child's birth to push her into making any final decisions about the religious identity of their family. She argued that it wouldn't be fair to either of them if they rushed into a decision now to try to resolve all of the issues they had avoided for so long. It would take some time to sort out all of their feelings, and they both agreed that they would continue to work toward a mutually acceptable agreement that respected the needs and wants of both of them.

- Because they were both religiously nonobservant when they met and had shared so much in terms of race, class, education, interests, and their attraction to each other, they hadn't anticipated that their different backgrounds would present any serious challenges to their relationship. Melissa was now better able to understand how Ed could feel so strongly about being Jewish even though he knew far less about his religion than she did about hers. And Ed began to realize how he had been projecting his feelings about Christians and the history of the persecution of the Jews onto Melissa. He could now see how, by casting Melissa in the role of the oppressor of the Jews, he had been making it impossible for her to consider any serious involvement in Jewish life. It was the first time that they had ever really recognized both the cultural and the religious asymmetries that were part of their relationship.

- They went on to decide to do something that they could never have previously imagined doing together: They would begin to study both Christianity and Judaism together so that they could make more informed decisions about the future religious identity of the family they had begun.

No Simple Answers

Creating a shared sense of family cultural and religious identity is a complex task for all couples in this era of rapid change. Today there are few simple answers to the question of Who am I? And there are no solutions to questions of religious practice and cultural-racial identity that are best for all couples.

In order to work with your partner on making decisions about the identity of your family, it's important that you first work to clarify your own individual sense of connection with your family traditions. By sorting out your relationship with your own past, you can begin to develop a better sense of what is culturally and religiously important to you. You will then be in a much better position to try to understand your partner's sense of identity and be better prepared to work on creating a vital and positive identity for your family.

CHAPTER 5

Creating a Family Identity

My father died the same year Dale and I had our first child, Dale, Jr. And it was also that year that Susan, Dale's daughter from his first marriage who lived with us, entered high school. Even though Dale and I had always agreed that neither of us was interested in practicing religion, almost every month that year felt like we were involved in a different religious crisis.

My mother is Filipino and a devoted Catholic. My father was a WASP from North Carolina who was basically an atheist. My parents met when my father was stationed in the navy in the Philippines. Somehow they learned to live with their differences, but I always felt some tension between them over Mom's pushing us to go to church all the time. I rejected my mother's Catholicism years ago when I was in college.

Dale is from a mixed Irish-Scotch-English background, and he was raised without much formal religious training. Part of what he and Betty, his ex, fought about was religion. She is a devout Irish-Catholic who constantly took Susan to Mass over Dale's objections. When we got together, we were both comforted by the fact that neither of us wanted to practice any religion. But we soon found out that our little bastion of secularity was to come under attack.

The first crisis came after our son was born. My mother began to put a lot of pressure on us to have Dale, Jr., baptized. She was really angry because she felt that we were putting his eternal soul at risk. We resisted for months, but my mother just wouldn't let up, so we finally decided to go through the motions to appease her. We thought that would be the end of our struggles over religion.

But then my father got very ill a few months later, and the religious wars started up again. He made it very clear before he died that he wanted to be cremated and didn't want any religious service performed for him. That was fine with me, but when he died, mother went ahead and found a priest who would perform a Catholic funeral for him. It seemed like a sham and really wrong not to grant him his last request. I talked to my mother about it shortly before my father died, but she didn't listen to a word I said.

Then my stepdaughter Susan's mother, Betty, began to insist that Susan go to classes to prepare her to be confirmed in the Church. We had zero interest in having her confirmed, and she wasn't very interested, either, but because she lived with us, we were pressured into pushing Susan to go to class. And to make things worse, Betty expected us to do a lot of the driving to Susan's classes because Betty lived so far away.

Against my wishes I was going back and forth to church more than I had since I was a child. I had always had a decent relationship with my mother and Dale's ex, but I really started to resent them both. And even Dale and I began to argue over where to draw the line with them. He accused me of not being willing to set any limits. I began to feel that trying to lead a secular life was ending up being my cross to bear.

ISABEL, A TWENTY-NINE-YEAR-OLD BIRACIAL FILIPINO-WASP WOMAN RAISED IN
AN INTERFAITH HOUSEHOLD, MARRIED TO DALE, A WASP MAN

In the English language, most of our associations with the word *crisis* are negative. Western cultures tend to define crises as situations involving peril and potential loss. But not all cultures describe dangerous situations in the same way. The Chinese, for example, have no single word for crisis. The closest translation in Mandarin is the pairing of two characters, *wei* and *ji*, which define a time that presents opportunity as well as danger. Language shapes thought, and the Chinese language encourages a less dualistic way of thinking about situations that we label as crises. Celebrations have their potential dangers, even as tragedies offer the possibility of growth and transcendence.

The important life-cycle events—marriage, birth, and death—present just such dangerous opportunities in couples' lives. The rituals that are part of these life passages are used to acknowledge and affirm bonds of community, blood, and belief. They reveal not only the warmth and connection in family relationships but the unresolved tensions and conflicts as well. Reaching across time and space, they bring together family and friends, often from long distances, and create a stage for us to act out our most passionate dramas. For partners in mixed matches these times can be particularly stressful when they highlight unsettled cultural or religious differences between partners or members of the extended family.

Less dramatic transitions also provide opportunities for working through unfinished cultural differences. Choosing a neighborhood to live in, a school for a child, or even places to visit on a vacation are all important, if less ritualistic, defining moments. When couples can approach any of these life-cycle events as "crises" in the Chinese sense of the word, they can use them to resolve differences and deepen their relationships.

In this chapter you will meet couples who have creatively used the dangerous opportunities presented by the life cycle to learn more about themselves and their partners. Because every relationship is unique, there is no simple road map that can guide every couple through all of the different situations they will face. But the following exercises will help you to acknowledge and deal with your differences more compassionately, as well as enhance your ability to find creative solutions to questions of family identity.

EXERCISES: Making Use of Opportunities
Each of the following four steps can help you use the inevitable passages of the life cycle to enrich and strengthen your relationship. They are tools that should be used repeatedly as you approach and go through important life transitions.

Step One: Acknowledge Imbalances

Openly and honestly review with your partner the differences in your identities that you learned about as you went through the exercises in Chapter 4. And remember to take into account the differences in your cultural communication codes that you learned about in Chapter 3. As you share more of your personal histories with each other, try to identify the following differences:

- How assimilated each of you is into the majority culture
- The historical experiences of your cultural groups
- How fluent each of you is in your religion
- Your past and current relationships with your own religion
- The definition of sex roles and the division of power in your family of origin and in your current relationship

Step Two: Practice Unconditional Experimentation

Often couples try to deal with the anxiety of a crisis by trying to reach decisions too quickly. Working through differences takes time, and taking a shortcut may result in an unstable temporary truce. One way to slow things down is to use a process called "Unconditional Experimentation." This involves agreeing to learn about each other's cultures and/or religions and to "try on" a variety of possible solutions to your situation without making any promises.

Try to approach understanding the cultural and religious roots of your two respective families as openly and respectfully as you might explore an interesting foreign country. This is the best way to discover new, creative possibilities. Remember, you are conducting experiments that involve learning and trying on different possibilities. Agree not to make commitments before you are both ready. This process will not provide you with any quick answers. But if you are hoping to spend a lifetime together, it is worth the work.

Here are some ways you can experiment:

- Learn about your own culture and religion and more about your partner's. Read and take classes. Study by yourself and together with your partner. Attend each other's cultural and religious celebrations.
- Travel to each other's neighborhoods where you each grew up and/or to your ancestral homelands.
- Interview family members together about their cultural histories. Look through photo albums together. Videotape or audiotape grandparents and other relatives telling stories about their personal and cultural journeys.
- As you conduct your experiments, make sure to set aside time to share your reactions to them with each other.

Step Three: Make Decisions and Choose a Path

Stick with the process of learning, talking, and negotiating until you are able to make some decisions. Discuss the advantages of having one family religion versus incorporating aspects of both of your religious backgrounds. Decide which religious practices you will incorporate into your life and teach to your children. Decide what kind of neighborhood you want to live in, how often to visit each of your families, the language to speak at home, and how you will honor your ancestors.

The only real way to find out if a decision is going to work is to try it. You will never have enough information ahead of time to be certain that you are making the right decision. Don't insist on working out every detail now. Most likely none of your decisions will be perfect, but the decision not to decide is also a decision, and it's usually an unstable one, because it is not really satisfying to anyone.

Remember that the most successful long-term contracts between partners are those where both parties feel that their interests have been adequately represented and where neither side feels that it has "won" the negotiation. Good negotiations usually result in each partner experiencing some sense of loss as well as gain. Everything can't be perfectly equal, but if you got "too good" a deal, it is probably not such a great deal for your relationship. Remember, you and your partner are interdependent. In the short term it may feel like a triumph to have "won" a negotiation, but if you have created a situation in which your partner is resentful, the chances are that your agreement is bad. It probably won't last, and if it does, you may wish it hadn't.

From the experiences of the couples you will meet in this chapter, it should begin to be clear that there are many different ways that people can handle the cultural and religious differences they bring to their relationships. In spite of what some may counsel you about the *best* solution, no one answer is right for all couples. There is, however, a consistently bad solution: avoiding the difficult issues and living with chronic resentment. What is really important is doing the work to discover which path will work best for you.

In broad terms most couples choose some version of one of the following paths. We will look at them more closely in the chapters on raising children, but for now it is useful to introduce the five different decisions that most couples choose from.

FIVE FAMILY-IDENTITY PATHS		
PATH	DESCRIPTION	OPPORTUNITIES AND DANGERS
THE UNIVERSALISTIC PATH	Couples create an identity that transcends the particular religious or cultural identity that either of them was raised with. Or they will take elements of their own as well as of other cultures to create a unique blend.	*Opportunity:* Families can find ways to positively relate to their own and others' cultures and religions. *Danger:* Some couples use this path as a way to avoid the anxiety of dealing with their differences.
THE MINIMALIST APPROACH	Families who create a family life that is largely secular in outlook. While some elements of either or both of the partners' cultures or religions may be integrated into family life, the main identity of the family is as a family or couple, not as part of a larger group.	*Opportunity:* Can work well when neither partner has a strong cultural or religious identity and the family has other meaningful activities with which to identify. *Danger:* Little sense of belonging for children.

THE BALANCED SOLUTION	Couples work to include important elements of the religions and cultures of both of them into the family life and try to find ways to balance their importance and resolve conflicts between the two when they arise.	*Opportunity:* Both partners' cultures and religions can be enjoyed and made part of family life. Neither partner has to give up his or her practice or identity. *Danger:* Diffuse or confused identity for children if parents are not clear about dealing with contradictions, especially between beliefs of their two religions.
TWO CULTURES, ONE RELIGION	In these families one partner either converts to the religion of the other or actively participates in the other partner's religion without conversion. The couples, however, find ways to acknowledge their different cultural roots even as they practice a single religion.	*Opportunity:* Allows for spiritual togetherness of family while incorporating both cultures. *Danger:* Resentment if the partner who gives up his or her religion does not do so wholeheartedly.
ONE CULTURE, ONE RELIGION	These couples immerse themselves in the cultural and religious life of a single community. The partner who moves into the new culture spends time and energy assimilating into the community, going through many of the stages that the immigrant goes through in adapting to a new nation.	*Opportunity:* Clear religious and cultural focus for the family. *Danger:* One partner may feel he has given up too much of his or her identity and will resent the solution.

Step Four: Make Provisions for Renegotiation

Things change. Successful contracts are designed to deal with the inevitability of change as well as with the need for stability and predictability. One of the big problems with marital contracts is that they are not explicitly renewable. We make the vow of *till death do us part* and then somehow expect that we have closed the deal on a lifetime contract. With over half of all marriages ending in divorce, that clearly is not a very safe assumption. It is unrealistic to act as if every agreement in a relationship can remain totally constant throughout life.

Our idealization of the marriage contract makes it seem "unromantic" or a "bad sign" to make it explicit now that there will be a future need to renegotiate. But sooner or later we discover we must renegotiate if we hope to keep our relationships alive and vital. One way we can make sure that we do renegotiate our relationships is by using life-cycle events and rituals as opportunities for assessing the success of past contracts and planning for the future.

Marriage and the Wedding

For almost all couples the period of being engaged is an emotionally charged time. Choosing someone as a life partner is an act thats importance is difficult to deny. People enter marriage with the idea that they have made a decision to try to merge their fate with that of another person for the rest of their lives. Whether they succeed in this plan depends on how well they deal with their differences as they encounter success and failure, child rearing, temptation, aging, and loss.

Some get being engaged over as quickly as possible; others make it into a way of life. Those who marry quickly may be impulsively swept away by the intensity of their romance. They may rush the process because they secretly fear that if they really face their differences, the bubble of romance may burst. Or they hurry into marriage to separate from unhappy family situations. At the other end of the spectrum are those couples who manage to be engaged for years, continually finding ways to put off the big day. They fear the burden of commitment or have not found ways to work out significant interpersonal, financial, cultural, or religious issues. Some of these couples finally take the plunge, exhausted by delays that have become increasingly demoralizing, even though they still have not worked out many of their differences.

When couples treat the state of being engaged as a time-limited, intensified period to deal with their differences, they build better marital contracts and create stronger relationships. While couples usually don't like to remind each other of this fact, being engaged is the escrow period of love—a time when it is difficult, but still possible, to back out of the deal. As such, the state of being engaged presents one of life's best opportunities to work through differences. It provides a socially sanctioned status of *in-betweenness*.

But couples often fail to make use of the opportunity because romantic expectations attached to the state of being engaged and getting married make acknowledging and dealing with differences difficult as the wedding date approaches. Burdened by the discrepancy between idealized images of being in love and a tumultuous emotional reality as the wedding day approaches, many couples simply try to avoid the hot topics, fearing that if they try to deal with them, everything will blow up. Engagement can then become a very lonely time when each partner silently struggles with doubts they don't have a way of expressing. *(How come we've been having such a hard time ever since we decided to get married? If we really love each other, why are we constantly bickering? If either of us is having such serious doubts about marriage, maybe it means the whole thing is a big mistake.)*

It would be far easier if couples would accept being engaged for what it really should be—a time to wrestle with and work through as many differences as possible.

Because bride and groom bring different traditions to their marriage, the wedding ceremony itself is a particularly important "dangerous opportunity" for mixed matches. Weddings symbolically condense and display how a couple intends to live their life in relationship to family, culture, friends, spirituality, and success. The ceremony is an event that is designed to honor tradition. By their very nature mixed matches are usually defying tradition. The couple can feel torn between their own different desires as well as those of their two families. But the wedding also presents an opportunity for the couple to start designing a blueprint and laying down the foundation for the future cultural and religious framework of their new family.

JANINE AND LANCE—ACCEPTING IMBALANCE

Janine and Lance's experience revealed how religious and cultural differences can affect the process of getting married and defining the identity of a family. When they met in 1973, they were both twenty-six-years old and living in Atlanta. Janine worked in a dental office and Lance had just finished medical school and was preparing to begin an army residency in medicine in Hawaii. They quickly and passionately fell in love.

Janine had grown up in Texas. Her mother, a Mexican-American Catholic, and her father, a white Southern Baptist, fought often. Her father often seemed on the fringes of the family's life. As a child she had been exposed primarily to her mother's Catholicism. She went to church every Sunday with her mother until she was a teenager. During the summers she was sent to stay with her father's parents in Alabama on their small farm. When she was on the farm, she would go with her grandparents to the local Baptist church. She shuddered a little even now when she recalled the fierce fire-and-brimstone sermons that frightened her so much as a little girl.

Lance had grown up in a small town in Georgia. His mother was a devout Baptist and would take Lance and his two brothers to church every Sunday. His father, who was neither very religious nor successful in his work as a carpenter, occasionally went with them.

In Lance and Janine's talks during the early months of their relationship, they both emphasized how much they had in common. They would make fun of the Baptist church they had both been exposed to as children. They discovered that they had each taken a family trip to New York as teenagers and joked about how intimidating the big city was and the strangeness of northern accents. And they both acknowledged how peripheral their fathers had seemed in their family lives.

They used whatever common experiences they had as a way of building a sense of having similar pasts. But most of all they took continual pleasure in marveling at how well they understood each other's feelings. They weren't trying to deceive each other by ignoring their differences. Like other young lovers they were enjoying the feelings of closeness that grew out of focusing on all that they shared in common.

Three months after they got involved, Janine and Lance decided they wanted to get married. Lance was going to be stationed in Hawaii in the fall, and they were both anxious to solidify their relationship and move in together. But when they got down to the mechanics of how and when to get married, they found themselves repeatedly getting stuck.

First Janine said that she wanted to get married in a civil ceremony. Lance agreed and they set a date, but as they started to plan the wedding, Janine changed her mind and said that she really would like to have a priest marry them. Lance seemed to accept the change, but a few days later he called Janine and said that he had second thoughts about getting married by a priest. They never got to the point of talking with a clergyman, their parents, or their friends about these aborted plans. After two more rounds of making and unmaking plans, they decided that marriage could wait awhile. "We have plenty of time," Janine reassured Lance after they had decided to put marriage on hold. She told him, "We love each other and that's what's important."

Deciding not to decide seemed to work—for a while. But two months later the marriage bug struck again. Lance told the story:

> It seemed like the only problem we had in an otherwise perfect relationship was in deciding about the details of getting married. I picked up the phone at 11:35. I have never forgotten that time, because I had been sitting there watching the clock for over an hour as if it held some secret information that would solve the riddle of our relationship.
>
> Janine answered and I said, "Let's do *it* right now." There was a one-second pause on the other end of the phone. Then she said, "Okay." We agreed to meet at the fountain that was a few blocks away from where each of us was working. We both arrived breathless several minutes later. Neither of us had uttered the word *marriage*, but we both knew exactly what we were intending to do during our lunch break that hot August day.
>
> We literally went running four blocks through downtown Atlanta looking for the office of this justice of the peace we knew about. We burst through the front door covered in sweat and begged his secretary to see him immediately. He came out and we told him we needed to get married right now, and that we

only had one hour. He looked at us as if we were a little nuts, but agreed to do the ceremony. We had to ask the secretary to act as a witness. We both made it back to work on time. No one in the world knew except Janine and me and the justice and the secretary that we were now husband and wife.

They soon discovered that the actual act of getting married had not resolved the issue of the wedding. They moved together to Hawaii, but every month or so they had what they both came to call "the talk," which always focused on the issue of a "real" wedding. For Janine it was becoming increasingly clear that only a wedding performed by a *real* priest could satisfy her need to feel that she had had a *real* wedding.

LANCE: I didn't understand why a religious wedding had suddenly become such a big deal. The differences in our religious backgrounds hadn't seemed very important up to the time we began to discuss a wedding. At first I thought it was Janine's way of expressing her reservations about me. I felt that even though she said she wanted a big wedding, she kept creating obstacles in order to not make our marriage public. But I slowly began to recognize that as unclear as she was about her Mexican Catholicism, it still held a great power in her life that she and I needed to come to terms with.

JANINE: The shift was subtle at first. It began the moment we began to talk about getting a church wedding. Even though I wasn't a "good" Catholic, I began to realize I still wanted a Catholic wedding. The church's decree at the time was still that the man had to sign papers assuring that the children would be brought up Catholic. Lance refused to sign, but said he would make a verbal agreement. That wasn't good enough for the Church. Another problem was that we wanted to get married outside in a natural setting, and the Church wouldn't permit it.

So we waited. We didn't have our wedding until the time came that the pope made a decree that signing the papers was no longer necessary. Then I had to petition the bishop in Hawaii, where we were living, for permission to marry outdoors. Having done all that, I still couldn't find a priest to marry us. They all wanted me to leave Lance for a "good Catholic man."

Finally we got permission to marry outdoors and found a priest who would do it. Here I was, a hardly practicing half Catholic, totally twisting my life around a Church I had such an ambivalent relationship with and giving the man I loved such a hard time about having a church wedding. I felt really bad, because I didn't have the words to explain why I felt so strongly about the whole thing, and I knew this was all very difficult for Lance.

LANCE: At first I got really upset with all of the changes that Janine kept making. But then I felt like maybe I should try to figure out what I wanted to do for our wedding. I started to try to reach back into my own past to identify what was important to me. But I couldn't quite find anything that had the importance to me that the Catholic and Mexican rituals had for Janine. My grandfather was important to me, and I knew a little bit about his Dutch heritage. But when I tried to reach to the cultural and religious level to find something meaningful to incorporate into our marriage, it was like trying to grab a hologram. There was an image, but no substance. So I ended up deferring to Janine.

The act of getting married is a kind of dress rehearsal for a shared life, and the issues that came up for Lance and Janine during the creation of their wedding kept reappearing as they tried to create a family.

> JANINE: My yearning to find ways to introduce religious and cultural symbols kept slowly breaking into my consciousness—first around the wedding, but, as the years went by, also around food, faith, festivals, and most of all raising children. I couldn't understand it when we got together, but it's now so clear to me that we are an interfaith *and* a cross-cultural couple. So were my parents. It has brought a lot of confusion into our lives as well as a lot of richness. I can see now that Lance and I did a lot of pretending about how similar we were when we first met. Maybe in the *Reader's Digest* condensed version we did have some things in common. But my real history took a lot longer to come out. As soon as we really got involved, I found myself moving, almost against my will, back toward feeling more Mexican and more Catholic. The more I tried to bury my past, the more it seemed to insist on coming back to life.

Their three children were born during the first seven years of their marriage. The basic differences in the intensities of their religious and cultural identities remained a source of some tension in their relationship. Janine's religious impulse remained strong, and over the years she tried to get Lance involved with her in religious practice, repeatedly asking him to go to church with her. Sometimes Lance agreed to go along with her requests; other times he resisted.

Janine was always the one who took the initiative, and she kept hoping Lance would be more interested in religious life with her and their children. While his occasional participation kept her hopes up, Lance never got involved enough at church for it to really feel satisfying to either of them. Finally, after ten years of marriage, Janine and Lance worked out a solution that helped them come to terms with and accept the differences in their feelings about religion. They created a kind of *balanced solution* that incorporated her strong religious feelings with Lance's more secular "religion."

> JANINE: It was only a couple of years ago that I finally realized that I would never succeed in getting Lance to feel the same way about religion that I do. In some ways I had to mourn the loss of us finding a unified family religious path. Now it's me and the kids, and sometimes Lance comes along. Even though I felt a lot of loss by giving up the dream of spiritual togetherness, it's helped us in some ways because I'm not continually pressuring him for something that he's not willing or able to give.
>
> LANCE: When Janine was finally able to understand and begin to accept my lack of strong feelings for religious practice, our marriage started to improve. It was okay with me for her to take the kids to church, and as I felt less pressured, I actually began to enjoy participating from time to time. We learned that we could be different and still have a good marriage and raise good kids.

The Birth of a Child

Nothing is more powerful in revealing the interplay of religious and cultural differences in a relationship than the process of having and raising a child. The birth of a child, especially a first child, is a dramatic reminder not only of new life but of our own mortality. The entrance of each new generation makes us aware of the passing of another.

But even as they remind us of death, children offer us solace in the special kind of immortality they symbolize. Children are our messengers to the future; they carry us beyond our death. But we realize that it's not enough for our children just to carry our genes. In order to make us truly immortal, they need to carry something even more important: our values, our traditions, our identity. And one of the most important ways we define and try to transmit those aspects of ourselves is through some combination of our religious and cultural identities.

RON AND JULIE—THE BIRTH OF A CHILD AND THE DEATH OF DENIAL

Ron and Julie's story illustrates the potential for deepening relationships when a couple uses the crisis of birth to clarify their own cultural confusion. Ron had called me from the hospital anxiously requesting a counseling session as soon as possible. One day after their son's birth he and Julie found themselves locked in a bitter argument over what to name him. The next day they came for their appointment with their unnamed three-day-old son.

Ron was a forty-six-year-old Japanese-American biologist, Julie a thirty-six-year-old teacher and self-described "generic white Protestant American." After a few minutes of introductions they plunged into the issue that had precipitated their crisis.

"It's very important to me," said Ron, "that we give our boy a name that honors my grandfather, Tomoji. I know I never made it clear during the pregnancy, but when I saw our son for the first time, I suddenly realized how important it is to me."

Julie had checked out of the hospital early that morning, and her response had a tired, angry edge to it: "You agreed that we could name the baby Sam if it was a boy or Samantha if it was a girl. I respect your feelings about your family traditions, but I don't want a name that labels our child as being from any particular culture."

Until the birth of their child Ron and Julie had always felt proud of their transcendence of the limiting identities of their birth cultures. They had often quoted John Lennon's song "Imagine," which looks forward to a better time when people have left behind the racial, cultural, and religious attachments that seemed to be the cause of so much conflict in the world. Even after Julie got pregnant, they never felt that it was necessary to talk about how they would shape the cultural identity of their biracial child.

When Julie went into preterm labor, she called Ron, who was at a conference in a nearby city. He quickly left the meeting to join her at the hospital, but their new son arrived before his father. As Ron ran into the delivery room, the first words that burst out of his mouth were "What shape are his eyes?" Julie looked up at him in shock and confusion. Several hours after the baby's birth Ron told Julie for the first time about his wish to name their child after his grandfather. In spite of their shared ideology emphasizing the universal, Ron found himself obsessed with the particular. Ron and Julie finally had to deal with old and deep cultural loyalties that do not simply disappear.

Talking openly about their cultural contrasts had always seemed dangerous rather than potentially enriching. They both feared that the past might highlight their differences and pull them apart. Underlying the bond of their common values, they each had very different feelings about their pasts. They both sensed that dealing directly with these issues might open old wounds from their own complicated and conflicted histories.

At this point Ron and Julie began to share the experiences that had shaped their cultural identities in their families of origin. They focused on their family's celebrations of holidays, the experiences they had had with members of other ethnic groups, and their families' own attitudes about their cultural identities. Exploring these experiences helped them to understand more clearly the cultural aspects of their childhoods that were painful as well as those that brought them a sense of meaning and belonging.

This process also helped de-escalate their conflict. When they were able to begin to see that at least some of the roots of their conflict lay in a larger cultural and historical framework, they became less angry about each other's behavior and less confused and guilty about their own. By taking the risk of lowering their defenses and by trying to understand their conflict in this larger framework, they began working toward more compassionate solutions to their differences.

As Julie and Ron began to explore their cultural pasts, they started to realize that their feelings were mirror images of each other. While Ron felt both burdened and enriched by his hidden, intense history, Julie hungered for a sense of belonging and cultural identity she had never experienced.

Julie volunteered to begin telling her story. She sounded a bit apologetic as she started:

> In a lot of ways I feel like my cultural heritage is of being a nothing. I mean, I guess I would be considered a white Protestant, but really I don't feel like I'm anything. I have always felt kind of pale and empty. I'm a "wannabe." I always wanted to be something distinct. I remember as a little girl visiting my Italian friend's family. They seemed lively, close, and at times combative. I wanted what they seemed to have, and when I was at their house, I used to pretend that I was a member of their family and

their culture. But then it would be time to leave, and I would feel like Cinderella at the stroke of midnight. I had to go back to being the ordinary me, the nothing.

Julie's father had been a career military officer, and her family had moved every two or three years all through her early childhood. The only sources of constancy in her life were her immediate family, the United States Army, and the Methodist church services she used to attend with her mother and sister near the bases where they had lived. Her isolated, quiet, and controlled family life as well as her cultural inheritance seemed more a void than a source of pleasure or pain.

After Julie stopped talking, Ron hesitantly began to speak:

> I feel really weird talking about my life history. I've never spoken in any real detail to anyone but my sister and a couple of friends in college about this stuff. But earlier in our relationship, when I implied that I was a generic Asian-American man and that my future was not determined by my past, I was really avoiding talking about what I've been through. I guess I thought I could just forget about it by thinking it isn't important to my life anymore.

Although Ron periodically paused to check out how Julie was responding, his hesitancy gave way as his life story began to spill out. His parents were Nisei, the first American-born generation. They were raised in Hawaii by their immigrant families, who had moved there from Japan shortly after World War I. Ron grew up as a Sansei, a grandchild of the immigrant generation. He was born in April 1940, two years after his parents had left Hawaii and moved to California to take advantage of the mainland's greater opportunities.

His mother and father invested their life savings in a small shop in Los Angeles, involved themselves in a thriving Japanese-American community, and were already doing better than they had expected, when a day came that changed their lives forever—December 7, 1941. The Japanese attack on Pearl Harbor resulted in the internment of thousands of West Coast Japanese-Americans, the majority of whom, like Ron and his family, were American citizens and guilty of nothing but their Japanese ancestry. His family was forced to sell their store at a fraction of its worth. Then they were transported to a desolate outpost in central California. They were devastated. Ron blinked back tears as he spoke:

> I have only three memories of the camps. The first is of the chain-link fence I used to hold on to and look through at the mountains in the distance. The second is of the shiny boots of the white guards, whose faces I never looked up at. And the third is of tears silently running down my mother's cheeks.

He looked shaken but relieved. Julie was clearly transfixed by his story. She had only heard small bits and pieces of Ron's history before now, and never with any feeling. He looked at Julie and went on:

> After we were released, we briefly moved back to Hawaii to live with my grandparents. When I was eight, we moved from a totally Japanese-American world in Honolulu to a neighborhood outside of San Francisco, where we were the only non-Caucasians. It was a tremendous shock. Some of the older white kids taunted me, and one of my classmates threw a rock at me and called me a dirty Jap. My mother waited at the bus stop with me every day for fear of leaving me alone.

Although Ron's parents continued to stress the importance of associating only with Japanese, there were no other Japanese to associate with. Even though they lived just a few miles from San Francisco, they made little effort to interact with the vital Japanese community up the road. They might as well have moved to a cornfield in Iowa. The disparity between their words and their actions was confusing and disturbing. But since it was against the rules to question elders, Ron and his brother and sister could not challenge their parents' mixed messages. They suffered in silence, condemned to a joyless social isolation.

Until Ron was eight, he had been a boisterous and well-liked child, even while his family was imprisoned in the detention camps. Freedom in the land of Caucasians proved more difficult. After entering school in California, where there were no other Asians besides his brother and sister, he became increasingly identified as a shy, studious, and sad little boy.

Julie and Ron now began to understand the problem with their agreement "to leave the past behind." By reviewing their cultural histories, we had learned that Julie actually longed for a sense of closeness and connection that she felt cultural rituals and traditions could provide. Ron had revealed that his disinterest in his history was designed to conceal a painful past that he needed to come to terms with. For the first time they could clearly see the connection between their failure to deal with the past and their current crisis over naming their child.

As Julie reviewed her own cultural choices, she realized she had done very little experimenting with and defining of her cultural and spiritual identity. As an adolescent she had become increasingly disillusioned with the Methodist church. In college she dabbled in Zen and New Age philosophies, but ultimately decided that just being a "good person" was a sufficient identity for her.

Julie felt that her last significant cultural decision was deciding to get involved with Ron. Describing the beginning of their relationship, she made it clear that she saw that the price of involvement with him was forgetting about both of their pasts:

> I was attracted to the fact that he had a close and large family with a distinct cultural identity. But one day, soon after we started dating, I asked him what proportion of his friends were Asian. He answered, "I have no idea, because for me people are people." Then he said, "I guess I could really think about it and recall which of my friends are Asian and which are Caucasian or black, but it would be an effort, because my mind just doesn't categorize people that way." I took his answer as a message that talking about his cultural roots was taboo.

Ron's description of his cultural choices as an adult was as brief as Julie's. Although both his brother and sister had married Japanese-Americans, he had done everything he could to distance himself from his roots. His choice of Julie, he began to realize, was part of his effort to erase his history. His intense feelings about naming his new son, though, showed him that his cultural odyssey was not yet over.

While they had been very anxious to settle on a name for their baby, by the end of the session Julie and Ron joked that their son probably wouldn't be too damaged by going without a name for a few weeks. They seemed visibly more relaxed, though the issues they faced were far from resolved. Ron looked at Julie and said,

Before we started this process, I was really afraid that talking about our differences would push us apart, that we would feel like we had nothing in common. But now I feel like we've discovered that instead of tearing us apart, talking about our differences is bringing us closer than before.

By delaying naming their son, Ron and Julie had spontaneously started the Step Two process of unconditional experimentation. They now realized that they could give themselves more time before making final choices about the cultural identity of their child and of their family.

The third week, they both came into my office smiling. They had made a decision about their son's name. They would name him Tomoji Sam. Until he started school, they would call him Tomi at home. But as he got older, they would give him a choice—he could be called Tomoji, Tomi, or Sam.

They decided to continue with their experiments without the help of therapy. Six months later they began to take oral histories of their families. Julie's parents were receptive to the idea, and they began with them. Ron and Julie were surprised to find out that Julie's cultural history was more complex and interesting than they had realized. She had several great-grandparents who had come to California in covered wagons. And to their astonishment they found out that one of Julie's great-grandparents was a Cherokee Indian, a fact that her parents "had never thought important enough to tell her."

Ron's parents were at first very reluctant to talk about the past, especially their wartime experiences. Although much of their social life revolved around relationships and organizations that had evolved out of their internment in the camps, they had created a

rigid barrier between the generations. They were wonderfully effective magicians and had made the past seem like it had disappeared—even from their own children. And they certainly had
never talked with Caucasians or other outsiders about their bitter
experiences.

They were so successful at adapting and fitting into American
life after the wartime betrayal by their own country that it almost
seemed as if the internment had never happened. Their children
were faced with the task of digesting an enormous history that
they were not even allowed to taste. His parents often used the expression *shogamai*, which roughly translates to "You can't do anything about it." Ron now realized that their attempts to make the
past invisible were consistent with the passive fatalism revealed
by the way they used the word *shogamai*.

After several months of brief and awkward conversations they
agreed to "tell a few stories." Their talks gradually evolved into a
series of deep, quietly intense, and very personal revelations
about their wartime experiences in the camps. These conversations brought them all closer than they ever imagined they could
be. After talking late into the evening one night, Ron's mother said
to Julie, "I never thought that someone who didn't go through it
could possibly understand. But you do." Ron and Julie's patience
and persistence had paid off.

The crisis brought on by the birth of their child revealed the
very different cultural roots they had always feared acknowledging. As their little unnamed infant pushed open the doors that had
hidden their pasts, their fears had seemed confirmed because of
the pain and conflict they experienced. But as they became less
anxious talking about their backgrounds with each other and with
their families, they each began to see that the cultural histories of
their childhoods contained healing and nurturing memories as

well as traumatic ones. Ron remembered the supportiveness and solidarity of the Japanese community through hard times. Julie began to appreciate the flexibility and freedom of her liberal Protestant background. They both experienced a sense of relief, and for the first time they began to see new possibilities and how they might actually find ways to use the past to enrich the future.

Choices for Children

There are other life-cycle passages linked to the growth and development of children that have no rituals to mark them. While not as dramatic as weddings or births, they can serve as forceful reminders of any unfinished business in defining the identity of a family. One of the most important of these passages occurs when the first child in a family enters school. This transition marks the entrance of the family into a community of families that are part of a school. Choosing a neighborhood and a school are decisions that will have a crucial impact on family identity. If parents have not already resolved the following questions, their child's entry into the larger world brings up several issues:

- Where are the best schools for our child?
- Are there religious institutions in the area that will meet our needs?
- What kind of cultural, religious, and racial neighborhood mix would feel comfortable for us?
- Will our children feel accepted for who they are?
- What kinds of compromises are we willing to make?
- Does one of us feel more comfortable than the other with the neighborhood we are considering? Does the less comfortable parent feel he or she could adapt?

- Is this a place where we would want to put down roots?

ALAN AND SARA—KINDERGARTEN AND COMMUNITY

Alan and Sara both brought to their relationship strong identities as members of two different minority groups. Alan felt as intensely about being African-American as Sara did about being Jewish. Rather than trying to escape the past, Alan and Sara were preoccupied with it.

When their son, Eli, was about to turn five, Alan and Sara found themselves stumbling over unfinished decisions about the identity of their family. Eli's life passage of entering school focused their attention on how important neighborhood and community are as shapers of identity. Since Eli's birth, they had lived in a flat in an inexpensive student neighborhood near the university where they had met. They both felt they now needed a larger house in a family neighborhood with more young children, but they couldn't agree about where to move.

They were very conscious of wanting to find ways to instill both African-American and Jewish identity in their son. Before they married, they agreed that they would expose their children to Jewish culture but that they would raise them in a predominantly black neighborhood. But now that it was time to make the move, Sara was no longer sure she wanted to keep her agreement.

SARA: Eli is the product of a biracial marriage, and to a certain extent he's going to feel different no matter where we live. Six years ago, when I agreed to live in a mostly black neighborhood, I had no idea how bad the public schools had become. We have to adjust to reality. I would like to live in the city, too, but we should move to the place where Eli can get the best education. Unfortunately the suburbs are the place. And there's a good Jewish community center there, too. Anyway he's so light, most people aren't going to even think he's black.

ALAN: I know the schools aren't perfect in the city. But the neighborhood I want to move to is mostly middle class and more than half black. Eli's going to be identified by the world as black and he should grow up in an environment where he doesn't feel different.

The conversation quickly turned into a heated debate. Each of them ended up arguing that the suffering of their ancestors somehow entitled them to a greater say in the decision they were going to make.

ALAN: How can you know what it means to be discriminated against? You grew up in a comfortable, safe neighborhood. You got to choose whether or not you revealed to others that you were Jewish. My ancestors were brought here as slaves.

SARA: I can't believe you're saying this stuff. You know that I lost great-aunts and great-uncles in the Holocaust. You don't have any monopoly on suffering. What right does the past give you to say how we lead our lives?

It's not unusual for couples to clash when their cultural differences are highlighted by a life passage. Alan and Sara's conversations about identity tapped into very complicated and intense sets of cultural and personal meanings and emotions. When I suggested that they slow down their decision-making process by first focusing on the personal experiences that had helped create each of their own sense of identity, they seemed to welcome the opportunity to stop fighting. As they shared their stories more openly, they found that they were able to begin to transform conflict into compassion.

Alan revealed that he himself was the product of an interracial marriage—his mother was black and his father Irish-American. The relationship was tumultuous, but they had remained married. The quiet but effective exclusion of his biracial family by neighbors and schoolmates in their predominantly white neighborhood made Alan feel uncomfortably different from his peers. His fair skin, blue eyes, and Anglo speech also separated him from his potential black friends on the other side of town.

Sara's relationship to her Jewishness was as problematic as Alan's was to being black. As she was growing up, her parents had focused on the Holocaust and the persecution of Jews as the center of their Jewish identity. Rather than celebrating Jewish holidays or actively participating in the Jewish community, their main connection to being Jews was through their identification with the suffering of other Jews. They often referred to the Holocaust and were quick to discover the anti-Semitic slant in every article about Israel in the newspaper. When Sara was an adolescent, she once asked her parents why they kept saying that it was so important to them that she marry another Jew when she grew up. Her mother's answer was one sentence long: "If you marry a goy, sooner or later he'll get angry with you and call you a dirty Jew."

When I asked Alan and Sara to review how their identities had changed since they had left home, they each seemed somewhat taken by surprise. A few minutes earlier, during their argument, each of them had been acting as if they were the official representatives of their respective cultural groups. Alan had cast himself as the protector of black pride, and Sara as the defender of the Jews. But when they started talking about the choices they had made, they were able to begin to see that even their marriage was one of a series of identity transformations they had each gone through.

> ALAN: My senior year in high school I really tried to fit in with the white kids on the tennis team. But it never felt quite right. In my first two years of college I got politically active in black causes. I got injured a few times by the police in anti-apartheid demonstrations, but it wasn't a big deal. But I resented having to "talk black" all the time with the other guys in the movement. It wasn't how I was raised and it wasn't me. Finally, I got interested in reggae music and Rastafarians and grew my hair. I was definitely the only graduate student in social work with dreadlocks.

Alan worked hard in all the arenas of his life, yet felt alienated and uncomfortable in each. Although his professors in college had respected his intellect, they felt vaguely uncomfortable with his appearance. He could speak in the ghetto language of the streets, but it was with the accent of one who had grown up in a more privileged neighborhood. Sara's parents seemed overtly tolerant of Alan, but subtly tried to undermine what they saw as their daughter's unconventional choice of a mate. With his Jamaican dreadlocks, his sixties radicalism, his ambiguous racial appearance, and his gentle demeanor, Alan seemed a part of so many worlds and yet a member of none.

When Sara talked about the choices she had made, it revealed that her Jewish identity was as complex and conflicted as Alan's black identity was to him.

> SARA: In college I became really disenchanted with what I saw as the materialistic and spiritually empty suburban Jewish world

I had come from. I was never interested in Judaism, but I became increasingly involved in Jewish culture. When I got together with Alan, I told him that it was really important to me to have kids who identified at least in part with being Jewish. He seemed sympathetic to the idea, but I don't think he really understood what I meant by "being Jewish," since at the time I wasn't doing much to define myself as a Jew. I guess it was just a feeling of connection that I was going after.

The root cause of Alan and Sara's earlier competition for title of "greatest victim" had been embedded in their unsuccessful attempts to resolve their own internal cultural confusion. By sharing more about their pasts they began to understand how they had each projected their own personal ambivalence about their group identity onto their partner. When Sara had felt certain that Alan was the one who had all the negative feelings about Jewishness, she didn't have to acknowledge her own. And when Alan saw Sara as being insensitive to the "black experience," he was able to avoid struggling with his own doubts and confusion about what it meant to be a biracial man. Just as Sara used her family's suffering under the Nazis to try to solidify and focus her identity, Alan had used slavery and the persecution of blacks as a way to simplify and clarify his complicated identity.

As they returned to their conversation about the future, they were noticeably less tense. They were now more aware that they had each been working on creating a clear sense of identity for years, even before they had met. And they also started to realize that being together did not mean the process had to end.

For Alan and Sara, reviewing the choices they had made as adults quickly evolved into Step Two, unconditional experimentation. They decided to take Eli on a summer trip to North Carolina, where Alan's black grandmother still lived in a quiet neighborhood in Charlotte. Alan had spent a number of his summers there as a teenager, and his memories were mostly positive.

At first Sara was reluctant to go on a trip to the South. She had never been there, and her images of the South were overwhelmingly negative. She was also frightened about how they would be treated there as an interracial family. Living in California seemed so safe. But Alan reassured her that his grandmother's neighborhood was safe, and they went ahead and planned the trip.

The first Sunday after they arrived, they all went together to Alan's grandmother's church. Sara had been in a few churches before, but had always been uncomfortable. Now she was not only the only Jew but the only white. It wasn't easy for her to go in. But the congregants all knew Alan's grandmother well and were gracious and welcoming.

"The singing was incredible," said Sara. "It was spring, and Easter was coming. I thought I would be squirming. But the choir sang so beautifully about the Hebrews going down from Egypt and leaving slavery that for a minute, when I closed my eyes, I thought I was in a synagogue—except that the singing was so communal and so moving."

For Alan and Sara one successful experiment led to another. Their crisis marked the beginning of a long series of discussions that led them to find meaningful ways to connect to each other's cultures as well as their own. Alan got involved in setting up a tutoring program for low-income children in a predominately black school. Sara started helping Soviet Jewish refugees with their housing needs and their problems in adapting to the United States. That year they helped a local synagogue and Baptist church organize an interracial

Passover dinner that highlighted the common symbols and experiences of slavery and liberation that were at the core of both African-
American and Jewish identities. Eventually they decided to move
to a middle-class neighborhood that had enough black families to
satisfy Alan and, as Sara put it, "good enough schools."

ADRIANA AND TERRY—THE DEATH OF A PARENT

Adriana was born in Cuba in 1957, two years before the revolution
that brought Fidel Castro to power. Before the revolution her parents had run a small candy business and had been very involved in
the practice of Catholicism. The new Communist economics disturbed them, but Castro's antagonism toward the church was intolerable. They managed to escape to South Florida in 1963, where they
raised Adriana in the large expatriate Cuban community. Adriana's
parents' new life remained so Cuban in character that they never became fluent in English. They were able to reestablish their business
and became even more devoted to the Church.

Adriana was an only child, and was the first person in her extended family to complete college. Her parents were proud of
their beloved daughter, but her art studies in New York City and
her immersion in English-speaking society led to a physical and
emotional separation that left them all a little sad and uncomfortable. At twenty-eight Adriana was a talented and successful young
woman in her family's adopted land. She had found exciting work
as a set designer for an off-Broadway theater when she met Terry.

Terry was a cardiologist who was raised in a very religiously committed and conservative Mormon family in Salt Lake City. He was
the oldest and the most gifted of their three sons and two daughters.
His parents were aware that Terry's intellectual abilities might lead
him away from them, and they had repeatedly told Terry all through

his adolescence that they hoped he would settle in Salt Lake and that they absolutely expected him to marry another Mormon. Terry was the "good son" in high school, and he had always assumed that he would fulfill his parents' wishes. He attended college and medical school in Utah but went to New York for his residency, after promising his parents that he would return to Utah as soon as his training was complete. He met Adriana at a party given by some mutual friends the last month of his residency. They fell in love and moved in together two months later.

They seemed to easily adapt to the cultural differences they brought to their relationship. Adriana was more expansive in her gestures and emotions, Terry more restrained and reserved. Rather than being a source of conflict, they savored their differences in style and felt that they were continually learning from each other. Living in New York, they thought of themselves as citizens of the world. Their religious backgrounds, they both agreed, were part of their past but not of their future.

But neither of them could bring themselves to tell their parents that they were "living in sin." To make matters worse, of course, was the fact that they were each living in sin with a person from an unacceptable religion. They kept separate phone lines and answering machines in their apartment so that when their parents called, they would not accidentally find out about their relationship.

Terry and Adriana both kept putting off telling their parents about their relationship. Terry told his parents that he had decided to stay in New York one more year to take a fellowship. Adriana's parents accepted that she was going to stay in New York, but she told them nothing about her relationship with Terry.

Terry described the incident that sparked his decision to tell his parents about his relationship with Adriana:

For a long time I was afraid that if I told my parents, it would kill my father. He had suffered from chronic colitis ever since I moved to New York, and last year he had been diagnosed with prostate cancer. I was really concerned about what would happen if he had to deal with the truth.

I think we were all invested in pretending that things were different than they actually were. They knew I had changed. They knew I had started dating a non-Mormon woman, and I think they even suspected that we had moved in together. When I would call them, they never asked about Adriana, which was their way of expressing their disapproval. But none of us addressed the issue, and our shared conspiracy of silence meant that we would all pretend that my relationship with Adriana wasn't really serious.

That year Paul, a gay colleague and friend of mine, died of AIDS. He had been brought up as a Mormon too. I was listening to a friend of his give testimony at his funeral. The man talked about how he had always felt inspired by Paul's courage in confronting difficult realities. He added that knowing Paul had helped him to take some important risks in his life and that he was really grateful to have been Paul's friend. And he said that even though Paul had lived a life that was very different from what his parents had expected, they had always maintained a close connection with him throughout his life and during his illness.

At that moment it really hit me. I realized how sad I felt that my relationship with my parents had become so superficial. What I was doing was absurd. My parents were getting old, and my father was approaching the end of his life. I really did love them. It hurt me and I think it must have also hurt them for us to be so emotionally distant. I was sick of living a lie and I decided to take the chance of telling them everything. I wrote them a letter and simply spelled out the whole situation that my parents and I had been hiding from.

At first it was really hard. We stopped talking for three months. My father's colitis flared up, and he was briefly hospitalized. I spent a lot of sleepless nights feeling that I was going to be responsible for my father's death. But then, two months later, I received a card from my father. He said that he had really been thinking a lot about me and that he had prayed a lot, and that he felt that even though he would never fully understand why I had left the Church, he was prepared to accept my decisions. And he went on to invite Adriana and me to visit them for Easter. I cried.

We went, and my father was true to his word. It was the best visit we had ever had. We didn't talk about religion, and we just seemed to enjoy one another for the first time in many years. And when I asked him about his colitis, he acted nonchalant and mentioned that he was symptom-free for the first time since he had developed the condition. I now think that all the pretending had taken a big toll.

The final chapter in every life is death. At the beginning of the next winter Terry's father died of cancer.

TERRY: When my father died of cancer later in the year, I felt at peace in my relationship with him. Adriana and I went to the funeral together, and my family was very gracious to us. I am very thankful for the last year we had of feeling so much closer.

ADRIANA: I was very upset by all of this. If I'm going to be honest, I think it was because I was jealous. I could not even contemplate telling my family. Cuban-American culture in general, and my family in particular, are in many ways very conservative. I don't know if it would kill my father if I had told him, but I almost felt afraid he might kill me. I just couldn't do it. And I didn't.

When my mother's sister got sick last year, Terry encouraged me to use the situation to be more honest with my parents. He reminded me of how his risk had paid off. I had never been more aware of the differences in our backgrounds. I just felt he couldn't possibly understand how and why it was so impossible for me to do what he had done. When my aunt died, I went to the funeral alone, even though Terry offered to come. I wanted Terry to be there for support, but I just couldn't imagine answering the questions that would be raised by our being there together.

We've talked about it a lot since then, and I think Terry understands better why I have to do things at my own pace. But I also realize that sooner or later I will have to deal with the situation.

Like other important life passages, the illness and deaths of a friend and family began a process of change. Even though Adriana decided that she was not yet ready to talk to her parents about the reality of her life, she decided that she didn't want to go on much longer without telling her parents about her real life. She began to realize that she couldn't always reconcile her wish to please her parents with her need to define a life of her own. Terry felt that his friend's death helped him take the risks that brought new life into his relationship with his family and most importantly with his father during the last year of his life.

Getting Help

If you find that you are stuck in the process of working out a mutually acceptable sense of religious and/or cultural identity for your family, you may benefit from counseling. You may actually be closer to making some good decisions than you realize, and sometimes a little help can go a long way toward making your relationship work.

In the past, couples turned to clergy for whatever counseling they might need as they approached marriage or having children. In more recent times psychotherapists are often called on to help couples with family conflicts over religious practice and cultural identity. But whomever you turn to, remember that no clergy or counselor is value-free. Don't turn to experts to tell you the best solution. They will all have their own opinions. Rather, find someone who can help you reach a decision that you feel comfortable enough with.

We don't expect clergy to be "value-free" in their approach to dealing with a couple's questions about religious practice. After all, clergy are in the business of promoting their own religion's particular view of how to create a moral universe. But even among clergy within any particular denomination, there is a wide range of approaches to the issues presented by interfaith marriage. While some clergy are more interested in "protecting" their religion than in helping couples, others are skillful at guiding couples in finding religious solutions that work best for them.

Some clergy err by being too rigid and doctrinaire in their approach to interfaith marriage. They see it as only a mistake for the couple and a threat to the integrity of their religious community. These clergy tend to be uncomfortable with or critical of couples even before they understand their particular concerns. But other clergy err in precisely the opposite way. They are so eager to be accepting and so anxious about the possibility of alienating anyone that they never question or challenge each partner's reasons for looking to the rituals of organized religion for guidance.

Even among those clergy who strongly believe that couples should practice only one religion in their household, there is a wide range of attitudes and approaches. I interviewed a rabbi and a priest together who were good friends and who constantly referred interfaith couples to each other. Neither of them would offi-ciate at interfaith marriages, and they both agreed that it was better for a couple to practice one religion, even if it wasn't the one that they represented. But they were open and respectful of each couple's decision. They simply asked that couples also re-spect their values as well and not ask them to create a composite Jewish-Christian religion by having them both officiate at a life-cycle ritual.

When either of them met with couples who were in a crisis over deciding which religion to practice or how to get married, each urged both partners to become as knowledgeable as possible about their own and their partner's faith before making important religious decisions. The couples who saw them were often sur-prised because they expected each clergyman to try to sell them on his own particular faith. Instead they each tried to promote the idea of a unified family religious practice.

Other clergy sincerely believe in the possibility of combining two (or more) kinds of religious practices in a single family. They had all co-officiated with clergy from other religions at life-cycle rituals. Even when they tried to teach about their own religious perspectives, they remained open to other possibilities. While groups such as the Unitarians are the most open to more "univer-salistic" approaches, I have spoken with rabbis, Catholic priests, Lutheran ministers, and others who have participated in compos-ite types of religious rituals.

Just as we sometimes mistakenly assume that clergy will be rigidly bound by preconceived notions, we can also err when we assume that therapists will be value-free. There is no such thing as a value-free therapist. Take your time and choose carefully when selecting a psychotherapist to assist you in the process of defining the religious or cultural identity of your family. Some therapists are extremely uncomfortable in dealing with religious and cultural issues. They may feel that they must behave in a totally neutral way when in fact they feel quite strongly about intermarriage, or they may simply be uncomfortable addressing issues of race, culture, and religion. They may also be inexperienced in dealing with complex family situations and prefer to see each person as an individual, which is usually not as effective in dealing with couples' issues. Find someone who understands religious and cultural issues, is willing and able to get involved in helping you as a couple, and has a background in family therapy in case you decide that it would be good to involve other members of your family in the counseling process.

What love conceals, time reveals. Important life-cycle passages inevitably illuminate the problem areas a couple has in defining a clear identity for their family. A wedding, a birth, a child's rite of passage, or the death of a parent can all bring unfinished business about identity into focus. These events can also expose generational conflicts by calling attention to the different religious and cultural choices made by parent and child. But as difficult as the crises catalyzed by life-cycle passages can be, they present crucial opportunities for people to confront really important issues and to build more solid and satisfying family relationships.

Because discussions about the religious, racial, and cultural identity of a family can be so complex and emotionally charged, many couples choose to avoid them. Putting off dealing with these issues, though, is like buying peace for your relationship on a credit card. You may enjoy the temporary freedom from anxiety you "purchased" by avoiding the difficult topics, but when the bill finally comes due, the "interest" that's accumulated in the form of resentment and regret may be devastating. Whether you use the help of clergy, psychotherapists, friends, family, or decide to do it on your own, the most important thing to remember is to do the work of creating a clear religious and cultural identity for your family. The sooner you do it, the greater the chances will be of your finding a path that works for your relationship. Pay as you go.

CHAPTER 6

Dealing with Parents, Family, Friends, and Foes

Yesterday I told my mother I would marry an Eta,
Today my mother told me I had died.
Yesterday I was part of a family,
Today I am an orphan.

POEM BY A JAPANESE WOMAN WHO MARRIED AN ETA MAN

Almost all mixed matches are seen by some members of both partners' cultures and communities as a betrayal of tradition. Although there are many places in the world that are more tolerant of cross-cultural marriages than they were a generation ago, ancient loyalties and prejudices have far from disappeared. Your relationship may be seen as a sin, an abomination, or, more benignly, an unconventional choice. But whenever others judge your love, you are faced with important decisions about how to respond.

The poem that began this chapter, by a Japanese woman who married one of modern Japan's two million *burakumin*, the leather tanners traditionally known as the Eta, illustrates the sad fact that some intermarriages almost inevitably lead to a total rupture of family ties. Although ethnically and religiously indistinguishable from other Japanese, the Eta throughout history have led lives almost totally segregated from the mainstream. They deal with dead animals in a largely vegetarian society. They are in effect the Japanese caste of untouchables. In a society concerned with cleanliness and belonging, they are the ones chosen to be the unclean outsiders.

Those who marry into the *burakumin* literally lose their families. One can enter into the *burakumin* but not exit it. The *buraku* example from Japan presents us with one end of the continuum of family and social reaction to intermarriage: the complete disowning of the intermarrying couple. There is no way to remove the invisible stain of Eta blood.

The few who marry into the Eta have only one advantage over those who intermarry in more open and diverse societies: They don't have to trouble themselves wondering if or why their family will object to their decision. They won't need to reflect on the subtleties of their parents' motivations for refusing to accept their relationship, because they are all too aware of having broken a fundamental social taboo. Banishment is not a surprise.

Couples who choose partners across religious, ethnic, and racial lines in Western cultures find that the reactions of family, friends, and society are usually less drastic, but often more confusing. One of the major challenges mixed matches face is finding ways to understand and deal with the complex responses of others to their relationships.

Sometimes partners in mixed matches are overly sensitive and misinterpret others' mild discomfort, awkwardness, or simple curiosity about cultural, religious, or racial differences as evidence of terrible intolerance. Or they may interpret the lack of civility of a stranger as disapproval of their interracial relationship when in fact they are dealing with an equal-opportunity boor whose bad manners are distributed evenly to everyone irrespective of race, creed, or color. Other couples err by being too patient with people who truly are biased and hateful. They tolerate abusive behavior that they should not put up with.

But one of the problems in understanding and responding to others' reactions to your relationship is that every reaction may be motivated by incredibly different values and emotions. The response to a special report, "Mixing Colors," in the February 9, 1992, issue of *Image* magazine in the *San Francisco Examiner*, was a dramatic illustration of this fact. One of the articles in that issue was entitled "You Can See the World in Their Faces," by Joan Walsh. It sympathetically explored issues facing the children of interracial marriage. Several weeks after its publication, a self-proclaimed white male "racist, redneck" and a black woman found unlikely common ground in their attacks on the article expressed in their letters to the editor.

> Call me a racist. Call me prejudiced. Call me a redneck. Call me whatever you like, but I believe in separation of the races. Your February 9 issue celebrated the mixing of races through miscegenation, and you are wrong. All races should remain pure and untainted by other races. Think I am alone in holding these views? I hate to disillusion you, but more people worldwide share my views than share your race-mixing views. Racial purity forever!
>
> TED BILBO III

> As a black woman, I am livid with your "Mixing Colors" issue of February 9. Virtually every day I see black men who have spurned

their black sisters to marry white women, which is a blatant slap in our faces. And now you come along encouraging and promoting mixed marriages. Your February 9 issue was a knife in the hearts of all black women.

ARTISHA HANKS
OAKLAND, CALIFORNIA

Mr. Bilbo and Ms. Hanks probably could find little else in life to agree on other than their anger about the article that they each saw as encouraging interracial marriage. Underlying Mr. Bilbo's call for racial purity, no doubt, are the fear and rage of those who require a scapegoat to organize their view of the world. Hatred requires an object for its passion.

Ms. Hanks' response, however, is motivated by the anger of those who want to marry within a culture and who have difficulty finding mates. Over the past three decades many black women, who have fought alongside their male counterparts for civil rights and economic justice, have been disturbed by one of the unintended by-products of their accomplishments: increasing rates of interracial marriage, especially between black men and white women. Two-thirds of African-American intermarriages involve a black man and a white woman. With increasing rates of middle-class, educated men marrying out of the African-American community and the high rates of young, lower-class black men who are unemployed or snarled in the criminal-justice system, it's no wonder that among black women, the absence of suitable mates and interracial marriage are topics that generate distress, anger, and pain.

Why Others React the Way They Do

People's responses to your relationship are inevitably a function of their own life experiences, the values of the cultures and families they were raised in, and the social climate they live in. The combination of these factors makes the important task of understanding others' reactions very difficult. When I spoke to Elena, a Chilean woman who had immigrated in 1976 to the United States with her husband to escape political oppression under the Pinochet regime, it became clear that her complex feelings about her daughter Maria's interracial relationship were intertwined with painful strands of her own history. Elena remembered the cautious way Maria first told her about Matt.

"Mom, how would you feel if I told you that I was going out with a guy who is getting all A's at Columbia?" Maria's tone instantly aroused Elena's curiosity and a little uneasiness—she sensed that Maria was bracing her for something. Not waiting for a response, Maria went on, "And, Mom, what if I told you that his mother is a Yale-trained physician and that his father has an MBA?" Maria was usually very direct, and Elena sensed that Maria's coy question-and-answer game must be the preamble to an uncomfortable topic. Elena responded cautiously, "Well, I'd have to get to know him before I could tell you how I felt."

Maria set up a lunch date for the three of them. They agreed to meet Matt at a newsstand right outside of Penn Station. When Maria and Elena arrived there in the middle of the afternoon, it was unusually quiet. After they had waited for a couple of minutes, two black men approached. One was a middle-aged businessman, walking quickly and carrying a briefcase. The other was a young man wearing a team jacket and a baseball cap. "Matt," Maria called out, and the young man came trotting toward them.

Elena now knew why Maria had been so coy about her new boyfriend. Maria had suspected that her mother might not approve of her dating a black, even though they had never talked about interracial dating. Elena was cautiously polite during that first encounter.

After Matt left, Maria turned to her mother and asked, "Why were you so quiet?" Elena responded softly, "You didn't tell me he was black." Maria abruptly stood up and snapped at Elena: "I can't believe how racist you are, Mother. Didn't you hear the things I told you about him and his family? I'm really disappointed in you."

Before Elena could say another word, Maria stormed off. When we spoke a few days later, Elena told me about a dream she awoke from in the middle of the night after her lunch with Maria and Matt.

> I am sitting in a small restaurant with my daughter, my husband, my grandson, and my son-in-law. I look at my two-year-old grandson. I have a warm feeling and think to myself, "This is my first grandchild." Then my pleasure dissolves into anxiety as I realize that everyone in the restaurant is looking at us. My grandson is brown. My son-in-law is black. And my daughter is no longer mine.

The dream and her reactions to meeting Matt revealed feelings that were far more complex than Maria's indictment of her mother had suggested. As our conversation continued, Elena leaned closer, as if telling me a dangerous secret:

> When I thought about the dream, I really started to feel guilty. I remembered how we had come to America as refugees from Chile. When Allende was assassinated and Pinochet took power in 1973, our lives totally changed. Jose, the man my husband's sister was married to, was declared an enemy of the state. One

day he was arrested by the military and taken to La Palacio de la Risa—the Palace of Laughter. It was a prison known for its torturer, who laughed as he tormented his victims. Jose never returned, and we were never able to discover his fate. My husband, who was not even political, suddenly began to be treated differently at work. He had been rapidly rising in his firm. He was on the fast track to become a vice president. Suddenly he was given the most menial assignments. And he was treated rudely by his boss.

Then one day my worst nightmare started to unfold. Early in the morning, on a Monday, the police came and took my husband. I thought I would never see him again. But after a month he returned from what they called camp. A week later, with the help of a well-connected friend, we were on a flight to Miami. We fled with fifty dollars in our pockets, the clothes we were wearing, and Maria, who was an infant, on my lap. We left everything else behind.

So you see, I know what it's like to be the victim of persecution. I have identified with the plight of the blacks ever since I realized what life was like for them in this country. But I can't help it if I have these reactions to my daughter's choice. I think I will just keep my mouth closed and hope that things work out for the best.

As we continued to talk, I could see that her complicated reactions to Maria's new relationship included fear, self-reproach, and uncertainty. On one level her response was simply protective. Having known persecution herself, she feared the difficulties her daughter might have to face as part of an interracial couple. She then launched into a monologue about the problem of black crime, seeming to have internalized a certain degree of the mixture of fear and hostility that is so prevalent in Americans' reactions to young black men. At that level of her response, Matt's qualities and his parents' accomplishments were irrelevant.

But the fact that she had herself been the victim of persecution also made her uncomfortable with her own discomfort. She wondered how she could be biased after what she had gone through in Chile. Matt seemed like a nice, intelligent, hardworking young man. But moments after she began to relax in thinking about her daughter's relationship, she anxiously switched to talking of concerns about how her friends and family would respond. As in the dream, the pleasure of the images of her daughter being happily married and of her first grandchild could quickly dissolve into the fear of others' judgments.

Elena's life experiences had taught her powerful lessons about the dangers of being identified as a member of a stigmatized group. She had lived in a culture where political turmoil and hatred led to the persecution and death of those she loved. While she felt safer in the United States, the traumas of her past did not just disappear. They were incorporated into the fabric of her life and affected every relationship she formed and each decision she made. Her reactions to Maria's relationship with Matt were motivated more by her concerns that her daughter and grandchildren might be the victims of the prejudice of others than out of any strong racial biases of her own.

That night Elena had a long conversation with her husband, Mario. He had several colleagues who were black and was much more relaxed than his wife about interracial relationships. He helped Elena to calm down, and after their talk she decided she would call Maria to talk to her about the incident. Early the next morning Elena's phone rang. She was relieved when she heard Maria's voice.

ELENA: I was just about to call you. I'm sorry about what happened yesterday. I've been thinking a lot about it. I want you
to understand that I don't have any objections to Matt as a
person. I was just concerned about you.

MARIA: I've been thinking a lot too. I think I sort of set you up by
telling you everything about Matt before you met him except
his race. I guess I was so worried about your reaction that I
felt I had to sell you on him ahead of time.

ELENA: You don't remember all that we went through in Chile. We
suffered a lot, and your father and I know how hard it can be
when you're on the wrong side of things. But if you really care
about Matt, I will be there for you no matter what happens.

Your family's cultural history can have a major effect on how they
respond to your choice of a partner. If they have been victims of
tyranny, they may fear and mistrust outsiders. If they are recent immigrants or refugees, they may be concerned about protecting what
feels like the threatened solidarity of their own cultural or religious
traditions in a new land where they are now part of a minority group.
Also your family may simply not be comfortable with people who
are culturally different than they are, especially when it comes to
marrying one of their own. The negative reaction of a family member
who has "never met one of them" may have more to do with anxiety
or discomfort than with unbending intolerance.

Perhaps the greatest difficulties are faced by *Romeo and Juliet*
couples, who come from cultures that are historically hostile to
one another. The Turkish woman quoted at the beginning of Chapter 1 and her Armenian fiancé were both painfully aware that their
families would oppose their relationship based on events that
occurred long before they were born. Likewise relationships between Germans and Jews or Chinese and Japanese may carry heavy

historical baggage. And while an interethnic, interreligious marriage of an Irish-American Catholic and a white Methodist in Iowa
doesn't raise many eyebrows these days, the marriage of an Irish
Protestant to an Irish Catholic in Northern Ireland certainly raises
more than eyebrows. A couple in love may believe that they have
transcended the hatreds and pain of the past. But their families
often have not.

Don't be too quick to condemn others' reactions to your relationship, especially those of family members. If they sense that
you are trying to understand their concerns, it can sometimes go a
long way toward helping them to try to understand yours. It demands a lot of maturity to take the time and emotional energy to
try to diagnose the underlying causes of the hostility, anger, or rejection of family members, friends, or others. Part of the difficulty
results from the fact that it's often a combination of two or more
of the following factors that influence family and social reaction
to your relationship:

- Prejudice
- Class differences
- Smoke screen
- Religious beliefs
- Genuine, unbiased concern

Prejudice: The Need to Create the "Other"

While we may take for granted a universal human need to love and
be loved, the *need* to hate may be just as common. How many individuals have gone through life never hating someone or something, what family does not have a "black sheep," in what land is
there not a despised race, culture, or caste, and which nation has

never had an enemy? Stereotyping others seems to be an inherent part of the human condition. Some of the negative reactions to your relationship may be a result of others' prejudice. Even the most tolerant of people occasionally find themselves thinking about another group (or even their own) in a negative and stereotyped manner.

- "Irish are a bunch of drunks."
- "Blacks are violent and dangerous."
- "Whites are blue-eyed devils."
- "Asians are sneaky and inscrutable."
- "Jews are greedy."
- "Conservative Christians are rigid and racist."
- "Muslims are terrorists."
- "Mexicans are lazy."

The one thing that all forms of hatred have in common is the projection of all that is bad onto someone who is not us: the "Other." We demonize the Other and label them as barbarians or subhuman animals who *deserve* to be attacked. We come up with reasons to justify our hatred; we persecute them because they have insulted our honor, have evil beliefs, are contaminating our pure blood, are threatening to harm us if we do not first destroy them, or because their ancestors have inflicted injuries upon ours.

The psychological process of scapegoating grows out of a very human need to see all that is unacceptable, evil, and impure embodied in someone or something else. The term *scapegoat* itself is derived from the Old Testament, where a goat was literally sent out into the desert to die after being ritually imbued with the group's sins. The sacrificial goat unburdened the community of its collective guilt, freeing it up to begin anew.

Some theorists of group process have suggested that *every* human group identifies others as alien in order to solidify a sense of its own identity. Whether it's an "undesirable alien," a despised race, or a dangerous enemy, the existence of the Other seems to satisfy a number of primal needs. It satisfies our competitive wish to feel superior by selecting others to label as inferior. The sense of threat attached to the outsider helps us define the boundaries of *our* world, which feels safer than the unknown dangers in the distance. The external danger presented by the Other helps us control the tensions and conflicts within our own group, because we must band together to protect ourselves from the evil they represent. We are the light, they are the shadow; we are good, they are evil; without the *them* we have nothing to form an identity against, and there is no *us*.

When you have chosen a partner from a widely scapegoated group, such as African-Americans, Latinos, or Jews, at least part of the reaction of family, friends, and society to your relationship results from your having violated a basic social taboo. One way or another others communicate their disapproval. In effect they are saying, *Loving the scapegoat is wrong. Even though I used to care for you, you must now be bad, because you have chosen one of them. You have forgotten our values and disgraced us. And I am angry with you because your choice has called into question something I hold dear—the totally negative image I have of my scapegoat.*

From the perspective of other members of the scapegoated group, the person who leaves the group to join those with more power and status has committed the ultimate sin: disloyalty. *How could you,* they ask, *abandon the group for someone who is one of our oppressors? You must be full of self-hate, or you are trying to pass because you want to escape our fate. Do you think you're better than we are? Some of them may try to act nice, but just beneath the skin they are all racists [or anti-Semites]. Don't you realize how evil they are? In the end you will be sorry that you have cut yourself off from your true roots, because they will never really accept you.*

Of all the contrasts that partners in a mixed match may bring to their relationship, race is the most visible and inescapable. It's the most likely to target a couple for others' intolerance. While Caucasian interethnic and interreligious couples can choose how and when they will reveal their differences to strangers, interracial couples don't have a choice. Their differences are written on their faces. More than any other kind of mixed match, interracial couples must find ways to deal with social as well as family reactions to their relationships. Even when couples share similar religious, cultural, class, and educational backgrounds, racial differences can lead to family and social opposition to a relationship.

No racial division in American society is sharper than the one that separates blacks from whites. Every other group besides African-Americans freely chose to come to America. And while non-Caucasians have not assimilated as rapidly as white ethnics, every group of immigrants has followed a similar path of adaptation over a period of two or three generations. Because of their history of slavery, however, assimilation into the mainstream culture has remained outside the grasp or desire of many blacks, in spite of the fact that they have been in America far longer than most immigrant groups. Interracial relationships involving a black partner therefore remain the least frequent and most stigmatized type of mixed match.

Cynthia, who is Chinese-American, and Tyrone, who is African-American, found that they had to deal with negative reactions to their interracial relationship from both family members and outsiders. Over the course of their years together they felt that they had learned from each other in developing a range of ways of dealing with the difficult situations they sometimes had to face.

They would often joke that it was a miracle that they were together at all, because they had come from such different worlds. Tyrone grew up poor, in a large Mississippi family, the second youngest of seven children. Born in 1950, he had memories of the segregated South. His parents were always struggling to make it, and they didn't have much time to focus on any one of their children. He felt loved, but on his own. He knew that the main things his parents expected were that he work hard and stay out of trouble.

His parents could never have predicted that their son would aspire as high and travel as far as he ultimately did. Always intense and driven, a very bright student and talented athlete, he was horrified and enraged by the violence of the local authorities toward the Freedom Riders and civil rights workers who came to Mississippi when he was a child. He was inspired by the courage of the young men and women who had put their lives on the line to end segregation. He remembers sitting in a class one day in sixth grade and deciding that he was going to get an education and make it out of poverty, and out of the South.

He earned a football scholarship to college and afterward went on to business school, where he did very well. Business and athletics weren't his only passions. After finishing graduate school he went on to learn how to speak Chinese and studied computer technology. He was a modern, self-made, Renaissance man.

Cynthia was raised in Hong Kong until she was twelve, when she immigrated to Seattle with her parents to start a new life. They developed a high-tech import business and were as successful as they had been in Asia. They also expected success from their children.

Cynthia met Tyrone at a lunchtime colloquium at her university, when she was twenty-five. At the time, she was finishing graduate school in business. They began seeing each other, but Cynthia realized, as she found herself falling in love with Tyrone, that they would not have an easy path to follow:

Telling my parents was a very long process. I knew Tyrone for five years before we decided that we wanted to get married. When my parents finally began to get the idea that we might be romantically involved, they started to work on me and say things like, "You don't understand his culture, and he's from a different race. Marriage is difficult enough anyway, and it will also be hard on your children."

When we finally decided we were going to get married, I went home and told my parents. My mom just broke down. She started crying and yelling and screaming. And then she tried to use guilt. "You don't care about us. We brought you up. You're doing this just to hurt us." The best thing for me to do at the time was to be silent. I didn't want to give them any indication that I might back down.

TYRONE: I never talked to Cynthia's mother, but I talked to her father and told him that I had hoped he would be able to accept our relationship even if he could not understand it. I wanted to make it clear that if we married, it was not out of a desire to hurt them or out of a lack of respect. He listened quietly, but that was the last time I spoke with either of Cynthia's parents for nearly three years. Neither of them nor anyone in Cynthia's family came to the wedding.

CYNTHIA: I didn't talk to my parents for a year and a half. Before, I had talked to my mom every day. We had been a very close family. When I got pregnant, we continued to not talk. My sister would tell them about me. My brother was very protective of my parents and very mad at me for the pain I caused them.

We were brought up to please our parents and make them proud. It's bred into your bones. I was the good, oldest daughter. To not follow my parents' wishes meant I was disloyal.

It's painful being part of two cultures. Because I was born and partially educated in China, I understand exactly how they feel. You may find this hard to believe, but I wasn't angry with them. But I went to college here, and I am part American too. I identify with both worlds, but I am not really totally in either. I just can't say that my parents don't matter, because they do. But I'm also not willing to give up the freedom I feel I've earned. It isn't easy.

More than any other event a grandchild's birth has the potential to melt barriers between the generations. Birth is a symbol of the connections between past and future generations. Families who disapprove of their child's cross-cultural relationship will often try to prevent the marriage and may even try to break up the marriage. But a grandchild's birth can change everything. It is their own flesh and blood, who will carry on their spirit.

CYNTHIA: Two months after our first child, Derrick, was born, I had this strong urge to see my parents. So I drove home with Derrick one day and just showed up. They were both kind of cold. My father didn't want to look, but he couldn't stop himself. Derrick was very light-skinned. I think that made it easier for him. He didn't want to hold him, though.

Then my mother said, "Let me see him." She held him for a minute, and then I took him and said I had to go. Gradually I started to go home more. And then, when Derrick was a year old, they even took care of him for the weekend. But it really bothered me that Tyrone still had not seen them or spoken with them since before we had married.

TYRONE: One day Cynthia had to drop Derrick off with her parents. I drove. Her father happened to be outside working in the yard. I thought about just continuing to drive and pretending that I didn't see him. But Cynthia said I needed to face him. I was afraid he would walk away. But when I got out, he walked over and hugged me and said, "We know that you're working hard to establish your business. Keep at it." I was totally dumbfounded. I was expecting something like "Get away from my house." Then her mother came out, and I said, "Hello, Mrs. Chang, how are you?" She nodded and mumbled something. Cynthia gave Derrick to her mother, and we drove away. I was shocked. I told Cynthia that it was a lot easier than I expected.

CYNTHIA: Later on my mom came to me and complained, "What's the matter with him, calling me Mrs. Chang? Doesn't he know he's supposed to call me Mom?" That was her way of tweaking me even as she was telling me that she was letting go of shutting us out. That moment was a turning point, and since then we have slowly been rebuilding our relationship with them.

TYRONE: My in-laws are not the only people we have had to deal with. My sister accused me of self-hate. She said, "What's the matter, aren't black women good enough for you?" It made me really angry. I said, "I'm old enough to know what I'm doing. I will try to explain my feelings to you, and hopefully you will understand. But if you can't, it's your problem." She eventually more or less accepted our relationship, but we had several confrontations, and they left some scars.

My mother is a very polite southern woman. She had no problem with Cynthia as a person. But when it came to marrying her son, she wasn't sure if we would make it or not. She resented my being put on probation for being black. That's what was happening, and I understood her anger, as well as my sister's. But now my mother is a lot more accepting, and we recently took a family vacation together.

Cynthia set limits with her parents by deciding to go ahead with the marriage in spite of their objections. But she was also patient with them and didn't escalate the conflict when they refused to talk to her. Her ability to understand and empathize with their point of view, even as she made decisions contrary to their wishes, kept open the possibility of reconnecting with them.

Tyrone was also able to set limits and to understand his sister's and mother's anger. And while his talk with Cynthia's father before they got married was not enough to prevent the original rupture of their relationship, it planted a seed of caring and respect that would later take root. It was this dual ability that Cynthia and Tyrone had, both to empathize with their families' reactions *and* to separate enough from them to make their own decisions, that was the key to their success. It was also their willingness to reach out in the face of rejection that led to re-establishing the family bonds that had been so strained by their marriage.

Cynthia and Tyrone also had to deal with the reactions of friends, colleagues, and even strangers to their relationship. They both had to find their own ways of confronting people's biases, and discovered that they could learn from each other through the process.

> CYNTHIA: At first I was very sensitive about others' reactions to our relationship. I was too sissy to come out and confront them. I would think, "You just can't change people." Or, "It's not worth your time."
>
> But there was this one situation where I knew I might be working with this one white woman in the future. She didn't know I was married to a black man and she was saying some negative stuff about adopting black children, so I decided I had to say something, because *I didn't want her to embarrass herself.* I told her that I understood what she was saying.

But then I told her that if it's wrong for her, it doesn't mean it is wrong for anyone else. I went on to tell her that I knew because my husband is black and my children are half black.

I am not always so gentle, though. I was working with this one very opinionated Chinese person. He was saying bad things about blacks. About them being lazy, and so on. I told him that my husband is a black businessman, that he works very hard, and that he doesn't have wealthy parents to support him. He was a customer of mine. He had confidence in me. He understood how hard I worked for him, and I had a lot of personal credibility. So he was embarrassed.

When I have to deal with other Chinese who were brought up in China, I know how they are thinking, because I was there once. I feel closer to them than I do to American-born Chinese. They are my brothers and sisters, and I feel like I'm sort of saying to them, *Don't be so ignorant, you're embarrassing me.* [laughs]

It all goes back to face and shame. It's hard to communicate this thinking pattern to people who don't understand it. Whether you're conscious of it or not, losing face breaks the power structure. If I hadn't let that woman who was talking about black adoption know that my husband was black, she might have said something that would embarrass her, which would also embarrass me. It throws the whole universe out of sync. When you cause someone to lose face, you disrupt the social network, this web that holds all people together. Therefore, I have to tell her to protect her, me, and the universe.

TYRONE: Cynthia is fatalistic. She feels that patience is the most important thing. I am much more likely to charge up the middle. It's one thing to have tolerated my in-laws' behavior, but I won't put up with it from others. Anybody else who offends me or Cynthia finds out very quickly that they had better stop.

Some things I have grown more tolerant of, like *the look* that people give us. I used to assume that anyone who stared at us was probably a bigot who didn't like that we were together. But then I began to think, hey, not only are we an unusual couple, we're also a pretty good-looking couple. It's no wonder people want to take a look. In any case I don't get all bent out of shape about it anymore. I've learned to take it in stride and save my anger for people who are really looking for trouble.

Our differences in style create conflict between us sometimes. Especially in the past I used to get frustrated with how much crap Cynthia would put up with, and she used to get upset with how quickly I would get angry. But our differences also complement each other and we have both changed. Cynthia has learned to be more direct, and I have learned to be more diplomatic.

Class Differences: Money Matters

The Brazilian saying "A rich Negro is a white and a poor white is a Negro" is a reflection of the fact that in some cultures, class and educational attainment are more important than race in determining family and social reactions to intermarriage. To varying degrees in different countries, wealth, and sometimes the lack of it, can erase other social distinctions. In many societies there is more intermixing of cultures and races at the top and, sometimes, at the bottom of the social ladder. Money lubricates social interactions in many groups, and the wealthy have been among the first to marry out. Similarly the shared burden of poverty and social stigma can sometimes minimize other social distinctions. Frequent intermarriage between blacks and native Americans in the years before and after the Civil War is one example of two low-status groups intermarrying.

Every family has its own unique set of priorities and values, but it's often difficult to discern exactly what they are, even for members of the family. If you think carefully about your family's reaction to people you have cared about, it should become clearer if it is race, religion, class, or education that is most important to them.

I spoke to one young woman from a white Protestant background whose parents were extremely upset when she began to date a Chinese-American man who worked as a landscaper.

> My parents worked hard to talk me out of my relationship. They never talked about his income, which wasn't great, but kept on focusing on the problems they claimed that most interracial couples had. They cited some statistics they had read somewhere about the incredibly high divorce rates of interracial couples. Two years later, after Bob and I broke up, I started going out with Alan, who happens to be Japanese-American and who also happens to be a physician. Suddenly my parents' racial concerns were forgotten. I never confronted them about their change of heart. It was weird. I always assumed that they were kind of racist, but now I realize that what they really are is *classist*.

Smoke Screen: Avoiding the Real Issues

Sometimes, as family therapist Edwin Friedman pointed out, the content of family objections is really a smoke screen used to disguise deeper issues. While parents in these families may use religion, class, race, or culture as the focus of their opposition to your relationship, what they are really opposed to is their child growing up.

Sophia's family presented a clear example of a "smoke screen" type of family. Sophia was a twenty-five-year-old Spanish-American woman who was the youngest of three children. Her father had suffered from heart disease from the time she was in third grade but was able to control his symptoms fairly well using medication. When Sophia began dating during her junior year in high school, every time she invited a boyfriend to dinner, her father would have chest pains and have to go to bed. Each time, her mother would take her aside and let her know that her father was upset with her choice of a boyfriend. When Sophia asked why, her mother gave her only vague answers. Sophia suspected that her father was using his angina attacks to try to undermine her relationships with her first two boyfriends because they weren't Catholic. But in her senior year in college, when she started to date Dan, a Catholic student, her father still had an attack when she brought him home to meet her parents at Thanksgiving break.

That year her mother began calling her and complaining about Sophia's father. When she would visit her parents, her father would sometimes talk to her about her mother's difficulties with menopause. More and more Sophia felt like it was her job to bridge the tension and emotional estrangement between her parents. Sophia began to suffer from insomnia and had increasing difficulty focusing on her studies. With the help of a counselor at the campus clinic, she began to realize that her parents were having a very hard time letting her separate from them.

Both her older sister and brother had married and moved far away, and she was the only child who was physically and emotionally available to her parents. The message behind her father's attacks began to become clear: *If you abandon us, it might kill me, or at least kill the marriage.* Even though her father's ill health made her very anxious, Sophia began to refuse to listen to her parents' complaints about each other. She was very relieved when, several months later, her parents went into couples therapy to find better ways of dealing with their problems.

Clearly this sort of problem can seldom be resolved by trying to address the cultural or religious content of your parents' objections. As soon as you respond to the supposed issues, they evapo-

rate and new ones appear. The constantly changing issues create a
smoke screen that prevents the more fundamental problems from
being addressed. In these situations it is important to confront in-
consistencies in your families' behavior and to set limits on how
much influence they have over you. Ultimately the unspoken rule
prohibiting separation will become clear, at least to you.

Smoke screens are used to express family anxieties and needs
in indirect and often confusing ways. But the smoke screen is not
always evidence of deeper psychological or marital problems;
sometimes it is a disguised request for help. Nam, a young Vietnamese man who had immigrated with his family to the United
States as a young child, talked about the way his mother had tried
to prevent him from growing up:

> My mother is a widow and I am an only child. My father died ten
> years ago when I was fifteen. My mother has objected to every girl-
> friend I had since then. My first girlfriend had two strikes against
> her: she was Japanese and she was a Christian. My mother said
> she did not trust the Japanese and that she had raised me to be a
> good Buddhist. My second girlfriend was no good because she was
> white, and my mother said she would never remain loyal to me.
> But last year, when I was twenty-eight, I fell in love with a Chinese
> woman and we got engaged. When my mother said that she was
> okay, except that her teeth were not straight enough, I suddenly
> realized that something else must be bothering my mother besides
> all of my girlfriends' imperfections.
>
> I talked to a Buddhist priest I knew, and he helped me realize how
> afraid my mother was of being alone. After talking with him I went
> to my mother and told her that I intended to marry the Chinese
> woman I loved. She started to get very upset, but when I also told
> her that we would be getting a house large enough for her to live
> with us, her objections to the relationship instantly evaporated.

Nam had not been able to separate from his mother because of his sense of obligation toward her that was so deeply culturally conditioned. But he had also been growing increasingly distressed with his mother's responses to each of his relationships. With the priest's help, Nam was finally able to accurately diagnose his mother's behavior, address her underlying concerns, and create a new life that allowed him greater autonomy even while honoring his love for his mother and his culturally shaped values about loyalty to one's parents.

Religious Beliefs: Keeping the Faith

Religion and the name of God are often invoked for ends that are hardly spiritual. Soldiers of two warring nations may share a common religion and yet both invoke the same God to pray for victory over one another. Just as nations sometimes use religion for narrow and nationalistic ends, families and institutions may use religion as a way to mask racist, classist, or ethnocentric objections to your relationship. God's will is always a popular tool for those seeking to justify their biases.

Some families' objections to intermarriage, though, are genuinely religious. For the truly religious, race, class, ethnicity, and nationality are not the important issues. What they do seek is to have their children carry on what they believe is God's truth. Genuinely religious families and clergy are often more than willing to accept intermarriage of people from different races or cultures as long as they share the same religion.

The great religions at their cores transcend national, racial, and class lines. In mosques, churches, and synagogues around the world, one can see rich and poor, black, white, and brown, and people born in different lands using the same words to worship a common god.

Even if you don't share their beliefs, it's important not to stereotype religious devotion as simply just another form of intolerance. If you do, you may be confusing belief with bigotry. They aren't the same, and it's important to be able to distinguish between them when deciding how to deal with objections to your relationship that are framed in religious terms.

Sometimes successful conflict resolution with parents and in-laws requires professional help. Ted and Erica were a couple who found that resolving their marital crisis was made much more difficult by Erica's parents' actions. Her parents were devout Lutherans, who had used Erica's marital problems to act out old, unresolved anger about her marriage to a nonbeliever. Their minister told about how he was able to help defuse this volatile family crisis:

I had a couple in the congregation who were going through a marital crisis. Ted had had an affair, and when Erica found out, it was very touch-and-go for a while. They saw a counselor, who helped them back from the brink of divorce. I was pleased that they had found a way to preserve their family, because they had three children and seemed to have had an otherwise decent relationship.

A month after they finished working with their therapist, Erica called me and said that they were having a very difficult time again. Her parents refused to let Ted come over to their house or to speak with him. She had asked her parents to go see the therapist with them, but they had refused. Erica was increasingly feeling trapped between Ted and her parents and was beginning to buckle under the strain. The progress they had made in reviving their marriage seemed to be unraveling, and she told Ted that she didn't know if she could go on with their reconciliation.

I remember when I performed their marriage twelve years ago. Ted's parents were Russian Orthodox, but he himself was an agnostic who refused to participate in organized religion except for going through with the motions of a Lutheran wedding ceremony. Her parents weren't thrilled about his lack of belief, but they accepted the marriage, more or less, and life went on. Ted and his in-laws maintained a polite but emotionally distant relationship. Erica learned to live with the subterranean tension between her husband and her parents.

Now the latent conflict over religion between Erica's parents and Ted had exploded into the open. To Erica's parents, Ted had finally proven himself to be the godless, immoral person they had always suspected he was. When they told Erica that they couldn't understand how she could forgive him for what he had done, they reopened marital wounds she had been working to heal. Maybe she should get a divorce.

Then she went home to Ted who further polarized the situation by telling Erica that he thought her parents were rigid, moralistic people who didn't care about anything but fanning their self-righteousness. Erica felt torn in two and asked if she and Ted could come and see me.

Ted reluctantly agreed to come to meet with me together with Erica. He had lumped me together with his in-laws and anticipated that I would be as moralistic and rigid as he believed they were. He had always experienced them as judgmental people, and their response to his and Erica's marital crisis only confirmed his judgment about them.

I knew Ted had apologized to Erica and asked for her forgiveness, but I felt that he would also have to apologize to his in-laws and that it wouldn't be easy for him. I wanted Ted to apologize to Erica in front of me, because I believed that this could be a dress rehearsal for a more difficult meeting to come with Erica's parents. I didn't want him to grovel, but I also didn't want him to get angry or defensive.

I'm not sure how I got his trust, but Ted decided to take the risk and told Erica a lot of important things that day. That he was truly sorry about what he had done and that he had the affair only because he hadn't known how to deal with the unhappiness they had both felt for a long time in their marriage. He said that he wasn't trying to justify what he had done, but that he needed her to know about what he had experienced. He said that he had learned through their counseling how much better it was to be direct about problems and that he was happy that they had been succeeding in working on making their marriage more vital and alive than it had ever been.

It was a good meeting, not only because of all the positive things that Ted had said, but also because I had failed to live up to his negative expectations of me.

I told Ted that I had known his in-laws a long time and that I understood how he could see them as severe. But I also said that I thought they were more complex people than he gave them credit for, and reminded him about their generosity with time and money in working for a local food bank. I suggested that even though they were angry and hurt, I thought they wanted what was best for Erica and their grandchildren, and yes, even for him. Ted silently listened. Before they left, he and Erica agreed to a meeting together with me and her parents if I was able to arrange it. I think that Ted was able to take in enough of what I said to be less anxious and to soften a little.

Later that week I met together with Erica and her parents. Her parents genuinely believed that Ted's breaking the commandment against adultery was an unforgivable sin. Their lives were built on a foundation of faith, and it had always been difficult for them to believe that a person could really deal with all the temptations that life presented without the guidance of religious belief. I suspected that there was also an element of perverse satisfaction around the margins of their anger: It seemed comforting to them to have their view of the universe proven true once again. Erica looked beaten down. Her parents didn't have to say the words that their pained and angry expressions made only too clear: *We told you so.*

I talked with them a long time that day. I tried to help them realize that even though what Ted did was wrong, his actions had called attention to serious marital problems that had existed before his affair, problems that both Ted and Erica had avoided dealing with. I was able to use my authority as a man of the cloth both to validate their religious beliefs *and* to challenge their righteous anger. I gently gave them permission to think about the other Christian values that had been in the background up until now: compassion and forgiveness. I didn't feel like I could come right out and tell the parents to "lighten up," but they seemed to get the message.

Erica seemed emboldened by my speech and told her parents that she and Ted had started to address their problems and were working toward having a more solid marriage and family than they had before his affair. She then asked her parents to trust her.

I was finally able to get everyone to agree to a family meeting. I think the preparation I had done worked. The parents expressed their hurt and anger directly to Ted. He was able genuinely to apologize without getting defensive. Erica was able to sit back and listen and get out from between Ted and her parents.

Ted and his in-laws began to speak again after that meeting, and a year later the marriage seems to be on the right track. What some of us ministers do behind closed doors is often a lot more flexible and creative than people give us credit for. We know that there are many paths to help along God's work.

Ted, Erica, and her parents needed assistance to make it through their family crisis. This was clearly a situation where an outsider was able to help family members get beyond seeing each other in stereotypical, two-dimensional ways and to help build a bridge of understanding between the generations. Many couples and families are understandably anxious about letting an outsider into the intimate and confusing center of their family life. But this was the kind of situation where a skilled person can not only help a family survive a crisis but can also help them create a better family life.

There are several ways to diagnose the sincerity of family objections to your relationship that are based on religious differences. Answer the following questions:

1. *Are the family members who are objecting to your relationship religiously observant in a meaningful way?* Do they contribute time and money to their church, synagogue, or mosque? Do they participate regularly in some religious community? Do they pray, believe in God, and act in ways that are consistent with their stated religious beliefs? Do they raise their children as active members of their religion?

If the answers to all of these questions is yes, then you are probably dealing with people who take their religious beliefs seriously and are sincerely concerned about perpetuating their faith. While you may not adhere to their beliefs or comply with their wish for you to practice their religion, their objections are far more worthy of respect than families who use their "faith" only when it suits their needs.

2. *Do family members who are concerned by your interreligious relationship accept converts as true members of the religion?* One of the best tests of religious authenticity is openness to converts. Religiously devout people tend to be far more concerned with their faith than with pure blood lines or cozy cultural clannishness. If they are accepting of converts, it is another indication that they are actually more concerned with religious issues than with race or ethnicity. A religious Jewish family I knew, for

example, strenuously objected to their daughter's relationship with an atheist man from a Jewish background but were later very open to her marriage with a black man who had converted to Judaism.

While secular and less religious Jews are often the most open to the idea of interfaith marriage, they often have the most difficulty emotionally accepting a convert as a "real" Jew. They experience their own Jewishness through a sense of ethnic-cultural commonality with other Jews. Often it's religiously observant Jews who are the most accepting of converts as genuine Jews, if they perceive the convert as sharing a common religious devotion. For the religious, once a partner has converted, it is no longer an intermarriage; it has become a marriage between two Jews.

Genuine, Unbiased Concern: Worrying for Real Reasons

Sometimes family objections are not so much a function of prejudice, class differences, smoke screens, or religious beliefs, but are primarily an expression of genuine concern. Ahmad and Helen brought so many differences to their relationship—age, race, religion, and nationality—that it was not surprising that both their families might disapprove of their match. They would not have to be bigots to be worried about their prospects for a happy marriage.

Ahmad is a Muslim from Kashmir in India who is an orthopedic surgeon affiliated with Western Reserve University in Cleveland. When he was in his late thirties, he and his Indonesian wife divorced and he received custody of their two children. He had settled into being a doctor and a father and feeling these roles were enough, until a conversation with a friend.

I had a very traumatic divorce and I had decided not to get married again. But then a friend of mine woke me up. He said, "You say you're not going to get married again. What are you going to do when your kids leave?" I had never, ever thought about the day that the kids would leave, because *back home we don't leave our families.* We live in the same house even though we're married. We have a really big house, and in the earlier days all my brothers, their wives, their children, and everybody lived in that house. Suddenly it dawned on me that this is true, these kids are going to leave me, and in my old age I'm going to be all by myself and I won't have anybody. And that's when I decided that I was going to get married again.

But getting married again wasn't so easy. His desire to wed the first woman he was interested in ran into the opposition of his older brother.

I was involved with a woman from Colombia whose parents lived in Texas. I asked her to go to talk to her parents about our getting married, and they gave their approval. But when I talked to my brother, who is fifteen years older and assumes a kind of parental role in the family, he was absolutely against it. "She is a Catholic, a Christian, she is a completely different kind of person, she will take advantage of you. *You are alone, you have no one to look after you.*" He made it seem like I was being drawn into something that I was not completely aware of because I had no family here to protect and guide me.

He was crying so hard on the telephone that I felt really bad for him. I told him, "I will not marry her unless you give me your blessings. I have just one condition. You have to write me and tell me your reasons." He wrote me a thirty-page letter, which was interesting for its lack of specifics, but just kept repeating in many different ways his opposition to the marriage. But I kept my vow and did not marry her.

His story, from the perspective of most Americans, especially those of northern European extraction, is almost completely incomprehensible. How could a competent, highly accomplished professional base a fundamental life decision on the wishes of a brother who lived twelve thousand miles away, who had never even met the woman Ahmad hoped to marry? The explanation lies in his brother's words: "You are alone, you have no one to look after you." The meaning of those words lies in the norms of the Kasmiri culture Ahmad had physically, but not emotionally, extracted himself from.

Even though his brothers were engineers and doctors, all of them were living in the same family complex in Kashmir. Ahmad's brother was appealing to their shared cultural values, in effect saying, *You have torn yourself from the body of our family. You are vulnerable because you are incomplete without us to help guide you. And, as your oldest brother, you owe it to me to respect my wishes.*

The conversations with his brother revealed important contrasts between the values of collective and individualistic cultures. In collective and communal cultures marriage symbolizes the joining of two families, not just two individuals. Love cannot be separated from the context of the family. And age carries with it respect and power.

The kinship bonds that are so powerful and influential in traditional cultures are often far more fragile in Western cultures. While family harmony is the most important consideration in collective cultures, individual happiness and the romantic love between two individuals is most valued in individualistic cultures.

Because the healers in any society both reflect and reinforce its values, from the perspective of many American family therapists Ahmad's behavior would be evidence of "unhealthy enmeshment" with his family of origin.

But what his deference to his brother's wishes really demonstrated is how emotionally and spiritually rooted he remained in the culture of his birth. In spite of his success and adaptation to American society, the idea of individual happiness remained in many ways alien to him. Describing himself as a "man who has seen both sides," he was free enough of his culture to emigrate and love an outsider, but so rooted in tradition that he would yield to his brother's demands.

He continued with his search for a wife, and a year later met Helen.

> I saw Helen for the first time in the chart room at the hospital, and somehow, this is true, when I saw her that first time, I knew that I was going to marry her. I didn't know who she was or if she was married. I didn't know anything about her except that she was also a doctor.

Helen, who was from an English-Scottish Presbyterian background, was a physician at the same hospital as Ahmad. When they met in 1979, she was twenty-seven years old and had never been married. They began to date. Even though Ahmad was very active in the local Islamic center at the time, he did not feel that his relationship with a non-Muslim would present a problem. While marrying an outsider was an unusual act, in Islamic tradition, women may not, but men can marry any woman who is from "people of the book"—meaning Jews or Christians, as well as Muslims. He once again consulted with his family about his desire to marry.

When I called my father in Kashmir to tell him about Helen, he gave me his blessing as he had in the past. And he told me to go ahead and do what I wanted and not to listen to my older brother. But I told him that I wanted my brother's blessings as well. I soon received a telegram from my brother approving of the match. I later found out that my father had gotten hold of him and told him not to try to stop this marriage from taking place.

Ahmad's deference to his brother's wishes undermined his first relationship, just as his older brother's submission to their father allowed him to move forward in his relationship with Helen. In doing so, he defined himself first as a member of his family and secondarily as an individual with the inalienable right to pursue his own happiness.

Helen's family, however, presented additional obstacles to their relationship. They lived several hundred miles away in Indianapolis, and Ahmad had met them only briefly at an anniversary party that Helen had brought him to. When she and Ahmad decided they wanted to get married, Helen went by herself to talk to them.

After I went to talk to them about our relationship, I called Ahmad and said it absolutely wasn't going to work. Even though we had carefully rehearsed what I would say to them, they wouldn't hear anything about it. They didn't want to talk about it.

Ahmad went on:

I told Helen that if we would not get the blessings of her father and mother, I would not marry her. I felt that the only thing they had in the world was this one daughter. She is an only child. I felt that if I pushed and she married me against their wishes, they would spend the rest of their lives being very sad.

I realized they must be thinking all kinds of things about me. On paper I could understand why our relationship looked awful. Here is this guy from some part of India who is seventeen years older than their daughter who wants to marry her, and he has a different religion, is divorced, and has two kids. It didn't look very good, but for some reason I felt there was something good about it.

So when Helen told me they were against it, I decided to go see them myself. I wanted them to know me, to know what my thinking was in regard to Helen, what I planned to do in the future, why I was divorced, and why I have these black spots on my résumé. I felt confident that if I had a chance to talk to them in person and openly, I would be successful in getting what I wanted.

We went and had a long talk. When I felt the ice melting on the other side, Helen whispered to me to stop while I was ahead. But I didn't want to stop. I told her parents that I didn't want them to just say "all right," but I wanted them to say that they were happy that we were marrying. It was at that point that Helen gave me a kick. She felt that I was pushing my luck.

But it ended up that they did say they were happy about it. I think they were very much moved by the fact that we had not done anything about getting engaged behind their backs and had come to them to ask for their permission. I brought the ring with me, and I told them that I wasn't going to put this ring on her unless they said okay. They did.

HELEN: When I talked to my mother later, she said, "That man could talk me into a hip replacement even if I didn't need one."

Helen's parents had initially objected to her relationship with Ahmad because of his different nationality and religion as well as his divorce and age. But her parents found one of the cultural differences that Ahmad brought to the relationship very appealing and uncharacteristic of young, individualistic, educated Americans:

his willingness to put their wishes before his own. Because of the values of the collective and communal culture in which he was raised, he shared more traditional values with Helen's parents and grandparents than with most of Helen's peers. Helen began college in the early 1970s and came of age when rebellion against authority and traditional values was at a peak. While Ahmad's obvious differences had frightened her parents, his respect for them as parents ultimately won them over.

In his dealings with Helen's parents' objections to their marriage, he used a skill that is effective in dealing with all conflictual situations: empathy. Not only did he put Helen's parents' needs and wishes before his own, as he had done with his own family, but he understood and empathized with them as well. He correctly diagnosed their objections as being based on genuine concern about the prospect of their daughter marrying someone so different. Rather than seeing them as biased, he simply saw them as concerned parents. It was this attitude that opened the door to Helen's family's acceptance.

EXERCISES: Dealing with Opposition to Your Relationship
There are a number of ways you can learn to deal more effectively with other people who are judgmental about your relationship.

1. *Face Your Own Biases*
It's much easier to understand and deal with others' biases if you are familiar with and have begun to deal with your own. We *cannot avoid* creating both positive and negative stereotypes. Even the most tolerant among us seems to find at least one category of humans to dislike or mistrust.

One way to get in touch with your conscious and unconscious images of different groups is to use what I call the Stereotype Exercise.

Write down the following categories on a piece of paper and leave room under each one. Add any other cultural or religious categories that you may have positive or negative feelings about, and make sure your own group is included. Then write down the first three words that come to mind after you think about each category.

You will probably find it difficult not to censor your first responses, even if you are alone when you do this exercise. But it's important to be as self-aware as possible and to acknowledge the complexity of your own internal images about your own and other cultural and religious groups.

HISPANICS	CHRISTIANS	BLACKS	ASIANS	WASPS
JEWS	ITALIANS	MUSLIMS	GERMANS	ENGLISH

2. Deal with Hatred

While many mixed matches have to deal with annoying reactions to their relationship, some have to deal with harassment and violence. According to the Southern Poverty Law Center, hate crimes in 1992 and 1993 in the United States reached record levels. While there is no single category to measure the number, some of those crimes were directed at interracial families. Behind each statistic is a real and disturbing story.

Marcia and Douglas Drumright are an interracial couple and the parents of four children. He is a black man, she a white woman. After a self-proclaimed Ku Klux Klan member moved next door to the Drumrights' house in a quiet suburban neighborhood outside of San Francisco in 1987, he spent the next four years harassing, intimidating, and making death threats against them and their children. Over fifteen calls to the county sheriff did not result in an arrest or stop his behavior. It was only after getting the help of the county Human Relations Commission that the Drumrights discovered that none of their calls had led to an official police report. Finally, with the help of the commission, they were able to get the authorities to arrest their tormentor. They also eventually filed a civil suit with the help of the San Francisco Lawyers' Committee and their Racial Violence Project.

In February 1993 Principal Hulond Humphries reportedly told students at the Randolph County High School in Wedowee, Alabama, that the senior prom would be canceled if interracial couples attended. When questioned by student ReVonda Bowen about how the ruling would affect her, as the child of an interracial couple, Humphries reportedly said that his ruling was to prevent more "mistakes" like her. A lawsuit was filed by the Southern Poverty Law Center on behalf of ReVonda Bowen charging that her civil rights had been violated under the U.S. Constitution and Title VI of the 1964 Civil Rights Act. If the case goes to court, it will represent the first time that any court has ruled on whether the civil rights laws apply to an interracial individual. It is another example of individuals and families working together with organizations to combat bias.

Hatred is hatred, whether it comes from family, friend, or stranger. It is not always possible to build bridges, and sometimes it is dangerous to try. Intolerance exists in every society, and in its ugliest forms it is easy to recognize and important to confront. Unfortunately there really is evil in the world, and it is important to be able to recognize it for what it is.

It is important to have considered a range of options to deal with the hostility, anger, or violence of others. Almost every interracial couple has encountered many curious stares, dirty looks, and rude behavior from strangers. These kinds of problems are relatively petty, but are annoying and can be demoralizing. Use every minor incident as an opportunity to work with your partner on developing a range of responses. Practice "diagnosing" the seriousness of each event. Develop a set of responses that you are both comfortable using: ignoring rude people, staring back at gawkers, or verbally confronting the unpleasant behavior of others.

If you find yourself confronted with anger or violence that seems threatening, get away from the offensive people if possible. Defend yourself emotionally, legally, and if necessary physically. It's dangerous to try to understand the causes of hate when you're the intended victim. Your job is simply to protect yourself, and if possible, find ways to right wrongs. Unfortunately in some cities there are some neighborhoods where you may be in danger because you are an interracial couple. It is best to identify these places and stay away from them.

The "Resources" section at the end of the book lists organizations that can help you if you are the victim of harassment, threats, job or housing discrimination, or other forms of discrimination because of the nature of your relationship. It is important to find ways to deal with prejudice and not feel like a helpless victim.

3. Decide How Important the Relationship Is

In deciding how to respond to opposition to your relationship, you first need to evaluate the nature of your relationship with the person who disapproves of you. How important is it to maintain the relationship? Ultimately you and your partner need to agree about which relationships are important enough to work on.

If you can't decide what your priorities are, you may have a major problem with your partner. One Mormon college student I knew refused to stop dating his Catholic girlfriend, in spite of his parents' strong objections to the relationship. But he also failed to confront or set limits on his parents' rude behavior toward her. Clearly the situation would remain unsatisfactory for everyone until he could decide what and who was most important.

You may encounter some family members whose prejudices are so deeply rooted that all of your efforts to understand and build bridges fail. There are times when it may be best to recognize the hopelessness of the situation. Sometimes it really does come down to choosing between family and beloved.

I spoke with Ana, a woman from a Mandarin Chinese background whose parents were totally opposed to her marriage to a Cantonese Chinese man. Every time the subject of her marriage came up, her parents would make some disparaging remark about the Cantonese in general or her husband in particular. After their first child's birth things did not get better. Ana became more and more upset, and the tension affected her relationship with her husband. She and her husband found themselves increasingly irritable with each other. Finally, after a major crisis during which she became very depressed, they decided to move out of the city where they had been living near her parents.

> It was very difficult for me, but I realized that I had to choose between my marriage and my family, and right now I don't feel that I can have both. I feel terribly guilty, but moving away from my parents seemed to be the only way to keep my own family together. Of course I never confronted them about what they were doing. I just told them that Ben had a good job opportunity in Boston, and we moved. I still cry every day and keep wishing that we can find some way to work it out, but we will have to see.

4. Develop Hidden Family Resources

Sometimes there may be other family members who can help you deal with the difficult situations. Grandparents can be particularly important. While some grandparents are more traditional and rigid than their children, others have mellowed with the years and are more flexible in their attitudes about their grandchildren than they were with their own children. While not all of them are as open-minded as the grandmother who said, "If God hadn't intended for the races to mix, he wouldn't have made body parts that fit," even more conservative grandparents can help build bridges between their children and their grandchildren who have intermarried.

Adam, who was from a German-Scotch background, felt that he and Rosie, his Korean-American wife, would never have married if it wasn't for her grandmother's intervention.

> When we were first going out, Rosie's parents were extremely upset by her dating a non-Korean. They refused to meet me. One day Rosie decided to take me to visit her grandmother, who lived only a few blocks from Rosie's parents. It was hard to read her reaction. She didn't speak much English, and I didn't speak Korean. She offered us tea, and after a half hour we left. We started to visit her regularly, and even though Rosie's parents wouldn't accept our relationship, it was clear that her grandmother enjoyed our coming over. Finally she had a talk with Rosie's mother, and soon after that we received our first invitation to the house.
>
> Now we have a child, and Rosie's parents have relaxed. I was really touched when her father said at the baby naming, "After a hundred generations our family tree has a different color branch grafted onto it. I was very worried about the colors harmonizing, but now that I can see the results, I am pleased."
>
> I think if it wasn't for her grandmother, we would never have made it as a couple. When I visit my in-laws these days, I take my mother-in-law's hands and kiss them in front of her friends.

She and her friends giggle like schoolgirls. In their culture they are not used to direct expressions of affection—especially between men and women. It wouldn't be considered proper nor would they tolerate that kind of behavior if Rosie had married another Korean. But my being white puts me in a different category. I think for them, as upset as they initially were by Rosie getting involved with me, they enjoy the novelty I have introduced into their lives.

Taking Risks: Courage and Persistence Pay Off

For too many couples the failure to work things out results from a failure to try. While some couples try for too long to negotiate with family and others who clearly will never accept their relationship, more often couples retreat in hurt and anger before the situation is truly hopeless.

You may have been hurt by others, especially if they have tried to reduce you and your relationship to a one-dimensional stereotype: "She's just doing this to rebel," or "He's just going through a stage that he will get over." You realize that your love for your partner is far more complex, and you may be understandably angry if you and your relationship are being treated disrespectfully. But it's important not to fall into the same trap by too quickly categorizing others' motivations. Not everyone who looks at you is a racist, and not every family expression of concern about your relationship is motivated by bias.

One white Protestant man who was treated very rudely by his fiancée's Mexican-American parents turned to her as they were driving away from her parents' home and said, "I plan to spend the rest of my life with you, and that means that even if they don't like me now, I intend to have them for my in-laws for the rest of my life."

At that moment he stopped the car, turned it around, and returned to their house to try to work things out. It marked the beginning of a sometimes bumpy but largely successful relationship with the people who did become his in-laws. That simple story of "turning the car around" is symbolic of the couples who have succeeded in building bridges where others have failed. They took risks and persisted with the people who are important to them.

CHAPTER 7

Split at the Root: The Children of Mixed Matches

They say the:
mocha, cafe con leche,
chocolate, brown sugar, high yellow,
banana, oreo, güera, negrita—
essence of your being—
should define exactly who you are.
Where you stand becomes truer the
lighter or
darker
you get
right?

And I say:
I don't buy it
You don't know who I am by
    looking at me.
I am a light skinned,
    conglomeration,
a wild rice mixture
a hot salsa blend,
of corridos de México;
of Califas and Aztlán;
of white trash incest;
of poverty in all colors;
of punk rock and hip hop;
of hippies and freaks;
of dykes, fags and bisexuals;
of TV and anarchy;
of the California fields and farm
    workers;
of Guanajuato and Chihuahua;
of Southern Ireland;
of Chicago, Illinois; Greely,
    Colorado;
Delano, California and
Hollywood, USA.
I am everything above and
everything below.
I accept those pieces I want
and reject what no longer works.
This is me,
take it or leave it.

A CRISIS OF COLOR BY
DAWN VALADEZ DALTON

This may be the first time in history when large numbers of people are able to shape and create their own sense of group identity. Cut loose from the moorings of community, religious institutions, and traditional family life, few can take a feeling of communal belonging for granted: it has to be constructed. No group is more aware of the process of creating an identity than the children of mixed matches. Born of parents who were raised in different worlds, children of interracial, interethnic, and interreligious unions begin to learn at an early age that identity is as much a matter of decision as of destiny.

In this chapter we will focus on the experiences of the children of mixed matches and learn from them about the challenges they face and the kinds of choices they make. The next chapter, "Helping Children Develop a Solid Identity," will look more directly at how parents can help and support their children's quest to create a healthy sense of identity.

The conventional wisdom about the children of intermarriage is that they suffer difficult and often tragic lives. Everett Stonequist, in his 1937 book *The Marginal Man*, wrote about how "halfbreeds" functioned as buffers between hostile and separate cultures that live side by side. He used the mixed-race "coloreds" of South Africa and the English-Indian mixed offspring in India as examples of people never fully accepted by the communities of either of their parents. Stonequist described them as wandering forever in an identity purgatory.

More recently J. R. Berzon studied the portrayal of the "tragic mulatto" figure in American fiction. She described how frequently these characters are portrayed as confused and pathetic, tortured by their inner racial disharmony, clash of blood, and unstable genetic constitution. She quotes from a 1950 novel, *Daughters of Strangers*, about the confusion of a biracial character: "The idea of the mixed river of her blood was whirling in her brain and in her troubled, uneasy frame of mind she had become a stranger to herself."

Cindy Nakashima, a doctoral student in ethnic studies at the University of California, observed the similarities between the portrayals of the mulatto offspring of black-white unions and those of mixed Japanese-European backgrounds in her study of people of mixed racial ancestry. She cites a description of a Eurasian character from the novel *Kimono* as representative of fictional portrayals of Eurasians' tortured dual identities: "A butterfly body with this cosmic war shaking it incessantly. Poor child! No wonder she seems always tired."

The only real body of literature on the children of interfaith marriages focuses on the offspring of Jewish-Christian couples. Almost all of the writing up until the last decade has been uniformly depressing in its description of *mischlings*. The review of psychological and sociological literature by James Bossard and Eleanor Boll in their 1957 book, *One Marriage, Two Faiths*, best sums up this body of writing:

> People who make interfaith marriages apparently realize that children will cause problems or will have problems. . . . When the parents are of different religions, the family is a cultural mixture and the child is torn, in choosing his religion and philosophy of life, between the two sides of the family. This results not only in "taking sides" within the family but in inner conflict for the child.

It is only recently that people have begun to speak and write about the positive aspects of embodying more than one background. A 1992 study by Ana Mari Cauce and her colleagues found that the social adjustment of biracial Asian-white and black-white youth did not significantly differ from their monoracial peers. Lee Gruzen, in her 1987 book *Raising Your Jewish/Christian Child*, wrote a hopeful commentary about the possibilities of interfaith couples raising children in either one faith or in two different faiths. She felt that the "talkativeness, vitality, and humor" of her interview subjects, who were the children of interfaith marriages, grew out of the stimulating task of integrating their parents' different heritages. Another researcher, Teresa Williams, who is herself the product of a Japanese mother and a Welsh-American father, noted that having roots in two worlds can be an asset as well as a liability. She points out that bicultural people can possess insight into "often antagonistic worlds." She goes on to say that their intimate knowledge about life on both sides of the fence "can enable [them] to lead the parent societies into transcending their differences."

Educator Christine Iijima Hall suggests that it should be obvious just what would motivate the bicultural person to want to fill the roll as mediator and bridge. The multicultural person can find intergroup conflict very painful, especially when one of their parents' cultures is involved. The offspring of a marriage between a black American master sergeant of the postwar occupation Army in Japan and a Japanese woman, Hall described the natural role of bicultural people as mediators in *Coloring Outside the Lines*. Writing about other multicultural people she has known, she observed that, "They, like me, despise the fighting among the different ethnic minority groups in America. They are able to act as bridges among groups, fostering communication and cooperation. The future of mixed people may be that of negotiators."

In a world of polarized groups in conflict with one another, the children of mixed matches are in perfect positions to be able to understand more than one side of an issue. Because they embody "twoness" or "manyness," their potential to see and be able to deal with the complexity of intergroup relations is literally in their bones, hearts, and minds. But like any potential power, the complicated task of integrating and incorporating multiple cultural legacies into a single life presents dangers to be avoided, as well as opportunities to be cultivated and developed.

The 150-Percent Person

Dr. Terry Wilson is a bicultural, biracial native-American–Caucasian professor of ethnic studies at the University of California at Berkeley. He has argued forcefully that multicultural people can actually be more than the sum of their parts, rather than be crippled by their split heritages. Wilson points out that multicultural individuals throughout history have served as cultural brokers, bridging gaps between groups that have difficulty understanding one another. He cites as an example Chief John Ross, one of many native-American treaty signers in the nineteenth century who had English names because they were themselves the products of intermarriage.

Chief John Ross, who represented the Cherokee nation in negotiations with the United States, was one-eighth Cherokee and seven-eighths white by blood. He looked white, and he spoke both English and the Cherokee language and was fluent in both cultures as well as both languages. He could have blended into the white world, but he chose to be a Cherokee. His tribe recognized that his understanding of both cultures gave him abilities that made him especially valuable to the tribe. Rather than condemning him to marginality, his dual heritage made him a leader.

The story of Chief Ross is a dramatic illustration of a fact that many have difficulty recognizing: Blood heritage does not determine identity. While historically "one drop" of black blood could result in a person being labeled as black, in today's society identity is a far more fluid phenomenon. Like Chief Ross, for many, self-perception, the choices we make, and the acceptance of others are what shape our cultural identity and our sense of community.

In 1980 Dr. Wilson proposed teaching a course on people of mixed racial descent. The idea initially was not well received. Some of his colleagues on the faculty warned that such a course might cause further racial divisiveness on an already tense campus. They also pointed out that there would not be enough available printed materials on such an esoteric topic to be able to teach the course. And finally, they predicted, there would not be sufficient student interest in the course to justify it. In a last-ditch attempt to convince the faculty of the need for the kind of course he was proposing, he told them about his own life experiences as a person of mixed racial ancestry:

I was born on a reservation in Kansas to my mother, who is a French-Canadian, one generation removed, and my father, who is a full-blooded Potawatami. When I was four, we moved from the reservation to a small town in western Oklahoma, where my mother had grown up, an area that could never be described as a hotbed of racial liberalism.

In many respects the reservation had been a safe place. Indians were a majority. It was bad enough that we moved off the reservation to a place where we were a minority. But to make things worse, the town we moved to had a substantial population of Cheyenne and Arapaho Indians, who just happened to be traditional enemies of our tribe. We were the only Potawatami family.

My older sister, I learned, was a lot smarter than I was. She happens to look like my father, short and dark-skinned. I am light-skinned and tall like my mother. As we went together through the public school system, she received a lot of unwanted attention from both the white and the Indian communities over the fact that she was a "half-breed" or "breed." But she had small ears and was smart enough to ignore it.

I had big ears. I wasn't able to ignore the taunts. From the time I began public school when I was six, I was very aggressive with anybody who called me a half-breed. My way of dealing with people who used that term was to get in their face and attempt to beat them to a pulp.

I would come home at least three times a week from school with my clothes torn and with marks of battle. All that time, from when I was six to sixteen, neither my mother nor my father ever once questioned me about what had happened. Can you imagine your kid coming home bloody three times a week every week and never saying anything about it?

Mom and Dad knew why I was fighting, but they didn't know how to help me deal with being mixed race because they were uncomfortable being a mixed couple themselves. So they didn't say anything. I love them both a great deal, but their silence did me a real disservice. My sister and I talked about it, but we knew we were never to talk about it in front of our parents. There didn't have to be a sign up in the kitchen that said, Do Not Talk About Being A Half-breed. We just knew.

When I was a sophomore in high school, my sister came home from college and we went to a movie. When we came out of the movie, three full-blooded Arapahos came after us. I knew these people. I had played ball with them and talked with them. But that night, as my sister and I walked along the three blocks of the main street to the ice-cream parlor, they followed us about ten yards behind and kept calling us half-breeds. My sister saw how angry I was getting and begged me to stay calm. But by the time we got to the ice-cream parlor, I just couldn't take it anymore. I ran back to the three boys, knocked the first one down, then the second, and jumped the third. By this time the other two had gotten up and they jumped me.

For the first time in my life I lost a fight. As I lay there in the gravel, I felt that I had lost my anger. I didn't want to get up and get hit again. Always before, near-maniacal anger caused me to win. I had never cared if I got hurt as long as I could knock that one single word out of their vocabulary—*half-breed*. I ended up with three broken ribs and my ear half torn off.

My father came by to see me at the hospital very early the next morning on his way to work. He looked at me and said, "Terry, I'm kind of glad you got beat up." That pissed me off. It wasn't what I wanted to hear. I was stiff and sore. But he went on to say, "I'm not glad that you're hurt. But you needed to learn that you can't whip everybody. You need to learn that you have to find a different way to deal with your 'problem.' " He never mentioned what the problem was, but we both knew.

I began to realize what my problem was: I was something that society had no supportive way of acknowledging. I was tired of being invisible, and I was tired of being put down for who and what I was. I finally began to understand that all the fighting that I was doing would never get anybody to say to me, "Isn't it great that you embody two cultures and that because you can see things from a white point of view as well as an Indian point of view, you are special."

I don't blame my parents. In their generation no one knew how to talk about these issues. But I wish that somebody had told me that there were advantages to being bicultural when I was six rather than having to begin to figure it out for myself after hundreds of fights when I was sixteen. It took me a long time to get to the place where I could celebrate it rather than be messed up about it.

This campus is full of young people, many of whom are bicultural. When I can help them place their experience in a social and historical context, they learn a lot sooner than I did to use understanding instead of avoidance, and humor rather than hitting, to deal with the fact that they are trying to bridge a lot of cultural gaps.

The story convinced the cautious faculty to give Dr. Wilson a chance to try out the course as an undergraduate seminar. There was no shortage of interest the first time he offered the seminar: Twenty-eight students enrolled, even though the class had originally been limited to twenty. And in spite of the faculty's concerns, the course did not catalyze any new outbreak of conflict on the campus. His colleagues had, however, been correct in saying that it would be difficult to find texts to use for the course. The history of "half-breeds" was not a popular topic among scholars or publishers. Dr. Wilson decided to use his own history and the personal experiences of the students as the historical data for the class.

One by one all of the students in that first class told their personal stories. Twenty-six of the students were from mixed-race backgrounds. The other two were in interracial relationships. For most of them it was the first time in their lives that they felt able to acknowledge their feelings about having their roots in more than one culture or about loving someone from another race. The first class was a success, and as word spread around campus, it eventually evolved into a large lecture class that was one of the most popular at the university.

By developing and teaching his course, Terry Wilson had taken down the invisible sign he had grown up with that had said, Do Not Talk About Being a Half-breed. In doing so he discovered the hunger of so many others to find a place to talk about and deal with the problem that had no name. He has become the mentor and faculty adviser to Miscellaneous, an organization for racially mixed students. By confronting the problem of invisibility that so many multicultural people experienced, he offered young people of mixed ancestry positive ways to validate their identities as people who have a special ability to bring people together.

Wilson uses the image of the creative 150-percent person to replace that of the tragic half-breed. The bicultural person, Wilson points out, is 50 percent of one culture and 50 percent of another. But a third 50 percent that a bicultural person *can* possess results from a unique synthesis and understanding of both cultures. In defending the idea that the bicultural person may develop special abilities and be "more" than others, he ironically reminds his students that the original United States Constitution counted slaves as three-fifths of a person. "If people could be comfortable with the idea that humans could be counted as less than a complete person because of their heritage," he asks with wry humor, "why can't they now be counted as more than a whole?"

The Development of Racial, Cultural, and Religious Identity

Identity, as we have seen, involves both fate and choice. The formation of a stable adult sense of group identity is the result of a dynamic developmental process. The children of mixed matches go through several stages in the development of a sense of identity. A number of important factors influence the process:

- The nature of the cultural, racial, religious, and class differences parents bring to a family's life
  —Does one parent have a greater intensity of identification with his or her cultural or racial group than the other?

—Does one parent have a greater intensity of religious
belief than the other?

—Does a child's racial appearance or use of language
affect how the social world labels him in spite of
how he labels himself?

• Whether a child is being raised by one parent or both or
with a stepparent of a third culture or religion

• The members of the immediate and extended families
that are involved in a child's life

• The cultural and religious composition of
neighborhood and schools

• How successful parents have been in reaching a
mutually satisfactory agreement about an identity path
for the family (for a description of the five family-
identity paths, see pages 149–50 in Chapter 5).

The Life-Cycle Development of Identity

The children of mixed matches face different issues in the development of their cultural-racial identity in each stage of growing
up. The progress through the following stages is greatly affected
by the factors listed above.

EARLY CHILDHOOD
Cultural-Racial-Identity Development
The early period between two and eight years old is one of experimentation. Psychologist James Jacobs's research showed that
biracial children go through several stages in the development of a
sense of identity. From approximately ages two to four years old,
children experiment freely with the idea of skin color. At this age

they do not yet rigidly categorize people by color, nor do they fully realize that skin color or culture is unchangeable.

Beginning at about four and a half years old children begin to realize that people's skin color does not change. They begin to grasp that the larger social world uses color, culture, and class as ways of dividing, separating, and assigning status to people. As they become aware of the social meaning of color, and especially of prejudice against darker-skinned people, biracial children begin to alternate between rejecting their own color first and then later rejecting whiteness. It is also during this period that biracial children become increasingly aware of their differences from monoracial individuals.

Religious-Identity Development

Young children inevitably want to know how the universe works. Right and wrong, truth and lies, death, sex, and the nature of God concern the young child. Children's thinking is largely concrete and not abstract, and at this age they hunger for simple answers to complex questions. Young children are willing and receptive learners. Strongly identifying with adults at this age, they tend to accept their parents' definitions of religious beliefs and morality.

PRETEEN

Cultural-Racial-Identity Development

Eight- to twelve-year-old biracial and bicultural children who have had adequate support begin to feel less conflicted about their own identity and are able to accept themselves as being biracial or bicultural. Preadolescent children are often able to use labels that acknowledge their dual heritage, even while at times expressing negative feelings about one-half of their background or the other. Many also develop an awareness that their color or culture affects their group and social identity but does not determine it. Depending on their social, family, and class environment, biracial children are able to use skin color as only one factor that defines identity. Light-skinned children who live in primarily black environments may find ways to be accepted as black, just as dark-skinned youth who live in primarily white environments find ways to identify with other white children with whom they live.

Religious-Identity Development

Eight- to twelve-year-old children have begun to develop the capacity to think somewhat abstractly and independently. They may question some of their parents' beliefs, but are usually still focused on adults as primary sources of information and approval. At this age they are very aware of any contradictions between each of their parents' religious beliefs. They may experiment with religious identity, first taking on one parent's identity, then the other's, just as they experimented earlier with cultural and racial identity.

ADOLESCENCE

Cultural-Racial-Identity Development

Adolescence is a time when the influence of the peer group often becomes paramount. During adolescence bicultural youths often struggle to be accepted by the group that represents one-half of their background or the other. Or they may move back and forth between groups that represent the different parts of their cultural background. Their success in finding an accepting social group depends to a great extent on their early family experiences and on their current social milieu. In later adolescence the cultural and religious backgrounds of dating partners becomes an important way of *trying on* different identities.

Religious-Identity Development

The job of the adolescent is to question, challenge, and begin to develop independent reasoning abilities. In single-religion homes adolescents will tend to identify with parents' beliefs. In homes with two religions or no clear religion, the adolescent will often either reject religion entirely or choose one as "the best."

LEAVING HOME

Cultural-Racial-Identity Development

Young adults make decisions during the period of establishing independence between the ages of eighteen and twenty-two that often shape identity for a lifetime. Since they are more free of the constraints of family, this period is often a time of renewed experimentation. Daniel Levinson observed, in *Seasons of a Man's Life*, that this is a time of separation, not only from one's family of origin but also from the cultural, religious, and community structures of one's youth. This period is so crucial, especially in a rapidly changing world, because it is a time of testing out the currents of social life, and of trying to get a bearing on the world as it is and as it is becoming.

This is still a time when peer-group influence is very powerful. One research project dramatically illustrated the distinctions between public and personal identity and the social difficulties of working out a clear sense of identity. When interviewed in a group setting, eight out of ten biracial black-white students said that they identified exclusively as black. But the results of one-to-one interviews with those same students yielded results that were exactly the opposite. Eight out of ten said that they identified primarily as biracial. Social science has long documented how susceptible humans are to group pressure, and these students were certainly not unique in the discrepancy between their public and private reports.

Religious-Identity Development

The ability to think abstractly and independently is now fairly well established. The period of forming an identity separate from family may lead to rejection of parental religious values, especially if the parents are not unified in their beliefs. During the period of leaving home, young adults are receptive and seek out religio-philosophical answers to the meaning of life. But young adults in the process of separating from home and parents still tend to think in either/or kinds of ways that may lead either to strongly embracing their parents' religious beliefs or to strongly rejecting them and choosing very different ones.

EARLY ADULTHOOD

Cultural-Racial-Identity Development

As young adults enter their middle and late twenties, they become more aware of how consequential their choices may be. They attempt to consolidate and create a stable life structure and cultural identity to help them make crucial decisions about love and work.

Dr. George Kitahara Kich, a biracial Japanese-Caucasian psychologist and researcher on racial identity, found that beginning in young adulthood those individuals who could find ways to assert their "biracialness" were better able to accept themselves and had higher self-esteem. He cautioned, however, that acknowledging and coming to terms with being biracial did not mean that one has to identify equally with both of his or her "halves." Physical appearance and relationships with both of their parents' cultural communities are factors that affect identity.

Religious-Identity Development

As they approach marriage and childrearing, many young adults begin to look back to their past religious training and family beliefs to reclaim at least some elements of one or both parents' religious traditions to help them face the task of beginning a new family. The death of aging family members can also stimulate religious questioning and experimentation.

Four Identity Forms

The work of childhood is play, and its function is to enable children to experiment with the whole range of human experience. Play allows children to create, discard, and re-create categories of belonging and identity. Just as preschoolers experiment with sexual identity and try on boys' and girls' clothing when given the chance, they also experiment with "trying on" different cultural, racial, and religious identities.

This experimentation may lead members of the same family in very different directions. One African-American woman I spoke with was raised in a middle-class, monoracial, monoreligious Baptist family from Charlotte, North Carolina. She had followed in her parents' footsteps, married a young man from their church, and settled down less than a mile from the home she grew up in. Her older brother, though, evolved into an Afro-centric and militant Black Muslim, while her younger sister married a white man and joined a Unitarian church. There is, in short, no simple way to totally control or predict the eventual adult form of a child's cultural, racial, or religious identity.

While most children of mixed matches eventually achieve a stable sense of identity, the process is usually complex. Some children always identify with the race, culture, or religion of one of their parents and not of the other. Others may radically alter their cultural identification or religious practices over the years. Experimentation and change are the rule rather than the exception.

The following four identity forms provide a model of the ways that the children of mixed matches identify. In any of the stages of identity development children may settle on one of these forms, move between them, or create their own unique combinations.

IDENTITY FORMS	
	CHARACTERISTICS
MAJORITY-GROUP IDENTIFIERS	Majority identifiers live and identify primarily with the identity of the parent who is from the dominant culture or religion. They may or may not publicly acknowledge the identity of their other parent who, in this case, is of a minority-group background.
MINORITY-GROUP IDENTIFIERS	Minority identifiers live and identify primarily within the ethnic, racial, or religious world of the one of their parents who is a minority-group member. They may acknowledge that their other parent is from a different background, or they may try to deny their dual heritage. In either case they minimize or avoid contact with the other parent's culture or religion.
UNIVERSALISTS/ DISAFFILIATES: "NONE OF THE ABOVE"	Universalists/disaffiliates choose to create their own values, rituals, and identity that are not based in any significant way upon either of their parents' backgrounds. They may refuse to accept any label that defines them as part of a racial, cultural, or religious group. Or they may create an alternative identification as part of a particular and distinct group that is not related to their own parents' backgrounds.
SYNTHESIZERS	Synthesizers are people who are able to bring together and integrate some version of what they actually are—composed of two or more cultures and/or religions. They are able to acknowledge that they are influenced by aspects of both of their parents' backgrounds. Even if their identifications with both sides of their family are not evenly balanced, they still acknowledge the importance of both "parts."

Divorce, remarriage, transracial adoption, and other twists of fate can further complicate the identity equation of a child's development. There are few reliable statistics comparing the relative stability of cross-cultural and monocultural families, but with high divorce rates among *all* couples, there are many children of mixed matches affected by divorce, who are raised primarily by a single parent or by one parent and a stepparent.

Some divorced parents are able to make the best of an often bad situation and to respect and support each other's desires to instill some of their own sense of identity into their children. Other divorced parents, especially those who had battled over their children's identity while they were still married, continue to do so after the divorce, to the great detriment of the children. Single parents who find themselves raising children alone sometimes honor the absent parent's culture or religion in raising their child. But sometimes that is difficult or impossible.

One African-American woman who had raised her biracial black-white son from birth said she could understand and respect the desire of some mixed matches to raise their children to identify with both sides of their background. But she went on to explain that as a single black mother, who was raising a child whom the outside world saw as black in a black neighborhood, it didn't make a lot of sense to try to get him in touch with the white half of his roots. She suggested that it certainly wouldn't endear him to his black friends, nor would it help him in a white world that would always label him as black.

Remarriage often leads to yet further racial-ethnic-religious combinations in a child's life. Intact families with two parents raising only their own biological children are becoming a minority group themselves, and for blended families flexibility and a good sense of humor are the keys to success. One woman, who was half Hawaiian and half Caucasian, was divorced from her Japanese husband and remarried a Caucasian man, who was divorced from his Mexican-American wife. They brought five children to their union. The kids used to joke when asked the "What are you?" question about their family: "Oh, we're a Jap-Beaner-Gringo-Haole-Hapa family."

The controversial issue of transracial adoption, which most often involves white parents adopting racial-minority children, adds even more complexity to the identity equation. The largest number of children in foster care for whom there are no adoptive homes are black. The lack of enough African-American adoptive families and the availability of white parents who want to adopt minority children have led to a high rate of transracial adoption. But interracial adoption has been strongly opposed by the National Association of Black Social Workers, some of whose leaders have labeled interracial adoption as a form of "cultural genocide." Not surprisingly groups like the Association of MultiEthnic Americans (AMEA), which is the parent organization of multiracial family groups across the country, as well as members of the Baha'i faith, which encourages interracial marriage as a path toward intergroup harmony, object to any moves to limit transracial adoption.

In spite of the debate, interracial adoption continues among monocultural families and mixed matches, and "What color is he/she?" is often the first question that others ask adoptive parents when others find out that they have adopted a child. It's a question that highlights the fact that there are many parents raising children who are not from their own racial background, and it points to the powerful and often painful politics of race.

Searching for a Solid Sense of Identity

It is important to try to understand the kinds of challenges the children of mixed matches face. The following excerpts are from interviews with young adults, who describe, in their own words, the stages they went through in the development of their identities. In these interviews I asked people to talk in the present tense, as if they were actually the age they were speaking about.

STEVE—RELIGION AS A UNIVERSALISTIC SOLUTION
Steve's journey through the stages of identity demonstrated the distinction between cultural and religious aspects of identity. He was raised in a secular, professional family. His parents' backgrounds included Filipino, Jewish, native American, and Irish strands, but in their family life they did nothing to acknowledge their families' pasts.

Childhood
Until Steve approached adolescence, his identity was primarily family-based. Like most children he strongly identified with his parents and their values and interests.

> I am seven years old and I am living in Delaware. I am sort of aware that my mother is part Filipino and part American Indian and that my father is Russian-Jewish and Irish. But I don't think of myself as different, and no one else does anything to make me feel different. My mom tells me that people think I'm Italian, but I'm not exactly sure what that means. The other kids never tease me.
>
> My mom is a social worker and helps people, and my father teaches psychology at the university. Their work seems real important to them, and I feel kind of proud because they seem like important people.

Preteen
By the time he was twelve, Steve's social world outside the family began to have as much influence over his developing identity as

his family. He lived in an area where many of his peers were involved in formal religious training, and he was increasingly disturbed by his lack of any clear sense of a religious identity. His family was not equipped to guide him, so he began to conduct experiments in belonging on his own.

> I start to feel jealous of the kids I know who have religious training. I have Jewish friends who are preparing for their bar mitzvahs and Christian friends preparing for their confirmations. My family seems totally disinterested in religion. My parents always talk about psychology over dinner, and I know about the concept of "penis envy" before I am twelve. But I think to myself that what I have is "piety envy." I want to believe and practice a religion, but I don't know how, and no one seems willing or able to show me the way.
>
> For a while I go to a local synagogue with a friend, but my parents give me absolutely no support, and I always feel out of place and different among the Jewish kids, so I stop going after a few months.

Adolescence

A dramatic revelation about his family's past—the imprisonment of a grandfather for interracial marriage—became a focal point for the ongoing process of Steve's identity development. Having found his attempts at creating a religious identity frustrating, he turned to an issue many teenagers are preoccupied with—justice. His cultural-racial background became the vehicle for his experimentation.

> A big turning point for me is learning more about my family's history. I am looking through some old family albums and see a picture of a young man leaving what looks like a prison. I go to

my mother, and she tells me it is my grandfather, her father. I ask her why she has never told me about this, and she responds, "It didn't seem that important." I begin to question her about it incessantly, and she begins reluctantly to answer my questions.

My grandfather was thrown in jail when he came to California for being with my maternal grandmother. Their marriage was a violation of the antimiscegenation laws. He was Filipino. My grandmother is mixed American Indian and white, but it said "white" on her birth certificate. My grandfather died three years ago. I never had any idea about that part of his history. I become obsessed with social injustice, and race suddenly seems like a very important issue. I don't know any other Filipino kids, but for a time I start to search the newspapers for stories about the Philippines and begin to think of myself as Filipino.

Leaving Home

Steve went through a period of development that was characterized by his attempts to create an identity as a synthesizer. He identified as a multicultural person, who incorporated several different backgrounds. His interest in religion resurfaced, but he was embarrassed about his spiritual quest because he felt that he would be stigmatized by his peers.

I am less political now than in high school and more concerned with my social life, succeeding, and fitting in. But the family albums I have always been so interested in remain a real force in my life. I don't like to describe my white relatives on my father's side as white. They are Irish and Jewish. My paternal grandmother escaped out of Kiev in an oxcart. That side is very important to me too. So when someone would ask me what I am, I would just say, "I'm me. I'm a mix of a lot of different things."

But I really don't feel like I belong anywhere. If I try to identify with my Russian-Jewish part, I keep on remembering that it is only a part. If I really try to identify with my Filipino part, it becomes problematic too. When I go to the meeting of a Filipino student group on campus, they look at me like I am weird. I don't look typically Filipino. I don't know very much about the culture. Yet it is an important part of my background. What am I going to do, say that I'm a FIT, a Filipino-in-Training?

In the last few years I've given up on trying to identify very strongly with any of my cultural parts, but religious faith has grown to be a strong force in my life. My last year in college I get more involved in Catholicism at the Newman Center on campus. At first I feel kind of embarrassed about it. I don't tell my parents, because I am afraid that they will label my religious explorations as some sort of neurosis if they find out about them. And not many of the students I know are practicing any religion, so I almost feel like I have to sneak to Mass and that it is a secret I have to keep.

Young Adulthood

It was only as Steve entered young adulthood that he felt free enough of family and peer influences to begin creating a form of identity that seemed right for him. Gradually he became more comfortable with his growing religious convictions. The different aspects of his cultural background became less important to him as he became involved in religious beliefs that transcend cultural borders.

After I graduated, got a job in the city, and began to make some new friends through the church I went to, I started to feel a lot more comfortable identifying myself as Catholic. I remember being at Mass one Sunday morning and looking around the big church and seeing a lot of Asian and white and black faces, and for the first time in my life I had this feeling of being at home in a group of people, of not feeling different. It was like I was a little bit of all of these people, and they were all a little bit of me.

CINDY—THE MAKING OF A MINORITY-GROUP IDENTIFIER
Cindy is a fair-skinned, blond woman. Both of her parents are half native American and half Caucasian. She found that the combination of her physical appearance, her parents' discomfort with their native-American pasts, growing up in a region where there was a large Indian population, and her growing fascination with a forbidden identity, made shaping her own sense of belonging a complicated process.

In her early childhood her parents' discomfort with their own mixed identities prevented them from helping her shape her own in any sort of meaningful way. But parents can paradoxically focus their children's attention on the very issues they try to avoid. Cindy's memory of their discomfort with the "Indian question" was probably typical of hundreds of small incidents that focused Cindy's attention on the taboo topic.

Childhood

I grew up in Oklahoma. Both of my parents are mixed-blood native Americans. My parents and grandparents work hard at and are successful at passing for white. One time my aunt and uncle are saying something about Indians at a family gathering, but when I ask them a question about what they are talking about, they look angry and stop talking. I learn quickly not to talk about certain subjects.

Preteen

Her parents' divorce and her mother's remarriage proved to be pivotal events in the development of Cindy's identity. Her troubled relationship with her stepfather actually helped to begin to consolidate her sense of being a member of an embattled minority group.

Now I am twelve years old. My parents divorced two years ago. We move to Seattle. My mother remarries—to a racist.

I am in eighth grade and I am twelve, and I'm starting to notice how many shades of color there are. I wasn't really aware of other native Americans back in Oklahoma. It's weird, because I actually grew up with a lot of native Americans around, but we never really talked about it. Now I'm noticing other native Americans around me and their cultural events. I start to pay attention. I begin feeling like maybe it has something to do with who I am.

But I am living with my mom and my stepdad, and he is really racist. He will not let us watch the Spanish TV station because he hates "spic talk." And we cannot watch the "Cosby" show because he says, "We're not going to watch niggers in my household." I just cringe.

Adolescence

All through high school I am really scared. But I am becoming more aware of this other part of me that's not white. My stepdad has me and my brother and sister really intimidated. My mother would never have put up with his behavior, but we are afraid to tell her about it. So we learn to keep all of our feelings about who we are hidden. My mom works seven days a week.

Leaving Home

Cindy went to college without any parental support. Between an academic scholarship she won, savings from summer jobs, and a college work-study grant, she put herself through college. But she discovered that even though she was now on her own, there were others besides her parents who felt entitled to try to limit her choices about her identity.

Among many racial-minority groups today there are vocal members who have appointed themselves as the guardians and gatekeepers of their groups' cultural and racial integrity. They feel that it is their job to decide who is entitled to identify themselves as a member of the group and who is not. And in college Cindy found that being accepted as a native American would not be easy. She learned that she would have to work and struggle to be recognized as a member of the group she now identified with.

When I come onto this campus, it is really racially and culturally balkanized, and the message is clear—*you must choose.* I feel forced to decide who I am. I get really confused. As you can see, I have blond hair and a fair complexion. When I walk out on the street, anyone who doesn't know me immediately registers *white woman.* No one spontaneously looks at me and asks, *Is she an Indian?* Sometimes I just feel like giving up trying to relate to any identity and just run around and say, *I'm a human, I'm a human. I love everyone.*

I think, *Oh, my God, who am I? What am I doing?* I get mad at my family. I feel, *Why did you put me in this situation?* Nobody ever tells me who I am. Now I've come here, and these people are in my face about it. So I just completely shut myself off from my family. I am mad at my mom, even though we were once close.

That's when I decide to be a Native American Studies major. It feels like a way to affirm some part of myself and get in touch with what my family has robbed me of. I find myself pulling away from white culture. It doesn't mean anything to me that I'm part Irish, except for the features I happen to have. I am the lightest of my brothers and sisters. I have green eyes and freckles and very fair skin. I used to be proud of it. Now I look at it and feel like it's a burden. I don't look like who I choose to be. Now I feel, *Why me, why do I have to look this way?*

People in the department look at me and say, "Oh, yeah, you're Indian, right. Tell me something else." Then the other students say, "You must be trying to get something out of pretending that you're Indian. Come off it." The fact of the matter is that I have never sought out or accepted any aid as a minority student. But that doesn't change what people choose to think.

Over the last two years, especially since I enrolled in the Native American Studies department, I have come to strongly identify as native American. I find out that most of the people in the department as well as most of the native Americans I meet outside of school are of mixed racial ancestry. Some of them were born on the reservation and had a much more powerful experience early in their lives of knowing who they were culturally, but I have come to feel that my choice is just as valid. I am who I choose to be.

At that moment Cindy paused, dug into her handbag, and pulled out a card laminated in red plastic. With an ironic grin she held it up and emphatically stated, "And I have my tribal card to prove it."

Cindy was an unusually resilient and determined young woman who was able to create a positive minority-group identity in spite of many obstacles. Neither her parents, her stepfather, nor many of the native Americans she encountered gave her encouragement. But in spite of all these obstacles Cindy persevered and was able to build a small group of loyal and accepting friends in the Native American Studies department who accepted her, blond hair and all.

WILLIE—SYNTHESIZING AN IDENTITY

Childhood

As a young child Willie remembered easy transitions between the Anglo and Mexican-American halves of his family. In these early years he didn't have to synthesize his parents' different cultures, because it seemed only natural to him that the two parts of his identity could live side by side without apparent conflict or contradiction.

> I live in a small New Mexico town of about thirteen thousand. When I go to my white grandparents, we speak English and learn about good manners. When I visit my Chicano grandparents and aunts and uncles, we speak Spanish and I hear a lot of *gumbuyas* and *corridas* and we listen to music and eat a lot. It seems natural and normal to me to be part of both of these very different families.

Preteen

As Willie moved into his preteen years, he became more aware of his father's mixed feelings about his Mexican heritage and at the same time was increasingly influenced by peers. As a result, the two sides of his identity no longer felt so easily compatible as they had been when he was younger. He had always felt close to his father and began to identify more with the Mexican-American side of his family. But his father also gave him mixed messages about the value of identifying as a Chicano.

> We don't speak much Spanish at home because my father is embarrassed about it. He was punished as a child for speaking Spanish in the schools. So the only words I learned when I was young were the hot, bad words that now come out in moments

of passion: "Sit down, shut up, get out of my face." Those are the words that come easily to me in Spanish.

I am in junior high now and we have moved to Sante Fe, and most of the kids in my class are Chicano. But a bunch of them get mad at me for being too smart and they want me to help them cheat, and I do. I am not very happy in school, but my parents just tell me not to worry and that things will get better. So after sixth grade I decide not to be smart anymore.

Adolescence

When Willie entered high school, he found a way to resolve his dilemma about what sort of identity he would take on—he would become a universalist and not be trapped by either side of what seemed like an increasingly problematic dual identity.

I meet this hippie girl and her hippie mother and I admire them, so I start to take on their identity. Now I am in tenth grade. I drop my Spanish surname. I am going to be an artist-poet known only by the name Willie. Even though I have always been very close with the Chicano side of my family and went to the festivals and celebrations and have lots of warm memories, I now have decided that I don't like either side of my family.

I start hanging out with college-bound white guys by tenth grade, even though I still have a lot of Chicano friends. I use my "artist identity" to explain why I had erased my Spanish last name. But now I am beginning to know why I do it. I want to distance myself from that half of my past.

Leaving Home

During the next two stages of his development Willie increasingly adopted a composite identity as a synthesizer that incorporated all the parts of his background. He learned to handle the complexity of being both, and no longer felt that he had to choose one, the other, or neither. He could be who he felt himself to be and was no longer as dependent on either family or peer group.

My mom and dad divorce when I go to college. Now my identity is as *coyote*. I am lucky that my *tio* (uncle) called me "coyote," which means "the youngest" but also means "mixed." My uncle and aunt are real fond of me and I love them, so his saying it becomes a good thing. "Coyote" becomes a term of endearment. So I am a coyote.

By the time I head off to college, I always check "Other" on the forms that we have to fill out that ask us about our racial background. If there is a blank space after "Other," I fill in "Mexican-American"-slash-white or -Anglo. I refuse to be forced into a box where I don't feel I belong. It's very important to me.

When people ask me about how I feel about something, I say in a kind of joking way, "Well, my Mexican half thinks this and my Anglo half thinks that." They laugh. It's a joke, but it is also my way of dealing with my halfness.

So I am able to flow in and out of all the groups. I am with the honkies, I am with the cholos, the jocks. I get along with everyone. By this time I am really feeling that I am lucky. That I have all these different things I can do and that I am able to bring all different kinds of people together.

Young Adulthood

Now I am twenty-eight and married. My wife is white. I am very much a part of her family. Now we're this huge family. I have a little boy. Trying to pass on my fractured Spanish half is very difficult. I have to go back and begin building on the broken shards of identity I have.

I'm still learning a lot about how my different cultural "parts" talk to each other. My Mexican and Anglo parts are getting to know each other, to make peace, and to go beyond making peace and starting to become friends. They are learning to work together and to become stronger than either of them would be alone. I feel like I'm working to create an identity for myself that is not just an alternation between the two parts but is a unified, complex, and creative whole.

NATASHA—AN ONGOING STRUGGLE FOR A SENSE OF IDENTITY

Natasha's white biological mother was eighteen years old when she got pregnant by her black boyfriend. When Natasha was born, her mother decided to put her up for adoption. She was adopted by a black professional couple and raised in neighborhoods that were almost exclusively white. Every step of the development of her identity was profoundly influenced by this unusual set of circumstances. Lighter in color than her parents, darker than her friends, living as part of a black family surrounded by a white world, Natasha had to constantly work to create a clear sense of identity.

Childhood

I am five years old. My parents, who are both black, have told me that I am adopted and that my biological mother is white and that my father is black. But it doesn't seem to mean too much to me at the time. I know that I am black because I have a black brother.

Preteen

The process of Natasha's identity formation was further complicated during the crucial preteen phase of her development, when peer-group acceptance becomes so important, by her family's relocation to Indianapolis. She was in seventh grade and found herself in an environment where she tried to fit in, even while feeling very different. Her attempts to identify as a member of the majority group were awkward. While the girls she met were friendly, she was also aware of the tension that was caused by her black family moving into a white, conservative neighborhood.

I have just moved from Detroit to Indiana, because my father has gotten a big promotion at work. Where I was living before was at least a little diverse. This new town is totally white, and everybody says "please" and "thank you" all the time. I am very depressed.

I never really know what to do with my hair. I try to make it like the other girls, but it never quite works. But I do my best and I'm wearing my hair parted down the middle, held back in barrettes with my name painted on them. Everyone wears her hair with the curled-under bang and the hair cultured in. Well, I have serious problems because I always have this ripple. My hair always curls the wrong way. I blow it straight so much, it really gets damaged. All my friends love my hair, but I am tortured and struggling with it like it's an obstinate living beast.

I know that I am mixed, but it never gets talked about at home. I know that somewhere out there I have a white birth mother. There is only one other black family in our upper-middle-class suburb. I find out later that a lot of families were upset when we moved in and tried to block the sale of the house to us, but at the time my parents didn't tell me, so I didn't know.

My friends back at school are all white. I have a personality that always wants to fit in. But I find out early that I can never fit in. I can never fit in with the Catholic midwestern German stock that I live around, even though the girls are nice and try to make me feel comfortable.

Adolescence

Adolescence was a very difficult time for Natasha. She felt that the color of her skin was a handicap she could not overcome. Her earlier attempts to be "just one of the girls" were becoming increasingly problematic. But during her junior and senior years she was able to begin conducting some experiments with her identity and for the first time try on a minority-group identity.

I have no boyfriends, and no boy is interested in me. I know it's because I'm different. A lot of my girlfriends are pretty average-looking and they all have boyfriends. They say, "You're so pretty, you're so beautiful." And I think to myself, *Then why don't any of the boys like me?* And I know the answer is *Race*. But we *never* talk about it. It is never acknowledged.

At the end of ninth grade I give up trying to be white and decide to become black. It isn't really that conscious, but now as I look back, I see that's what I did. I'm *all* black. I start hanging out in the poor black section of town and go to my first party. I dance and try to learn what black people do at a party. I don't really know how to dance. Some of them think I'm stuck up because I'm really shy.

I go back to school and begin talking black slang to my white friends. They start to look at me really funny. They don't know what I am talking about. And they are shocked. But by my junior year I finally give up trying to be white or black, and I decide to be *different*. I'm still not dating at all, even though a lot of the girls tell me I am one of the prettiest girls in the school.

People always ask, "What are you?" When I was younger, I hated the question so much. Sometimes I say I am American. But usually I say I am black. Sometimes I let them guess. They go through a huge list; Italian, Greek, Jewish, Mexican, Filipino. Everything, everything but what I am. Even though I make a game out of it, sometimes it really angers me so much. Why can't people just know me? Why do they have to label and categorize me? It affects my self-image. If I was darker, it would be easier

and clearer. But because I look the way that I do, I always have
to deal with the "What are you?" question.

The frequently asked "What are you?" question was disturbing to
Natasha, as it is to many children of mixed matches. It was an intrusive question, and one strangers often feel entitled to ask. It
tapped into her own uncertainty about her identity. She wanted to
conduct her identity experiments at her own pace and didn't want
to be forced to answer questions before she was ready.

Leaving Home

When Natasha left for college, she felt safe enough to intensify her
experimentation with her minority-group sense of identity. While
it was confusing and painful at times, it was crucial to her to begin
to find ways to create an identity that she felt comfortable with.

> I go to Cornell University and now I identify totally as black.
> But I really have to conform. It is so rigid. Fitting in with the
> black students means I have to "speak." If I don't "speak," it means
> I'm not black. "Speaking" means you have to say "hi" to every
> black person. It is the thing. And if you don't speak, it is "Oh, she
> doesn't speak, she's not black." There's so much pressure. Just to
> walk across campus, you have to say "hi" or nod or smile every-
> where you go.
>
> I worry a lot about if people know I am black. I feel that I have
> to start over every year with the younger class and do something
> to prove to everyone that I am "really" black. When I am a se-
> nior, I worry about how the freshmen see me. Sometimes I feel
> like I am a reverse "wannabe." You know, some blacks want to
> pass for white. But I worry if I will be acknowledged as black.
>
> Even though I am the lightest one in my family because I am

biracial, I'm now the blackest of the black in the way I see my-self. All my friends are black. Anything in my life that is black I grasp at. Anything black I have experienced I remember and bring up now—even though there isn't really much to draw upon. I'm very good at adapting. I start racial conflict in my dorms—get whitey. We put up sexy pictures of black men all over the bathroom stalls. That creates a big uproar. Everybody I go out with now is black. I feel like whites are "boogeymen"—like my white blood taints me because of all the bad things white people have done to blacks.

I am very popular with the men because I am light-skinned, plus I act sexy. I am taking African-American studies courses. I become a sweetheart of one of the black fraternities. I go to all the black parties. I don't have any problem with talking bad about whites, even though my birth mother and half of my blood is white. I am trying so hard.

I finally start identifying as more biracial my junior and senior years. I am afraid to start working on a biracial identity because I am afraid of the reactions of my black friends. I am afraid to do it because they will think I am trying to do some sort of elitist thing. But I'm doing it anyway, at my own pace.

My racial sense of self is not all that constant. It can still change from hour to hour. Sometimes I feel good about being mixed, and then I realize I'm back to square one. Some days I'm on top of the world; then there are other days when I feel really confused. Overall I have become more biracial in my identity, even as I lean toward the black side. Since I got involved with a very Afro-centric guy, I've started to feel more black again. But then some days he seems so self-righteously "pure" in his black-ness that being with him actually makes me feel less black. I know that I'm a successful, good, and productive person. But it's still hard to be brown in a black-and-white world.

Natasha's life and identity were too complicated for her to force into some neat category. As a young adult she adapted a primarily minority-group identity, but she was secure enough to acknowledge that even at this point in her life her identity would change. She sometimes found the process difficult, but she felt her struggles with her identity were ultimately a source of creative inspiration in her life.

Experiments in Identity

In spite of all the difficulties of integrating and synthesizing more than one culture, many bicultural and multicultural people reported that they had grown increasingly comfortable with the idea that they didn't have to force their identity into some neat little box. As they approached their middle twenties, most began to work toward healing the splits inside of them. Rather than feeling compelled to have to identify entirely with one aspect of their background or the other, they found ways to acknowledge and embrace the different cultural currents that ran through their veins. As one young woman said, "I think the older I get and the less I try to conform to other people's definitions of who I'm supposed to be, the more comfortable I feel being who I am."

Each person's path through the process of creating an identity is unique, and all involve a process of experimentation and change. Many of the young people I spoke with felt that the struggles they had gone through in clarifying their identity had helped them become better and more interesting people. Rather than the "marginal man" of an earlier era, these were complex and interesting men and women with broad views on the human situation and a commitment to bridging social chasms. With roots in more than one tradition, many of them felt the need to find ways to heal racial, religious, and ethnic conflicts.

The following chapter builds on our understanding of these bicultural, bireligious, and biracial people and explores ways that parents and families can help children develop solid identities in a complicated world.

CHAPTER 8

Helping Children Develop a Solid Identity

ANNA: We were driving home from preschool one day when Teddy was four, and out of the blue he says, "White people are better than black people." I got really upset, but I tried to bite my tongue. "Who told you that?" I asked him. "Nobody," he said. "Your daddy is black, what about him?" I asked. Teddy said, "He's okay."

I resisted my impulse to jump on the soapbox and deliver a speech about how all people are the same. I didn't know what to do about it, so I waited to talk to my husband, Charles. I felt bad. Like I must have done something wrong.

CHARLES: When Anna and I talked about it, she agreed that the best way to deal with it was to just let Teddy talk and express himself and listen to what he had to say. He simply repeated himself and said that being white was better than being black.

Then I told him what I feel. I said that I have known a lot of people both black and white and that I can't really see anything that makes one better than the other. Then I talked about individuals I have known who have been good blacks and bad blacks and good whites and bad whites. We have had to go through different versions of this as he grew older, and I accept that it's an important thing to do.

ANNA AND CHARLES, TALKING ABOUT THEIR BIRACIAL SON, TEDDY. ANNA IS WHITE AND CHARLES IS BLACK

265

Parents of cross-cultural children often ask questions that are actually thinly veiled statements: *Don't you think that it's better for children to have a single religion practiced in the home? Aren't the children of intercultural marriages more likely to develop positive self-esteem if they learn to identify equally with both of their cultural heritages? Isn't it better for biracial children to identify primarily with the minority parent, because that's the way the world is going to identify them anyway?* But the truth is there are no definitive answers. Approaches that work well for some families spell disaster for others.

There are no simple formulas for raising children, because the best path for any particular family depends on so many variables. Children and families living in more tolerant environments face different issues from those living in areas plagued by pervasive racial and social tensions. Wealthy families may be able to afford a lifestyle that insulates them from the harsher aspects of life that families of more modest means may not be able to avoid. Single parents have different concerns than parents with intact marriages. Stepparents and blended families may introduce even more complexity into a family situation, creating a rainbow array of cultures in one household. And while many children do better having a unified family faith, some children thrive without any organized religion or in families that practice a blend of religions.

Even though there is no one route to successful child rearing, there are a number of basic principles for helping your children develop solid identities:

- Make working out your differences with your partner about the cultural and religious identity of your family an ongoing process

- Listen to your children and try to understand their experiences
- See your children's ambivalence about their identity as a normal developmental stage
- Provide your children with positive experiences that reflect who they are
- Help your children deal with prejudice
- Recognize that your children will grow up and choose their own paths

Work Out Differences with Your Partner

One of the mysterious facts about the world that children discover, even before they enter kindergarten, is that people are divided and categorized by race, language, and religion. They naturally turn to adults to help them figure out where they fit in the complex social matrix they struggle to understand. When parents are unable to agree wholeheartedly on how to define their family's religious and cultural identity, it's very difficult for them to provide their children with the guidance they need. In chapters 3 and 5 I described methods for making decisions about your family's identity. In order to help your children develop a clear sense of who they are, it's crucial that you work on the tasks laid out in those chapters.

ESTHER AND GUY—WUDAROO
Sylvia, the four-year-old daughter of an interfaith, cross-cultural couple, dramatically illustrated the kinds of problems that can result when parents do not deal with their differences. Her mother, Esther, was Jewish, and her father, Guy, was a Puerto Rican Catholic. Guy

had moved with his family from Puerto Rico to New York when he was eight years old. Esther's grandparents had immigrated to America in 1908 to escape persecution in Russia.

Esther and Guy were worried by Sylvia's strange behavior. She had wandered away from her backyard on a number of occasions. Each time she left, she would ring the doorbell of a different neighbor's house. When a surprised adult answered the door, Sylvia would usually look up and mumble a word that most of the neighbors described as "wudaroo."

Her parents were upset about Sylvia leaving the yard without permission, and couldn't get her to explain her actions. When they became anxious and irritated with her, she would fall silent. And when they asked her what "wudaroo" meant, she would hang her head and begin to cry.

Esther and Guy were still struggling to reconcile their cultural and religious differences. Six years earlier, when they had gotten married, they hadn't been able to agree on which religious or cultural symbols to include in their ceremony, so they chose not to include any.

Guy went to a local Catholic church almost every Sunday morning and often took Sylvia with him. Esther took Sylvia to synagogue once a year on the high holidays, more to "balance" her husband's influence than out of any real religious convictions of her own. Neither Guy nor Esther had ever entered the other's house of worship. The past summer Guy had taken Sylvia on a trip with him for a week to visit his grandparents in Puerto Rico. That fall Esther took her on several excursions she called "cultural field trips" to a Jewish neighborhood on the Lower East Side of New York City.

The one thing that Guy and Esther could agree on was their shared reluctance to discuss their differences. They were both very devoted to Sylvia and wanted their marriage to work. While neither of them was happy with silence as a solution to their problems, they felt it was the best way they had found. They had agreed to disagree and not to discuss the issues surrounding their different cultural loyalties and religious beliefs.

Sylvia was a friendly, if somewhat shy, child. After she and I had played together for a while with some plastic characters, I picked up a toy dog and used it to talk to the duck she was playing with. "Wudaroo," the dog said to the duck.

Without missing a beat the duck replied, "Can't you see, you silly dog? I'm a duck." "Wudaroo," it turned out, was her way of asking, "What are you?"

While it was clear to her that a duck was a duck, she was far less clear about her own identity. Sylvia had turned to neighbors to help her understand what her parents could not. If they had answers to the question of "Wudaroo," then perhaps they could help answer her unspoken question: What am I?

Esther and Guy were genuinely shocked by Sylvia's confusion. They had never even imagined that their unfinished negotiations about the religious identity of their interfaith family could so strongly affect a child as young as Sylvia. The incident led to a process of soul-searching and experimentation. After several long talks with a rabbi who was a family friend, Esther made a decision that surprised everyone:

> I've really thought about this a lot. But the turning point for me was some talks I had with Rabbi Stern. I told him that I felt strongly about my ethnic identity as a Jew, but that I had almost no religious training or real feeling for the practice of Judaism. I also told him that Guy had always been very involved in his Catholicism and about my fear that if we really faced our differ-

ences, it might destroy our marriage. He suggested some reading for me about Judaism and asked me to come back to talk to him in a couple of weeks.

When we met a few weeks later, I felt kind of embarrassed to admit to him that I hadn't read any of the books. I told him that I didn't feel that I had the time or energy to invest in learning about how to practice Judaism at this point in my life. I work full-time, and our life is very stressful. The rabbi talked to me about participating in some child-centered holiday celebrations at the synagogue and some other low-key ways I could introduce Sylvia and myself to Jewish life. But then he went on to tell me about how important he felt it was for children to have some real grounding in a religious tradition. He asked me if I had ever considered letting Guy take primary responsibility for Sylvia's spiritual education since he was so much more involved in his Catholicism than I was in Judaism.

I was shocked. Here was a conservative rabbi indirectly suggesting that I think about letting my child be raised as a Christian. But over the next couple of weeks, the more I thought about it, the more I felt it might be the best choice. I chose to marry Guy knowing how important his Catholicism was to him. We chose to have a child without really thinking about the implications of our differences. I guess we were naive in thinking it would all work itself out without any sacrifice. I'm not exactly sure how my parents or how I am going to deal with this decision, but we're going to start sending Sylvia to Sunday school at Guy's church beginning this fall. We'll take it one step at a time.

One of the reasons that couples have difficulties making decisions is that they want to avoid the losses that are part of every choice. *Suicide*, *homicide*, and *decide* all have the same root, *cide*, which is derived from the Latin *caedere* and means "to cut" or "to kill." The decision to raise a child in one culture or religion, in both, or in neither, does kill other options. The difficult truth is that even the best of decisions creates some risk and some loss, requires compromise, and is never perfectly balanced.

The better able you and your partner are at deciding which aspects of your different cultural and religious backgrounds you want to bring into your family life, the more successful you will be in helping your children create a solid sense of belonging.

Listen to Your Children's Experience

The children of mixed matches need to feel that their identity—who and what they are with all of its complexities—is a safe subject. When children sense that race, culture, and religion are topics their parents are uncomfortable with, they will tend to communicate their concerns about their identities indirectly. If parents don't pick up on their oblique communications, children will often retreat to the use of more troubling and provocative ways to address the issue of belonging.

When parents say, "If only he had brought it up, we would have been glad to talk about it," what they usually mean is that they would have responded to their children's questions if they had been directly asked. But it is a very unusual child who approaches his parents by saying, "Mom and Dad, I have some concerns about the effect that being bicultural has on my identity and on my self-esteem." When parents can pick up on their children's indirect communications about their identities, they can head off lots of problems.

Unfortunately we are often tempted to avoid dealing with the really tough issues. At one time or another, most of us have sidestepped discussing emotionally charged subjects with our children by using a variety of rationalizations: "We're waiting until he's old enough," or "We don't want to put any ideas into her head," or simply, "I'm too busy." *Later* almost always seems like a better time than *now* to deal with the most difficult topics. The problem is once we put a task in the "later" box, "later" often becomes never. "We always meant to talk about (sex, race, religion, etc.), but I guess we never got around to it."

And when we do have conversations with our children, we often find that the talking side of the equation is far easier than the listening. Really listening means we have to try to grasp our children's understanding of their world, which inevitably includes feelings, experiences, and questions that we are uncomfortable with. If listening were simple, the psychotherapy industry wouldn't exist. In reality it's the ability of the therapist to listen that enables the "talking cure" to work. And it's parents' ability to listen that allows their children to open up about their doubts and fears.

They express it in different ways, but many children of crosscultural marriages say the same thing: "My parents didn't listen; they didn't want to hear what I have had to deal with." Sometimes parents' failure to listen was a result of their indifference. But more often it was not a lack of caring that motivated the parents' avoidance but a desire to avoid their own anxiety and helplessness in dealing with their children's pain or confusion.

MORIA AND ELIZABETH—THE POWER OF LISTENING

Moria's experience illustrates the kinds of problems that can arise in the best of parent-child relationships when a parent has difficulty listening. But it also illustrates the possibilities of building bridges when parents and children find the courage to confront difficult realities, to talk *and* to listen.

Moria is a bright, attractive, twenty-five-year-old, biracial woman. She has dark brown skin and brown eyes, and most people, when they first see her, assume that she is African-American. Her mother is a hazel-eyed, brown-haired Irish-Italian woman who works as an executive for a large, nonprofit organization. Her father has the typical appearance of people from Cochin, in southern India, where he was born—almost-black skin and delicate features. He came to the United States from India as a child with his family and is now a successful businessman. At the time I interviewed Moria, she was working as a staff member at an environmental organization and preparing to go to graduate school.

Moria's parents divorced when she was six years old, and she was raised primarily by her mother, Elizabeth. After the divorce they moved from Boston to Denver. Moria had been very close to her mother all of her life, but was concerned that she and her mother had begun to grow more distant. As she thought about the reasons behind their increasing separateness, she realized that her mother's difficulty acknowledging Moria's experience around the issue of race had become a problem in their relationship.

I love my mother more than anything in this world. I always told my mom everything. But in the past couple of years I feel that there's more and more I can't say, especially about race, because it will hurt her. I know I am biracial and I also realize that I have been raised by a white mother in a mostly white neighborhood like any other middle-class, educated child. But even though I identify far more with my mother than with my father doesn't mean that the world knows that by looking at me. They don't.

I started talking to her about it last week when I was home, but it was too painful for her, so I changed the subject. I saw in her eyes that it hurt her so bad to hear the truth. What I was trying to explain to her was that no matter how I see myself, in America I am initially seen as a twenty-five-year-old *black* woman, even though I am not culturally African-American. She doesn't want to admit that I get treated differently than white people. She is a very worldly person and knows better, but she just can't bring herself to accept reality. When I try to talk about it, she thinks I am saying that I am rejecting her and everything that is like her and white about me. I'm not, but she can't hear it.

I tell her, "Mom, I go into stores and the shop owners follow me." She says, "No, they don't, you're my daughter. Of course they don't." If I push it, she says, "Well, it's probably because you're young." Then she goes on and asks me what I was wearing when the shopkeeper followed me. I know exactly what she is getting at. She was hoping I had been dressed all grungy so that she could attribute the shopkeeper's behavior to my clothes rather than to my color. I told her I was wearing a work outfit that was very nice and quite expensive. She was real quiet for a moment in a way that's unusual for her, because she's such an outspoken and articulate woman. Then she launched into her denial again. "This is the nineties, this can't be happening." That's when I stopped talking.

Elizabeth's attempts to reassure Moria were motivated both by her love for her daughter and by her desire to avoid her own sense of helplessness. It was difficult for her to accept how powerless she was to change painful social realities that affected her daughter. Her denial of Moria's experiences of racism, though, began to create problems. Fortunately Moria cared enough to find a way to deal with the barrier that had been growing between them.

Finally I decided that I needed to confront her. It was real hard for me, but we had always been so close, and I didn't like feeling so distant. I arranged a special time for us to go for a walk where we wouldn't be disturbed. We sat down on a big rock next to a stream in a beautiful place, and I launched into my speech that I had rehearsed ten times:

"Mom, just because I speak good English, just because I did well in college, just because you raised me and you love me and your love sees no color doesn't mean that I don't have to deal with being labeled and seen and treated as a black woman every day of my life. You know it's true, but you don't seem to be able to tolerate the idea. It doesn't matter how I talk, dress, identify myself, or feel in my heart. Until someone gets to know me well, I am seen as just another young black woman with all the stereotypes that go with that label. What am I supposed to do, wear a sign on my forehead saying, 'I'm okay because I'm not like *them*. I was raised by my white mother.' We both know what I'm saying is true and I need you to stop pretending, because if you won't, it means I can't talk to you about what my life is really like—the good and the bad. I am not rejecting you, but when you don't listen to what I am trying to say, I feel like you are rejecting me."

We both did a lot of crying that day, but it seemed to break down a barrier between us, and we have been a lot closer ever since. I think it really helped when my mother learned that listening is a lot more important than reassurance.

Just as Moria had to find the courage to confront difficult and painful issues, Elizabeth had to find the courage to listen. Elizabeth was all too aware of the racism that existed in society, but, until now, had been unable to bear the thought that it affected her daughter. Their talk made her realize that she *was* able to help Moria in a simple and powerful way: by trying to understand her daughter's experience.

Normalize Ambivalence

Children, as well as adults, naturally like to be on the "winning" side. Biracial, religious, and racial-minority-group children feel disturbed when they become aware of the disadvantages and vulnerabilities attached to their group status. They often go through periods of identity experimentation, rejecting and accentuating different parts of their identities. This experimentation is important for children in building a solid and healthy identity. But the process that children go through can be very difficult for parents, especially when they feel that their children's apparent confusion is a result of something they may have done wrong.

RALPH—A TEACHER'S EXPERIENCE

No one knows young children better than teachers who spend their days orchestrating the social lives of the young. Ralph, an observant and dedicated African-American preschool teacher, had developed an interesting and useful perspective on the whole issue of children's identity development. He and his white Protestant wife, Beverly, were raising two biracial children. Ralph had taught for twelve years in a preschool that served a culturally and racially diverse working-class population. Over the years he had helped many families deal with their children's personal conflicts about their identities. He felt that for minority and bicultural children ultimately to feel good about themselves, they needed to feel free to describe the world as they perceived it and to express both their positive and their negative feelings about who they were.

> I see all of my black kids, and to a lesser extent my Hispanic kids, go through a stage where they try to reject their own racial identity. It's what society teaches them. My attitude about it is

that it doesn't do the child any good to make him feel bad about having that perception. Because from the child's perspective, the perception that it's better to be white is logically correct.

When the kids look out on the school yard and all the teachers are white and all the janitors are Mexicans or blacks, they don't need to be told which is better to be. They put two and two together.

In many ways children are smarter than we are. They are not clouded by conditional thinking. We grown-ups have an awful lot of "It's not nice to think that" rules that put a stricture on the ways we think. A child just walks down the street and sees the way things are, and he draws conclusions from what he sees.

When their parents say that "everybody's the same," children start getting confused because they realize that their parents are not telling them the truth. They don't know how to deal with the contradictions between what their parents tell them and what they see. They love their parents and they sense that they should not challenge their presentation of reality. That's why and when they start to fit things into the "It's not nice to think that" adult rules. They sense their parents' discomfort, so they start to distort their own perceptions.

Ralph observed that in spite of "learning the adult rules," which require pretending not to notice the obvious, minority and biracial children's play reveals their keen awareness of racial categories and society's bias in favor of whiteness. Children's play often reflects their fears and wishes, and Ralph had observed that minority four-year-old children would consistently choose to play with white dolls, even when they had plenty of brown and black dolls to choose from as well. He felt that through their choice of dolls, minority children demonstrated their understanding of the social advantages of being white and their wish to be part of that favored category.

The white kids will play with black dolls. But the Mexican and black kids will only play with the white dolls for a long time. It doesn't matter. We have very ethnically and racially conscious parents who give kids all the dolls at home that match their own color. *But when they're given the choice, they choose the white dolls.*

Some parents would get upset with Ralph's accepting attitude about their children's expression of racial ambivalence. But Ralph felt that allowing children to express their feelings and perceptions would open up possibilities for healthier and more positive minority or biracial identities later in life. Ralph worked hard to help parents see their children's behavior as part of a necessary and inevitable stage that they were going through.

It just really upsets parents when I tell them about how their children are dealing with the issue of race. A person's racial self is one of the most vulnerable, touchy things that they have. It's very difficult for parents to hear their own children express negative feelings about their color and deal with it with anything approaching objectivity or compassion or understanding. They immediately take offense. They get angry. They want to lecture their child or blame someone for putting these ideas in their heads.

I understand the anger. I know how they feel. I can't say to the parent, "Don't feel the anger because it will make things worse." The only thing I can do is to try to help them understand that their kids are going through a normal process.

Ralph found that when parents reacted to their biracial children's initial preference for being white with alarm, children took the process of working out their concerns about identity underground and began to feel that there was something wrong about their racial characteristics. When parents were accepting of their children's feelings and experiences of "racial ambivalence," they were ultimately better able to help them achieve positive racial identities.

Provide Your Children with Positive Experiences

It's important to go beyond the acceptance of children's negative feelings about their identity. All children need positive cultural or religious experiences so that they can find ways to be proud of who they are.

ED AND MIMI—BUILDING A SENSE OF COMMUNITY
Ed and Mimi lived in a suburb outside of Washington, D.C. Ed is a businessman. Originally from England, he came to the United States as a college student. He had lived in the States for the past seventeen years. Mimi's family was originally from Brazil. She was fluent in Portuguese and worked as a translator for a company involved in international trade. They had two children, Cheree who was nine, and Steven, who was eight. Cheree was the more fair-skinned of the two, and everyone said that she looked like her father. Steven was a short, thin boy and was almost as dark as his brown-skinned mother. They lived in a middle-class neighborhood that was mostly white, with a fair number of black families. They didn't know any other English or Brazilian families in the area.

Cheree was a very outgoing child, made friends quickly, and adjusted easily to her school when she entered kindergarten. A year later, Steven's entrance to school was more tentative. He seemed to be worried about where he fit in with the other children and sometimes acted a little sad and withdrawn during his first two years of school. Ed and Mimi were loving parents and noticed his difficulties, but they both felt that it was just a stage he was going through.

During the summer before Steven was going to enter third grade, Ed took a three-week "stay home" vacation. He was able to spend more time with the family than he ever had before. Steven loved books, and Ed began to go with him to the library regularly. One day they found a beautifully illustrated book, *Dancing with Indians*, a story about runaway slaves who were taken in by the Seminole tribe. They read it together, and when they finished it, Steven wanted to read it again. He took it out of the library and reread it over and over.

One night Ed and Mimi talked about Steven's love for *Dancing*. Mimi said that she thought Steven identified with the theme of being an outsider finding acceptance among a tribe of insiders. Ed agreed that it was probably an important part of why the book had become his Bible.

They began to talk for the first time about the nature of their own social world. Between work, the children's school, after-school lessons, family visits, and a few casual friends in the neighborhood, their lives seemed more than full. But as they talked, they began to realize that they had really kept themselves separate from close connections with other families. Ed wondered if it was because they themselves were from two different tribes and had never found a community that they easily and comfortably identified with.

Ed remembered that a co-worker had mentioned an organization of cross-cultural families in the area. The next day Ed found him at work and asked him for the name of the group. A few weeks later they went to a picnic organized by the Interracial

Family Circle, a group consisting of all sorts of cross-cultural and interracial families in the area.

They began to get involved in the Circle. The social gatherings became a source of new friends and a way to normalize the fact that they were from two different worlds. They began to plan monthly dinners with a group of four other Circle families. Each month the couple who hosted the dinner prepared foods from their culture. Eda and Irene, an Indonesian-Dutch couple they met through the group, lived only a mile from them and also had an eight-year-old boy, Kitab. The two families started spending more time together, and the two boys quickly became friends.

Ed and Mimi also started to make a point of talking more to each other and to their children about their different cultural backgrounds. Ed brought home books from the library about England and began to talk more about his childhood. One day Mimi took Steven and Cheree to the office where she worked, introduced them to her co-workers for the first time, and let them try the word processor she used for translating documents back and forth between English and Portuguese. Steven was interested in learning some Portuguese, and Mimi worked with him on writing a letter in Portuguese to his cousins in Brazil, who were planning to visit them in Washington the next summer.

Ed and Mimi noticed that over the course of the summer Steven seemed happier. One day toward the end of the summer Ed and Steven went on a bike ride. When they stopped to rest, Steven told his father, "I'm lucky because I'm part of two tribes." Ed smiled and told him that he agreed. The next day Steven returned *Dancing* and took out a book about his new hobby, which Kitab had interested him in—collecting stamps from around the world.

DOREE—COMFORTABLE WITH ALL OF HER FAMILY

One of the most important ways that mixed matches can help their children feel comfortable with all of their roots is to maintain close contact with each parent's extended family. As an interracial black-white couple, Lana and Chuck felt a special obligation to make sure their eleven-year-old daughter, Doree, would be "culturally bilingual." Lana was a light-skinned African-American who had grown up in south-central Los Angeles. Chuck was a Greek-American who had lived in Minneapolis until he was twelve, when he moved with his family to southern California. They lived outside of Los Angeles, over thirty miles from each of their families, in a neighborhood that was about 90 percent white. Most of the nonwhites who lived there were Asian, and Lana and Chuck were well aware that Doree would not develop the complex biracial identity they wanted her to have without their active intervention.

> LANA: We've always looked at Doree as being a child from two backgrounds. We have always tried to make sure that her experiences are balanced. I am aware of the fact that we live in a predominantly white neighborhood and that she goes to a predominantly white school, and our feeling is that we don't want her to forget that she is an African-American child and that that is the way she will be viewed by the rest of the world. You can say that you're mixed and all that, and she is, but what happens when you are out in the rest of the world is you are treated as you appear. We have always maintained lots of contact with both sides of the family and with both cultures. There are a lot of African-American kids who grow up in predominantly white neighborhoods and who are totally out of touch with the black community. And I definitely don't want that to happen.
>
> I went through a period of being "high yellow"—meaning identifying with being a light-skinned black. I got hassled for

it. When she gets out in the world, she needs to know who she is—and how others will see her. She can't go out in the world and be high yellow and cute and not in touch with being black. Other blacks will eat her alive in any situation in college and in work. I'm not going to put her out there unprepared. She needs to know all these parts of her. When you're light and cute, you have to be careful, because other blacks are going to assume you think you're superior no matter what you really feel. And even though she hasn't run into it yet, she is going to run into whites who treat her differently because she doesn't fit into any neat racial category.

Yesterday morning she went to a birthday party in Malibu at a big, swanky place with almost all white kids and then in the afternoon she went to my auntie's party in not-so-swanky south-central Los Angeles to be with her cousin, and she felt fine going there as well. But the only way that we've made that happen is by spending enough time with her cousins so that the inner city feels as familiar as the suburbs.

She noticed the differences between the two worlds when she was really young. The small apartment that her cousin lives in and our house with a swimming pool are definitely different. I give her information about why the inner city is the way it is. About discrimination, and the lack of job opportunities, and the poor school funding. I have to be careful not to totally describe the black community as victims, though. It's a very difficult balancing act.

But the most important thing in helping her to feel comfortable in both worlds is that we feel comfortable in both. We are blessed to have loving and supportive families that are comfortable with us and our marriage. There's nothing like having fun with your family that gives your child the message that both worlds are okay. We end up driving a lot to give her the kind of experiences that we think are good for her, but to us it's worth it.

There are many ways to help your children feel good about themselves. No set of guidelines will work for all families, but consider the following list and discuss which will work best for you:

- Maintain positive relationships with both of your families and involve your children in as many of their cultural celebrations as possible.
- Teach your children about the cultural histories of both sides of their family.
- If you choose only to practice the religion of one parent, find ways to help your children feel comfortable with the religion of the other parent's family. Explain their beliefs to your children, even though they are different from your own.
- If both of your extended families are respectful of your religious and cultural choices, you don't need to separate your children from those who love them for fear of confusing their identity. Children are able to deal with lots of complexity if their parents lead the way. If you have relatives who try to impose religious or other views on your children that you are uncomfortable with, be very clear about your expectations.
- Live in a neighborhood that has at least some cultural diversity that in some way reflects your own as a couple.
- If possible, choose an area where the schools are tolerant and respectful of cultural and racial differences.
- Children cannot feel proud if they feel invisible. Make sure that your children have dolls and other toys that

look like them. All children need to feel that their identity is seen and validated.

- Provide your children with books and artwork that reflect the traditions of the cultures they are part of.
- Take your children to cultural festivals, museums, and other events that teach them about their different heritages.
- Even if you are trying to ground your children in one or both of your cultures, expose them to other people's traditions and celebrations as well so that they are comfortable with the idea of living in a culturally complex world.

See the "Resources" section at the end of the book for a listing of organizations, books, and magazines for cross-cultural families.

Help Your Children Deal with Prejudice

Few of us are happy about it, but we live in a world where people constantly categorize and often judge one another by the color of their skin, the religion they practice, or the accent they speak with. We can work toward the day when rigid and negative stereotyping of differences is no longer so common, but we cannot transform society by ignoring the obvious. Our children need to learn how to understand and deal with the problems of today's world even as we work to create a better one.

Kurt Lewin, the pioneer in the field of group relations, described the problems that can result when well-meaning parents do not prepare their children for the existence of disturbing realities. He argued that children need to be prepared early and repeatedly, in age-appropriate ways, to deal with life as it is. Shielding children

from difficult truths in the hope that they can deal with them better when they are older inevitably results in pain and confusion
rather than stability and security. He presented several anecdotes
that reinforced the same basic point: The emotional world of the
most lovingly raised children could collapse from the shock of
finding that they had been deprived of crucial information by the
people they trusted the most—their parents.

He described the experience of a young African-American
woman who had grown up in an unusually tolerant integrated
neighborhood, where she had been protected from encounters
with any serious racism. She had always been a very competent
and successful student, but she began to suffer from a major depression after she was the victim of her first racist incident.

Her reaction was typical of what Lewin described happening to
minority children who had experienced *little* prejudice in their
lives. Her parents and her immediate environment had shielded
her from virulent forms of racism. Like a person who travels to an
exotic tropical country and suffers terribly from diseases she had
never before been exposed to or inoculated against, the young
woman was devastated by the racism she had never directly experienced or been warned about. She had no emotional antibodies to
protect her from the plague of racially based hatred.

Teach your children about the nature of the world they live in.
Help them learn to begin to make sense of the senseless. Books,
museums, the stories of grandparents, and carefully selected movies
and television programs can be important sources of information
about the never-ending battles that have always raged between
good and evil.

As important as it is to prepare your children to deal with unpleasant realities, don't overwhelm them with too much too soon.
Like most things for children, learning about hatred in the world

needs to be graduated. A five-year-old is not ready for overly graphic lectures on the history of racism and ethnic hatred. The four-foot walls around some of the most horrific exhibits at the Holocaust Museum in Washington, D.C., are designed to protect young children from being flooded with images they are not yet prepared to face. The museum's "Daniel's Story," a re-creation of the house a Jewish boy lived in during the Nazi onslaught, allows children to begin to develop an awareness of history without over-whelming them.

Every culture has rituals that allow parents and children to ac-knowledge painful parts of their group's history in ways that can help build a sense of community, connection, and meaning. Memorial Day pays homage to soldiers who have died in battle and is a ritual that allows Americans to create a feeling of com-monality based on shared sacrifice. For African-Americans the celebration of Juneteenth Day acknowledges their history of slav-ery and celebrates its end. Yom Hashoah is a day that Jews use to commemorate and remember the Holocaust. Each of these days uses a sense of collective loss as one of the building blocks of identity.

KAMI AND HEIDI—HELPING A CHILD DEAL WITH BEING TEASED
Humanity's capacity for cruelty begins early in life. Sometimes, though, it can be dealt with in gentle ways. Kami, an Indian Sikh biologist whose family was originally from the Punjab state in northern India, married Heidi, an Anglo-American teacher he met during his training. Kami wore the traditional Sikh turban and metal bracelet and followed the tradition of not cutting his hair. They were raising their one child, Magi, to identify and be familiar with both his father's Sikh traditions and his mother's Presbyter-ian faith. But they raised Magi in a mostly Americanized fashion,

and he dressed like all of the other children at his public school, not wearing anything to identify him as being half Sikh.

Living in the relatively tolerant and incredibly diverse city of San Francisco, they hadn't ever faced any significant prejudice as a cross-cultural couple. They knew several other Sikh families who lived nearby, and Magi had gone to nursery school together with two other Sikh boys. Heidi had actively participated in Sikh rituals and felt accepted at the local temple. But the summer before Magi entered kindergarten, Kami was offered a new research position at a growing pharmaceutical company, and they moved to a suburban neighborhood.

Magi started school in September and seemed to be adjusting well. But after three weeks he started to complain of stomachaches and said that he felt too sick to go to school. At first Heidi and Kami assumed that he had a mild flu. But after their pediatrician couldn't find anything wrong with Magi, they started to suspect that he might be having problems at school.

They made an appointment with his teacher and met with her the next day. She told them that two of the boys in the class had said something that had apparently upset Magi the week before around the time he had developed his stomachaches. But neither of the boys nor Magi would give her any information. The teacher told Heidi and Kami that the incident had seemed so minor that she had not bothered to call them about it.

After dinner that night they both sat down and talked to Magi: "Miss Ellington told us that Kevin and John said something to you the other day that seemed to upset you."

Magi said he didn't remember. It was clear that he was trying not to answer their questions. Kami and Heidi patiently and gently persisted. Finally the story came spilling out: "Kevin and John teased me about you, Daddy. They saw you drive me to school the other day and saw your turban. They said that you wear bandages on your head because your brains are loose and that I need one, too, because I am stupid. And they said you were a sissy because you wear a bracelet."

After Magi went to bed, Kami told Heidi how angry he was about the other children's behavior. He wanted to call up the boys' parents and confront them about their sons' cruelty. But talking to Heidi helped him calm down, and over the next hour they worked out a plan to deal with the situation.

The next day after school they rehearsed with Magi what to say if any of the children teased him again. He practiced saying, "My dad is very special, and he wears his turban because of his religion. And if you don't leave me alone, I'm going to tell Miss Ellington." He went to school the next day, armed with his new response and his parents' support. Perhaps because he carried himself more confidently, he didn't have to use it.

That same day Kami called Miss Ellington to ask if he could do a little presentation about Sikhs in the class. She readily agreed, and the following day he came to class equipped with slides of his family home in India and of his experiences as a member of the Indian Army. He was the tallest soldier standing in a formation of rather fierce-looking Sikh soldiers. He told the class a story about the proud military tradition of the Sikhs. Then he showed the children his *kara*, his steel bracelet, and his *kirpan*, his ritual dagger. He also told them about his work as a biologist working on developing medicines that helped make children healthy when they got sick. And he brought some sweet Indian treats for everyone to taste. The children were very impressed.

Kami had presented himself—with his turban and his bracelet— as a strong and positive male role model. Through his manner he showed his son how to be proud and relaxed about who he is and who his parents are. After his father's dramatic classroom presentation, Magi's stomachaches spontaneously disappeared and he began to enjoy school again. He started to play at recess with the two boys who had teased him and, a few weeks later, asked if he could invite one of them over for dinner. Kami and Heidi quickly agreed, and they made a point of cooking a delicious Sikh dinner for Magi and his new friend, which they all enjoyed. In this situation Kami and Heidi's simple and positive ways of dealing with their child's problem were very effective. Even though Kami's first response had been anger, he realized in retrospect that this time finesse worked a lot better than fighting.

AL AND DENISE—CONFRONTING PREJUDICE

Not all prejudice is as benign or as easily dealt with as the teasing by Magi's five-year-old schoolmates. Because they spend so much of their time in school, all of your efforts to help your children develop positive identities can be either reinforced or undermined by their educational environment. One of the most important ways to prepare your children to deal with bigotry and bias in the world is to confront them when they affect your children's education. This can not only help your child through a current difficulty, but also models the importance of confronting and dealing with troubling situations.

Al and Denise's experience with their son Evan's school shows just how important parent involvement and awareness can be in dealing with more difficult situations. Denise is from a white Protestant background. Al's ancestry was Mexican-American. Al's family had lived in California for three generations and he was raised speaking only English in his home. But his surname, Hernandez, and his dark complexion marked him and his family as

Latino. Their son, Evan, an eleven-year-old child, had been in gifted (GATE) programs since first grade.

When Evan was about to start fourth grade last year, Al and I found out that we had the option of having him bussed to a school that we heard had an excellent GATE program. The school served primarily upper-middle-class children in a wealthy neighborhood, and we found out that it had so few minority students that the board of education was considering shutting it down if they couldn't or wouldn't integrate the school. The school's very existence was dependent on being able to attract enough minority kids.

We had been frustrated with our local school, because its resources were really limited. We wanted Evan to be able to go further academically, but we couldn't afford private school. We thought a long time about the decision, because it meant an hour a day on a bus and taking Evan away from many of his neighborhood friends, who went to our local elementary school. But it seemed like the opportunity we had been waiting for.

At the new school there were enough kids for one fourth- and one fifth-grade class. But instead of doing the usual thing of having one class at each grade level, they took all the kids from both grades and created two combined fourth- and fifth-grade classes. They designated one as a "bilingual" class and the other as a GATE class for "gifted" kids. I assumed that the "bilingual" class would be for kids who spoke English as a second language or who needed other kinds of remedial help. I was excited that Evan was going to get to be in a really excellent GATE program, and the loss of his going to our neighborhood school seemed worth the sacrifice to me.

When he came home from school after the first day, Evan seemed really unhappy. He told me he had been placed in the bilingual class. I was upset too. The only language we had ever spoken at home was English, and Evan definitely didn't need remedial help. I decided to drive him to school the next day and see if I could straighten out what I thought must have been a misunderstanding.

First I went to his class to talk to the teacher. She was busy, so I just watched for a few minutes. I saw the kids file into the two classes. I quickly noticed that *every* kid in Evan's class was brown or black and that every kid in the other class was white, except for one black boy, Donald. The second day of school Donald was transferred into the "bilingual" class. They had put all of the bussed-in minority kids into one class. Was it possible that *all* of the white kids were gifted and *none* of the minority kids?

I went to the principal and told her that Evan had been identified as gifted by district testing and that he had one of the best academic records in his old school. She seemed irritated with me for asking, but said she would look into the situation. Finally, after waiting a couple of days, Evan asked me, "Was I put in this class because I am brown?" I didn't know what to say, but it really upset me. I told him that I would work really hard to find out why he had been placed in the class he had been put in.

The principal was supposed to make a decision by Friday. I ran into her on Thursday and asked her if she had decided yet. She started snapping at me saying how much stuff she had to deal with. I then told her that my son asked if he was placed in the bilingual class because he was brown. Then she really blew up and started yelling.

Up until that point I had begun to doubt myself. Was I just making this whole thing up? But when the principal went off on me about what I had said, it helped me to trust myself more. I called my local councilwoman and the board of education to complain about what had happened.

The next day we were really surprised when we received a

call telling us that Evan was being transferred to the GATE class immediately. He came home from his first day in it and told us that he was really glad he got out of the "bilingual" class because the teacher had started to pull kids' hair and ears. I asked him how his friend Carlos was doing and he told me that Carlos's name was now Carl. The bilingual teacher made all the Spanish kids use "American" names.

Evan was much happier in his new class. But the incident with the principal made me aware of how prejudiced the whole system is. That's going to ultimately affect Evan too. So we started talking to other parents of children in both classes and we found out that we weren't the only ones who were upset about how the children had been divided up. We organized several meetings, and we are scheduled to make a presentation before the school board in a few weeks. Evan has been aware of how much time we've spent on the phone, and we've told him about what we're doing. I think he's proud of us for not just giving in and for thinking about the other children too.

Denise's involvement and persistence in dealing with a difficult school situation helped Evan in both direct and indirect ways. First, it resulted in his transfer into a class with a better teacher. But equally important, the process of involving other parents served as a model for confronting prejudice in a constructive way. It helped Evan begin to understand the power of working together with other people to right wrongs.

Let Your Children Grow Up to Choose Their Own Path

As children move through adolescence and approach young adulthood, they increasingly make their own decisions. It is an unstable period marking the transition between the dependency of child-hood and the greater freedom and responsibility of adult life. It is often a difficult time for both parents and their children, because adolescents seem to seek their parents' approval even as they question and challenge their parents' values.

While you may still be able to—and need to—control your seventeen-year-old's finances, curfew, and some of their more outrageous behavior, you cannot control who and what they identify with or what they believe: Their hearts and minds are their own. Ultimately the best way to influence your children's sense of identity is to set a positive example for them. Keeping a dialogue open is what is truly important.

LUCY AND CLARA—VERY DIFFERENT LIVES

An argument between Lucy and her daughter, Clara, illustrated just how different a parent's and a child's sense of identity can be in a cross-cultural family. Lucy was Guatemalan. She and her parents had immigrated to the United States when she was ten years old. She worked hard in high school, mastered English, and after starting at a small community college, was eventually able to attend a prestigious state university.

As the only Hispanic in most of her college classes in the mid-1960s, she was aware that classmates and professors viewed her as inferior because of her accent and her Spanish surname. She constantly struggled to prove to her instructors as well as to herself that she was competent. Lucy did well in her studies and became the first person in her extended family to graduate from college. Her successful struggles as an immigrant served to increase Lucy's feelings of pride in her Latin American background. Her experiences also created a strong sense of connection to and identification with members of other minority groups.

After college she found a job as a business manager for a small, rapidly growing company. In her late twenties she married a white Protestant man and moved to an upper-middle-class, predominantly Caucasian neighborhood. Her children, Clara and Robert, were born during the next three years.

In spite of the cultural chasms separating her early life from that of her children, Lucy tried to teach them about the importance of their Central American backgrounds through yearly visits to her parents in Houston and by taking them to Latin-American festivals. When Lucy's daughter, Clara, transferred to an elite private high school in her junior year, the school sent her an invitation to a special reception to welcome minority students. Lucy was very pleased that the school was reaching out to minorities and was excited about the event. But when Clara came home that afternoon and Lucy told her about the reception, Clara said that she wasn't interested in going.

Lucy couldn't understand why Clara would turn down the welcome that she herself could only have dreamed about when she was a student. When Lucy began to lecture her about how lucky she was, Clara became enraged. In the argument that followed, Clara's confrontation helped Lucy recognize and begin to accept how different her daughter's life had been from her own: "Mom, how can you insist that I go to that party? Look how and where we live. Look who you married and who my father is. Remember, I am only half Hispanic. And I don't want to be labeled as different from the other kids. If you think the party is so important, you go."

Even though they felt a deep bond as mother and daughter, Lucy's and Clara's life experiences were very different. Lucy was proud of what she had accomplished as an immigrant Hispanic woman. She identified strongly with her Guatemalan roots. Clara had grown up in an upper-middle-class American neighborhood and was the child of parents from two different cultures. Her daily life contained little to remind her of her mother's past. Their argument helped Lucy to face a reality that was difficult for her to accept, but impossible to deny: They could share a common love for each other but not a similar cultural identity.

Lucy and Clara were able to transform this crisis in their relationship into an opportunity to get closer. Lucy apologized for pushing Clara to go to the reception. Clara apologized for getting so angry. They began to talk more often about how different their lives had been.

Over time Clara grew more relaxed about identifying—in some limited ways—with her mother's heritage. One day Lucy and Clara went shopping together, and Clara pointed out a beautiful wall hanging from Guatemala they saw in a small shop. She told Clara that if she liked it, she would like to buy it for her birthday. In the past Lucy would have just bought the weaving and given it to Clara, and Clara would have refused to put it up. This time she showed greater respect for Clara's autonomy and her need to define her own identity; Clara responded by being more open. Clara thanked her mother and told her she would love to have it.

Lucy began to realize just how "American" her daughter was. But it seemed that her increasing acceptance of Clara's "American-ness" helped Clara relax more about the Latina part of her identity that was her legacy from her mother. She hung the weaving over her bed on her birthday, and it became a symbol of the bridge that she and her mother had begun to build.

We can guide our children, teach them, and expose them to the cultural and religious worlds we hope they will embrace. But no matter how carefully we orchestrate our children's experiences, we can never control or even predict how they will identify as they approach adulthood.

Just as we have broken with some of the traditions and ways of our parents and ancestors, so too will our children change with the new world they are helping to create. This doesn't mean that we have to give up our beliefs or change our identities to accommodate our children's wishes. When we reflect on our own lives, though, we may realize that our parents were no more able to control our choices than we are our children's. The best we can do is to provide them with a secure home, sources of pride and self-esteem, and meaningful ways to relate to who they are and are becoming. We can teach our children about the lessons of the past; ultimately they are the ones who will teach us about the future.

Beyond Categories

Those of us involved in the Association of MultiEthnic Americans (AMEA) have been working for years to get a multiracial category as one of the options that would be placed on the year 2000 census. The current governmental system of racial classification has led to situations where parents have been told that their biracial children would be denied admission to public schools unless they agreed to check *only one* of the five approved racial categories on school forms. Education is supposed to help develop a respect for the truth, but these rules force children to lie about the most basic of facts—their own sense of identity and the identities of their parents. Not being allowed to acknowledge all of who they are damages the very foundation of a healthy and positive sense of self-esteem. What right does the government have to categorize my children against my will, and inaccurately to boot?

Representing AMEA, we were finally able to get an appointment for our first face-to-face meeting with an aide to Congressman Tom Sawyer (D.-Ohio), who is the chair of the Census subcommittee. The aide was a very businesslike white woman. We proceeded to state our dissatisfaction with the current format of the census, the laws regarding racial classification, and how people of mixed race are counted and classified.

She acknowledged our concerns and then proceeded to give us a hard time. We had hoped she would at least be neutral, but she bombarded us with questions we expected our opposition would ask: Wouldn't this interfere with various minority programs? What about the concerns of the civil rights groups? Are we going to cause their numbers to be undercounted and thereby cause harm? This went on for what seemed like a half-hour. We responded to her questions vehemently, picking up on her confrontational tone. My voice was rising and I was getting very emotional about the whole process.

She paused at the most intense moment in the meeting, reached into her purse, pulled out a photograph, and handed it to me. It was a picture of a pretty young girl who appeared to be biracial. She told us it was her daughter. Then she sort of smiled, and as we all sat back in our chairs, she said, "Actually I hear what you're saying, and as you can see, I have a personal interest in what you are doing." She had been grilling us to see if we could take the heat and deal with the kinds of questions we would face at a real congressional hearing.

CARLOS A. FERNÁNDEZ, ON HIS MEETING WITH AN AIDE TO
CONGRESSMAN THOMAS SAWYER
(Mr. Fernández eventually testified before the U.S. House of Representatives
Subcommittee on Census, Statistics, and Postal Personnel on June 30, 1993,
as the president of the Association of MultiEthnic Americans [AMEA].)

It's not just the Census Bureau that likes to divide everything into as few neat and clean little boxes as possible. We are all tempted to reduce the complexity of life into the simplicity of either-or categories. At a certain primal level we are comforted when we can clearly and unambiguously define people and situations as either one way or the other. He is either black or white, she is either right or wrong, they are either with us or against us. For at least a moment we create order out of the chaos and uncertainty of life.

The passion for creating categories is built into us. During the first year of life babies spend increasing amounts of energy learning about the world by creating categories, the most basic of which are that of the *familiar* and of the *unfamiliar*. This normal and necessary developmental achievement, though, results in the infant's expulsion from the primal garden of innocence.

The two-month-old is a universalist and seems only to care about *how* she is held. All people are potentially good as long as they are gentle and soothing. But by eight months she has become more concerned about *who* is holding her than by how she is being held. She has already begun to create prototypes of *my people* and of *not my people*, of *us* and of *them*. The world has been divided into tribes and is never again as simple and pure as it once was just a few short weeks ago.

Our capacity—and compulsion—to create categories makes us human. Our skill in building systems of classification makes us the most powerful of creatures. But this power has no inherent ethics. The benefits of the most important scientific discoveries as well as the pure evil of Hitler's attempts to create racial purity derive from our ability and desire to separate this from that.

The problem isn't that we create categories. We have to. There is no way to deal with the overwhelming amount of information that bombards us every second without having ways of sorting it into a manageable number of cubbyholes. Our troubles begin when our categories become too rigid and we begin to reject information that does not fit into them. That is when we begin to distort the complexity of our relationships by stereotyping others in narrow and destructive ways. Whether we are talking about racism, anti-Semitism, the hatred of one nation for the next, or a battle between lovers, we are inevitably dealing with the problem of inflexible and oversimplified categories.

Married life sometimes seems, by its very design, to encourage spouses to eventually reduce each other into two-dimensional stereotypes. Repetition, boredom, and especially the stress of raising children have a way of turning exciting contrasts that were initially sources of attraction in a relationship into the focus of conflict. The words "you always" and "you never" are the danger signs that warn of rigidifying categories and hardening hearts.

When couples are unhappy in their relationship, it is usually because they are locked into depressingly repetitive conflicts. Their arguments become as predictable and stereotyped as their views of each other. Like actors trapped in an awful play they cannot leave, they feel compelled to repeat the same demoralizing dialogue. They can agree on the fact that they hate the play, but not on how to improve it. We humans are basically conservative creatures, and for many, predictable unhappiness is in some ways preferable to the uncertainty and anxiety of change.

But change *is* possible when people are able to take the risks of questioning the categories they have created. For all of their diversity the couples who successfully find ways to bridge their differences and build successful relationships travel down common paths. They all discover that good relationships require hard work, that patience and tolerance are crucial in dealing with cultural and religious differences, and that simple answers usually don't work in complicated lives. At their best they learn to approach their relationships like travelers on a long trip to a new, interesting, and unfamiliar land. The pleasures and rewards of discovery more than compensate for the occasional hardships of the journey.

The experiences of the couples and families we have met in this book hold important lessons for all of us. When we are willing to explore our own pasts, to question the beliefs we take for granted, and to accept our own complexity, new possibilities open up. As we begin to let go of rigid ways of seeing ourselves and our intimate partners, we discover opportunities to find common ground. We share more of our own experiences, and we start to listen with curiosity instead of contempt. With a better understanding of each other's points of view we find new ways to use our differences as sources of strength in our relationships.

Cross-cultural relationships reveal the kinds of problems and possibilities that are created when people bring different pasts to the task of shaping a new future. As the cultural mosaic of the larger social world grows increasingly diverse and complex, we all need to find better ways of dealing with our differences. Mixed matches present us with a microcosm of the larger world, a most human scale model of cross-cultural conflict and cooperation as played out in its most intimate forum. Learning about the struggles and triumphs of mixed matches can help all of us who believe that the everyday human concerns we all share are far greater than the racial, religious, and cultural differences that divide us.

NOTES

PAGE 3: Deborah Tannen, *You Just Don't Understand* (New York: Ballantine, 1991).

PAGE 6: Joel Crohn, *The Myth of the Melting Pot Marriage: Ethnotherapy with Jewish-Gentile Couples* (New York: The American Jewish Committee, 1985). A number of vignettes throughout this book are adapted from that study and used with permission of the AJC. Also see, Joel Crohn, *Ethnic Identity and Marital Conflict: Jews, Italians, and WASPs* (New York: The American Jewish Committee, 1986).

PAGE 7: Marc Zborowski, *People in Pain* (San Francisco, Jossey-Bass, 1969).

PAGE 7: For an excellent study of the sociology of Jewish-gentile marriage, see Egon Mayer's book, *Love and Tradition: Marriage Between Jews and Christians* (New York: Plenum, 1985), from which I borrowed this phrase.

PAGE 11: Michael Novak, *The Rise of the Unmeltable Ethnics: Politics and Culture in the Seventies* (New York: The Macmillan Co., 1971).

PAGE 11: Nathan Glazer and Daniel Moynihan, *Beyond the Melting Pot* (Cambridge, Mass.: MIT Press, 1972).

PAGE 11: Richard Alba, *Italian Americans: Into the Twilight of Ethnicity* (Englewood Cliffs, N.J.: Prentice-Hall, 1985).

PAGE 12: Quoted by Ronald Takaki, *A Different Mirror: A History of Multicultural America* (Boston: Little Brown & Co., 1993), p. 305.

PAGE 12: Andrew M. Greeley, *The Catholic Myth: The Behavior and Beliefs of American Catholics* (New York: Collier Books, 1990).

PAGE 13: Barry A. Kosmin and Seymour P. Lachman, *One Nation Under God: Religion in Contemporary American Society* (New York: Harmony Books, 1993), p. 242.

PAGE 13: Statistical Abstract of the United States. U.S. Bureau of Current Population Statistics, pp. 20–468, 1993.

PAGE 15: *Population Today* 20, no. 12 (December 1992), Population Reference Bureau, Inc.

PAGE 15: Gary A. Crester "Intermarriage Between 'White' Britons and Immigrants from the New Commonwealth and Pakistan," *Journal of Comparative Family Studies* 21, no. 2 (Summer 1990).

PAGE 15: Karen Breslau, "When Marriage Is Sleeping with the Enemy: Intermarriage in the Former Yugoslavia," *Newsweek* 120, no. 14 (October 5, 1992), pp. 52–53.

PAGE 20: M. McGoldrick, J. K. Pearce, and J. Giordano, *Ethnicity and Family Therapy* (New York: Guilford Press, 1982).

PAGE 30: From "The Reluctant Princess," about the Harvard-trained bride of the future emperor and giving up modern freedoms for tradition, *Newsweek*, May 24, 1993, p. 34.

PAGE 35: *Loving v. Commonwealth of Virginia*, United States Supreme Court, 1967.

PAGE 36: "Klanwatch Intelligence Report," Southern Poverty Law Center, Montgomery, Ala., no. 65, February 1994.

PAGE 38: Paul R. Spickard, *Mixed Blood: Intermarriage and Ethnic Identity in Twentieth-Century America* (Madison, Wisc.: University of Wisconsin Press, 1989).

PAGE 42: John Nichols, *The Milagro Beanfield War* (New York: Henry Holt & Co., 1974).

PAGE 42: Plato, *Symposium*, in *The Portable Plato*, ed. Scott Buchanan (New York: The Viking Press, 1948).

PAGE 44: Samuel R. Lehrman, "Psychopathology in Mixed Marriages." *Psychoanalytic Quarterly* 36 (1967), pp. 67–82.

PAGE 46: Paul R. Spickard, *Mixed Blood*. 1970 census (Madison, Wisc.: The University of Wisconsin Press, 1989).

PAGE 46: Gary A. Crester, "Intermarriage Between 'White' Britons and Immigrants from the New Commonwealth and Pakistan," *Journal of Comparative Family Studies* 21, no. 2 (Summer, 1990), p. 227.

PAGE 50: J. Klein, *Jewish Identity and Self Esteem: Healing Wounds Through Ethnotherapy* (New York: The American Jewish Committee, 1980).

PAGE 52: Robert C. Christopher, *Crashing the Gates: The De-WASPing of America's Power Elite* (New York: Simon and Schuster, 1989).

PAGE 53: E. Friedman, "The Myth of the Shiksa," in M. McGoldrick et al., eds., *Ethnicity and Family Therapy*.

PAGE 54: Alexis de Tocqueville, *Democracy in America*, trans. George Lawrence, ed. J. P. Mayer (New York: Doubleday, Anchor Books, 1969).

PAGE 54: Robert N. Bellah, Richard Madsen, William M. Sullivan, Ann Swidler, Steven M. Tipton. *Habits of the Heart: Individualism and Commitment in American Life* (Berkeley: University of California Press, 1985).

PAGE 55: Egon Mayer, *Love and Tradition: Marriage Between Jews and Christians* (New York: Plenum, 1985).

PAGE 56: Karen K. Dion and Kenneth L. Dion, "Individualistic and Collectivistic Perspectives on Gender and the Cultural Context of Intimacy," *Journal of Social Issues.* 49, no. 3 (1993), pp. 53–69.

PAGE 76: Carlos E. Sluzki, "The Latin Lover Revisited," in M. McGoldrick et al., eds., *Ethnicity and Family Therapy.*

PAGE 78: D. Morris, P. Collett, P. Marsh, and M. O'Shaughnessy, *Gestures: Their Origins and Distribution* (New York: Stein and Day, 1979). For example, while the thumbs-up gesture in most parts of Europe signified approval, the same gesture in rural sections of Greece is taken as a sexual insult that can easily catalyze a violent conflict.

PAGE 79: This framework is adapted from John Papajohn and John Spiegel, *Transactions in Families* (San Francisco: Jossey-Bass, 1975).

PAGE 103: This exercise is adapted from J. Petsonk and J. Remsen, *The Intermarriage Handbook* (New York: Morrow, 1988). As these authors note, the work of Esther Perel, Monica McGoldrick, Carol and Peter Schreck, and Joseph Giordano was important in their development of this exercise.

PAGE 108: David L. Kirp, "The Many Masks of Richard Rodriguez," *Image* magazine, *San Francisco Examiner*, Nov. 15, 1992.

PAGE 110: Paul Cowan with Rachel Cowan, *Mixed Blessings: Marriage Between Jews and Christians* (New York: Doubleday, 1987).

PAGE 113: A number of talks with New York psychotherapist and psychodramatist Esther Perel were of great help in the formulation of the psychodramatic exercises described in this chapter.

PAGE 114: Much of the development of this exercise has been done working together with Judith Weinstein Klein.

PAGE 120: Andrew Hacker, *Two Nations: Black and White, Separate, Hostile, Unequal* (New York: Charles Scribner's Sons, 1992), p. 233.

PAGE 123: The idea for this model of cultural connectedness grew out of the work of Evelyn Lee, editor of *Clinical Guide to Working with Asian Americans* (New York: Guilford Press, in press).

PAGE 124: Cowan, *Mixed Blessings*.

PAGE 151: A. J. Norton and J. E. Moorman, "Current Trends in Marriage and Divorce Among American Women," *Journal of Marriage and the Family* 49 (February 1987), pp. 3–14.

PAGE 188: U.S. Census, 1992.

PAGE 204: Terry P. Wilson, "Blood Quantum: Native American Mixed Bloods," in Maria P.P. Root, ed., *Racially Mixed People in America* (Newbury Park, Calif.: Sage Publications, 1992).

PAGE 205: E. Friedman, "The Myth of the Shiksa," in McGoldrick et al., eds., *Ethnicity and Family Therapy*.

PAGE 221: *Klanwatch Intelligence Report*, Southern Poverty Law Center, Montgomery, Ala., February 1993, # 65; *Klanwatch In-*

telligence Report, Southern Poverty Law Center, Montgomery, Ala., February 1994, # 71.

PAGE 222: "Principal Roils Southern Town with Remarks on Race, Dating," *San Francisco Chronicle,* March 16, 1994; "Mixed Race Student Sues Principal," *San Francisco Chronicle,* March 17, 1994.

PAGE 224: Joan Walsh, "The World Is in Their Faces," *Image* magazine, *San Francisco Examiner,* February 9, 1992.

PAGE 229: J. R. Berzon, *Neither White Nor Black: The Mulatto Character in American Fiction* (New York: New York University Press, 1978), p. 104.

PAGE 229: Everett Stonequist, *The Marginal Man: A Study in Personality and Culture Conflict* (New York: Russell and Russell, 1937).

PAGE 230: James H. S. Bossard and Eleanor Stoker Boll, *One Marriage, Two Faiths* (New York: The Ronald Press Co., 1957), cited in Lee Gruzen, *Raising Your Jewish/Christian Child: Wise Choices for Interfaith Parents* (New York: Dodd, Mead & Co., 1987), pp. 3–4.

PAGE 230: Ana Mari Cauce, Yumi Hiraga, Craig Mason, Tanya Aguilar, Nydia Ordonex, and Nancy Gonzales, "Between a Rock and a Hard Place: Social Adjustment of Biracial Youth" in M. Root, ed., *Racially Mixed People in America,* pp. 207–222.

PAGE 230: Cynthia L. Nakashima. "An Invisible Monster: The Creation and Denial of Mixed-Race People in America," in M. Root, ed. *Racially Mixed People in America,* pp. 229–230. This chapter and the sources it led me to were crucial in the development of my ideas about the children of intermarriage.

PAGE 231: Lee F. Gruzen, *Raising Your Jewish/Christian Child: Wise Choices for Interfaith Parents* (New York: Dodd, Mead & Co. 1987).

PAGE 231: Teresa Kay Williams, "Prism Lives: Identity of Binational Amerasians," in M. Root, ed., *Racially Mixed People in America.*

PAGE 231: Christine C. Iijima Hall, "Please Choose One: Ethnic Identity Choices for Biracial Individuals," in M. Root, ed., *Racially Mixed People in America*, p. 329.

PAGE 236: Based on a talk given at the annual Multiracial Association of Southern California Kaleidoscope conference, October 17, 1992, and on my further personal conversations with Dr. Wilson.

PAGE 237: Personal communication. Dr. Wilson points out that the concept of the 150-percent person was originally developed by social scientist Malcolm McFee in his article "The 150% Man: A Product of Blackfeet Acculturation," *American Anthropologist* 70, pp. 1096–1103.

PAGE 238: James H. Jacobs, "Identity Development in Biracial Children," in M. Root, ed., *Racially Mixed People in America.*

PAGE 240: D. Levinson et al., *Seasons of a Man's Life* (New York: Ballantine, 1979).

PAGE 241: Terry Wilson, Personal communication, 1993.

PAGE 242: George Kitahara Kich, "The Developmental Process of Asserting a Biracial, Bicultural Identity," in M. Root, ed., *Racially Mixed People in America.*

PAGE 285: K. Lewin, "Bringing Up the Jewish Child." in R. P. Bulka and M. H. Spero, *A Psychology-Judaism Reader* (Springfield, Ill.: Charles C. Thomas, 1982).

For Interfaith Couples

Jewish Outreach Instititute
33 W. 42nd St.
New York, NY 10036
212-642-2181
http://www.joi.org/

Commision on Reform Jewish
Outreach
Union of American Hebrew
Congregations
838 Fifth Ave.
New York, NY 10021-7064
212-249-0100

Unitarian Universalist
Association
25 Beacon St.
Boston, MA 02108
617-742-2100

Dovetail Magazine
P.O. Box 11945
Kalamazoo, MI 49019
800-222-0070

http://www.mich.com/
%7Edovetail/index.html

For Information on Teaching Tolerance

Southern Poverty Law Center
400 Washington Ave.
Montgomery, AL 36104

Magazines

Interrace Magazine
P.O. Box 12048
Atlanta, GA 30355
http://members.aol.com/intrace

Support and Advocacy Groups

AMEA Association of
MultiEthnic Americans
P.O. Box 191726
San Francisco, CA 94119-1726
http://www.ameasite.org

Following listings are adapted with permission from:

INTERRACIAL VOICE
P.O. Box 560185
College Point, NY 11356-0185
212-539-3872
*http://www.webcom.com/
~intvoice/*

ARKANSAS

A Place For Us
c/o Rita Bowens
P.O. Box 104
Little Rock, AR 72203
501-791-0988

CALIFORNIA

A Place For Us
Box 357
Gardena, CA 90248-7857
213-779-1717
(24-hour Message Center)

I-PRIDE (Interracial
Intercultural Pride)
Box 11811
Berkeley, CA 94712-11811
510-986-9120

MASC (Multiracial Americans
of Southern California)
12228 Venice Blvd., #452
Los Angeles, CA 90066
310-836-1535

Race Unity—Matters!
of Northern California
4309 Linda Vista Ave.
Napa, CA 94558

National Multi-Ethnic
Families Association
(NaMEFA)
2073 N. Oxnard Blvd, Suite 172
Oxnard, CA 93030
*http://www.latinoweb.com/
nuestram/*

COLORADO

F.C. (Families of Color)
Communiqué
c/o Dr. C. Lessman
Box 478
Fort Collins, CO 80522
303-223-9658

Center for the Study of
Biracial Children
c/o Francis Wardle, Ph.D.
2300 South Krameria St.
Denver, CO 80222
303-692-9008

Humanity
c/o Martin L. Scruggs
P.O. Box 481692
Denver, CO 80248-1692
303-832-6269

DISTRICT OF COLUMBIA

The Interracial Family Circle
of Washington

Box 53291
Washington, DC 20009
Voicemail: 202-393-7866 or
1-800-500-9040

FLORIDA

Unity Multiracial Social Group
P.O. Box 2902
Orange Park, FL 32073-2902
904-276-6668

BRANCH (Biracial & Natural
Children)
Box 50051
Lighthouse Point, FL 33074
305-781-6798

Interracial Couple & Family
Network of Tallahassee
2001 Holmes St.
Tallahassee, FL 32310
904-576-6734

A Place For Us
Naples, Florida, Chapter
c/o Cherie Byrd
813-732-6996

Harmony
Box 16996
W. Palm Beach, FL 33416
407-582-2182

Tallahassee Multiracial
Connection
2001 Holmes St.
Tallahassee, FL 32310
904-576-6734

GEORGIA

Project Race (Reclassify All
Children Equally, Inc.)
c/o Susan Graham
1425 Market Blvd.,
Ste 330-E6
Roswell, GA 30076
770-433-6076
E-mail: *ProjRACE@aol.com*

Interracial Family Alliance
Box 450473
Atlanta, GA 31145

Interracial Family Alliance
Box 9117
Augusta, GA 30906
404-793-8547

Interracial Family Alliance
c/o Tonia and Glenn Thomas
Athens, GA
706-353-0640

ILLINOIS

Biracial Family Network
Box 3214
Chicago, IL 60654
773-288-3644

Families for Interracial
Awareness
Northern Chicago area
c/o Linda Thomas
708-869-7117

Sherry Blass
c/o Tapestry
40 Francis Ave.
Crystal Lake, IL 60014

Interracial Family Network
c/o Dickelle Fonda
Box 5380
Evanston, IL 60204-5380
708-491-9748

Child International
4121 Crestwood
Northbrook, IL 60062

Linda Russo
c/o Adoptive Parents
Together
427 N. Wheaton Ave.
Wheaton, IL 60187

North Shore Race Unity Task
Force
536 Sheridan Rd.
Wilmette, IL 60091

Dialogue Racism, Inc.
c/o Charles Young
P.O. Box 110
Evanston, IL 60204
708-492-0123

KENTUCKY

Northern Kentucky
Multiracial Alliance
Pat DiMartile
502-331-2373

MARYLAND

Interracial Military Families
P.O. Box 1015
Upper Marlboro, MD 20773

MASSACHUSETTS

Students of Mixed Heritage
SU 3187, Williams College
Williamstown, MA 01267
413-597-3354

New England Alliance of
Multiracial Families
P.O. Box 148
West Medford, MA 02156
617-965-3287

Multiracial Family Group of
Western Massachusetts
P.O. Box 1216
Amherst, MA 01004-1216
413-256-0502

MICHIGAN

Multiracial Group at U. of
Michigan
c/o Karen E. Downing
122 Undergraduate Library
Ann Arbor, MI 48109-1185
313-763-5084 or 313-764-4479

Biracial and Interracial
Family & Friends (BIFF)
c/o Dr. Zawdie K. Abiade
Burton Heights U.M.C.
100 Burton St., SE
Grand Rapids, MI 49507

Society for Interracial Families
Box 4942
Troy, MI 48099

MISSOURI

Healing Racism, Inc.
(chapters nationwide)
P.O. Box 16015
St. Louis, MO 63105
314-727-6665
http://www.healingracism.org

Multiracial Family Circle of
Kansas City
P.O. Box 32414
Kansas City, MO 64171
Contact: Kevin 816-353-8689
E-mail: *MFCircle@aol.com*

NEW JERSEY

Multiracial Family Support
Group
c/o Bobbi Joels
265 Hempstead Drive
Somerset, NJ 08873
732-296-0734

G.I.F.T. (Getting
Interracial/cultural Families
Together)
P.O. Box 1281
Montclair, NJ 07042
c/o Irene Rottenberg
973-783-0083
E-mail: *NJGIFT@aol.com*

Web profile:
*http://members.aol.com/
NJGIFT/index.html*

G.I.F.T. (Getting
Interracial/cultural Families
Together)
P.O. Box 811
Lakewood, NJ 08701
c/o Betty Turko
908-364-8136
908-367-2755 (fax)

InterRacial Life
c/o Dave Seibel
2 George St.
East Brunswick, NJ 08816
908-390-7316

4C (Cross Cultural Couples &
Children) of Plainsboro, NJ
P.O. Box 8
Plainsboro, NJ 08536-4104
c/o Lisa Edwards
609-275-9352 (eve)

NEW YORK

BIRONY (Bi-Racials Of
New York)
212-979-0967

Interracial Identity
c/o Noel A. Trowers
228-26 Edgewood Ave.
Rosedale, NY 11413
718-978-6524

A Place For Us
c/o Valerie Wilkins-Godbee
P.O. Box 859
Peekskill, NY 10566
914-736-0536

Creole-American
Genealogical Socety, Inc.
c/o Ms. P. Fontaine, Director
Box 3215, Church Street
Station
New York, NY 10008

Interracial Club of Buffalo
Box 400 (Amherst Branch)
Buffalo, NY 14226
716-875-6958

Multiethnic Women for Media
Fairness
P.O. Box 859
Peekskill, NY 10566

Multiracial Americans of
New York
c/o Lynn Jordan
302 E. 94 St., Suite 1D
New York, NY 10128

NORTH CAROLINA

Interracial Ministries of
America
5805 Aqua Court
Charlotte, NC 28215

LIFE
Box 14123
Raleigh, NC 27620

T.I.M.E. (Triangle Interracial
and Multicultural Experience)
c/o Marsha Alston
15A Woodbridge Dr.
Chapel Hill, NC 27516

OHIO

Cincinnati Multiracial
Alliance
Box 17163
St. Bernard, OH 45217
513-791-6023

SWIRLS Ministry
Bob & Gerry Schneider
132 E. South St.
Fostoria, OH 44830
419-435-0325

Heights Multicultural Group
c/o Sylvia Billups
South Euclid, OH 44121
216-382-7912

Rainbow Families of Toledo
(adoption support group)
c/o Nancy Shanks
1920 S. Shore Blvd.
Oregon, OH 43618
419-693-9259

OREGON

Honor Our New Ethnic Youth
(HONEY)
454 Willamette Ave., #213
Eugene, OR 97401
503-342-3908

Interracial Family Network
Box 12505
Portland, OR 97212

PENNSYLVANIA

Multiracial Americans of
Philadelphia
c/o Joycelyn Damita
Box 58722
Philadelphia, PA 19102-8722
215-492-8761, Ext. 2

Rainbow Circle
Broadfield Association
Box 242
Chester, PA 19016

SOME Families
1798 Unionville-Lenape Rd.
West Chester, PA 19382
215-793-1533

One Race
P.O. Box 58722
Philadelphia, PA 19102-8722

TEXAS

The Interracial Family and
Social Alliance of Dallas-Ft.
Worth
Box 35109
Dallas, TX 75235-0109

214-559-6929
*http://www.flash.net/~mata9/
ifsa.htm*

A Place For Us
Dallas, Texas, Chapter
c/o Brad & Amy Russell
214-517-1498

Interracial Family Alliance
Box 16248
Houston, TX 77222-6248

Center for the Healing of
Racism
Box 27327
Houston, TX 77227

VERMONT

International Institute for the
Healing of Racism
Route 113, Box 232
Thetford, VT 05074
802-785-2627

WASHINGTON

Interracial Network
Box 344
Auburn, WA 98071-0344
The Interracial Family
Network of Seattle-King County
c/o John Duncan

Bill of Rights for Racially Mixed People

I HAVE THE RIGHT . . .

Not to justify my existence in this world.

Not to keep the races separate within me.

Not to be responsible for people's discomfort with my physical ambiguity.

Not to justify my ethnic legitimacy.

I HAVE THE RIGHT . . .

To identify myself differently than strangers expect me to identify.

To identify myself differently from how my parents identify me.

To identify myself differently from my brothers and sisters.

To identify myself differently in different situations.

I HAVE THE RIGHT . . .

To create a vocabulary to communicate about being multiracial.

To change my identity over my lifetime—and more than once.

To have loyalties and identification with more than one group of people.

To freely choose whom I befriend and love.

Racially Mixed People in America by Maria Root (ed.), published by Sage Publications (Newbury Park, CA, 1992), is a very useful book that explores in depth the issues facing biracial children.

Books for Young People

PICTURE BOOKS/EARLY CHILDHOOD

Garland, Sarah. *Billy and Belle*. New York: Viking Penguin, 1992.

An amusing story about Billy and Belle's day at school while their mother is in the hospital delivering a new baby. Illustrations provide the only clue that this family is interracial.

Heath, Amy. *Sofie's Role*. New York: Four Winds Books, 1992.
An outstanding and lovely tale about a biracial family living in a middle American city. The story involves a little girl's first day of work in the family's bakery. Superb illustrations.

Loh, Morag. *Tucking Mommy In*. New York: Orchard Books, 1987.
A beautifully illustrated picture book with an amusing twist where a mother attempting to put her daughters to sleep instead falls asleep herself. The mother is Asian and the father is European.

McKee, David. *Tusk, Tusk*. New York: Kane Miller Publishers, 1990.
A funny and upbeat story that pokes fun at a conflict between black and white herds of elephants.

Williams, Garth. *The Rabbits' Wedding*. New York: Harper, 1958.
When this beautiful book about the marriage of a black rabbit and a white rabbit was first published in 1958 it was controversial. Many libraries in the South refused to include it in their collections.

Williams, Very B. *More More More Said the Baby*. New York: Greenwillow Books, 1990.
This Caldecott Honor Book contains three short stories, the second of which features a child of mixed ethnic heritage. No big message. Just a cheerful, colorful book portraying loving families.

JUVENILE/SCHOOL AGE

(These works are generally intended for preteen readers.)

Blume, Judy. *Are You There God? It's Me Margaret*. New York: Dell Publishing, 1970.

An eleven-year-old child is subjected to pressure by grandparents of different religious beliefs. This book was controversial both because of the religious issues it raised and because of the protagonist's impatience for the onset of her menses.

Friedman, Ina R. *How My Parents Learned to Eat*. Boston: Houghton Mifflin, 1984.

A picture book tale told by the child of a Japanese mother and a European-American father recounting how her parents met in Japan, and the two traditions of eating that her family maintains.

Medaris, Angela Shelf. *Dancing with the Indians*. New York: Holiday House, 1991.

A tale set in the 1930s revolving around a historical account of runaway slaves who were accepted into the Seminole tribe. Beautiful illustrations.

Nichols, Joan Kane. *All But the Right Folks*. Owings Mills, Maryland: Stemmer House Publishers, Inc., 1985.

This tale involves a boy's discovery of his "white" ancestry when his grandmother invites him to spend the summer in New York City. An exciting, well-written adventure with vivid characters.

Simon, Charnan. *Wilma Mankiller: Chief of the Cherokee*. Chicago: Children's Press, 1991.

A very short biography of the Principal Chief of the Cherokee Nation of Oklahoma, who is a woman whose mother was "Dutch-Irish" and father was "full-blooded Cherokee Indian."

YOUNG ADULT
(These works address the concerns and aspirations of young adults.)

Garland, Sherry. *The Song of Buffalo Boy*. New York: Harcourt, Brace, Jovanovich, 1992.
A seventeen-year-old Amerasian in Vietnam is promised in marriage to a repellent suitor. She escapes to Ho Chi Minh City and applies for the Amerasian Homecoming Program. The portrayal of Amerasians in postwar Vietnam is heartrending, as is the description of the Vietnamese peoples' suffering due to the polluting and persistent effects of modern warfare and chemical defoliants.

Gay, Kathlyn. *The Rainbow Effect: Interracial Families*. New York: Franklin Watts, 1987.
The author interviewed interracial and interethnic families about growing up as "Children of the Rainbow." The major theme of this work is that people of mixed race and/or ethnicity need and deserve positive recognition.

Irwin, Hadley. *Kim/Kimi*. New York: M. K. McElderry Books, 1987.
Sixteen-year-old Kim seeks information concerning her deceased Japanese-American father who died before she was born. During a brief vacation she flies to Sacramento, where she first experiences Japanese culture by meeting for the first time her Japanese relatives. She learns of WW II and the U.S. government's Japanese internment camps of that period.

Lipsyte, Robert. *The Brave*. New York: HarperCollins, 1991.
Sonny Bear lives on the margins of Moscandaga and white cul-

ture. His mixed heritage is ultimately a source of strength as he learns to channel his energy as a boxer.

Pullman, Phillip. *The Broken Bridge*. New York: Alfred A. Knopf, 1992.
A compelling contemporary novel set in Wales, this is the account of a sixteen-year-old girl's search for knowledge of her Haitian mother, her father's parents, and his first wife. Her discoveries are painful, yet strengthening.

Rinaldi, Ann. *Wolf by the Ears*. New York: Scholastic Hardcover, 1991.
A fictionalized biography of a 3/4-white slave on Thomas Jefferson's plantation. Persistent rumors suggest that the protagonist is one of Jefferson's children by Sally Hemings.

Robinson, Margaret A. *A Woman of Her Tribe*. New York: Fawcett Juniper Books, 1990.
This tale begins with the departure of fifteen-year-old Annette and her widowed mother from her father's Nootka Indian village. Annette has been awarded a scholarship to an exclusive private school, where she will unravel the social mysteries of an unfamiliar white world.

The above annotated bibliography was used with permission: It is adapted from a larger list by Dildar Gartenberg, 1994.
The complete bibliography can be obtained for $1.00 to cover postage and handling from:

I-Pride
P.O. Box 191752
San Francisco, CA 94119-1752

BIBLIOGRAPHY

Alba, Richard. *Ethnic Identity: The Transformation of White America*. New Haven: Yale University Press, 1990.

———. *Italian Americans: Into the Twilight of Ethnicity*. Englewood Cliffs, NJ: Prentice-Hall, 1985.

Allen, James Paul and Turner, Eugene James. *We the People: An Atlas of America's Ethnic Diversity*. New York: Macmillan Publishing, 1988.

Armstrong, Karen. *A History of God: The 4000-Year Quest of Judaism, Christianity, and Islam*. New York: Alfred A. Knopf, 1994.

Boyd-Franklin, Nancy. *Black Families in Therapy: A Multisystems Approach*. New York: Guilford Press, 1989.

Choing, Jane. *Racial Categorization of Multiracial Children in the Schools*. Westport, CT: Greenwood Publishing.

Christopher, Robert C. *Crashing the Gates: The De-WASPing of America's Power Elite*. New York: Simon & Schuster, 1989.

Corner, James P. and Poussaint, Alvin F. *Raising Black Children*. New York: Plume, 1992.

Cowan, Paul and Cowan, Rachel. *Mixed Blessings: Marriage Between Jews and Christians*. New York: Doubleday, 1987.

Fisher, Roger and Brown, Scott. *Getting Together: Building Relationships as We Negotiate.* New York: Penguin, 1989.

Ford, Clyde W. *We Can All Get Along.* New York: Dell, 1994.

Gambino, Richard. *Blood of My Blood: The Dilemma of the Italian-Americans.* New York: Doubleday, 1974.

Gay, Kathlyn. *The Rainbow Effect.* New York: Franklin Watts, 1987.

Gibbs, Jewelle and Huang, L. N. *Children of Color* (chapter on interracial adolescents). San Francisco: Jossey-Bass Publishers, 1989.

Glazer, Nathan and Moynihan, Daniel. *Beyond the Melting Pot.* Cambridge, MA: MIT Press, 1972.

Greeley, Andrew M. *The Catholic Myth: The Behavior and Beliefs of American Catholics.* New York: Collier Books, 1990.

Grier, William H. and Cobbs, Price M. *Black Rage.* New York: Basic Books, 1968.

Gruzen, Lee F. *Raising Your Jewish/Christian Child: Wise Choices for Interfaith Parents.* New York: Dodd, Mead & Co., 1987.

Hacker, Andrew. *Two Nations: Black and White, Separate, Hostile, Unequal.* New York: Charles Scribner's Sons, 1992, p. 233.

Haizlip, Shirlee Taylor. *The Sweeter the Juice.* New York: Simon & Schuster, 1994.

Harrington, Walt. *Crossings: A White Man's Journey into Black America.* New York: HarperCollins, 1993.

Jones, Lisa. *Bulletproof diva: tales of race, sex, and hair.* New York: Doubleday, 1994.

Klein, Judith Weinstein. *Jewish Identity and Self Esteem: Healing Wounds through Ethnotherapy.* New York: American Jewish Committee, 1980.

Kosmin, Barry A. and Lachman, Seymour P. *One Nation Under God: Religion in Contemporary American Society.* New York: Harmony Books, 1993.

Levin, Sunie. *Mingled Roots: A Guide for Jewish Grandparents of Interfaith Grandchildren.* Washington, D.C.: B'nai B'rith Women, 1991.

Mathabane, Mark and Gail. *Love in Black and White.* New York: HarperCollins, 1992.

Mayer, Egon. *Love and Tradition: Marriage Between Jews and Christians.* New York: Plenum, 1985.

McCord, David and Cleveland, William. *Black and Red: The Historical Meeting of Africans and Native Americans.* Atlanta: Dreamkeeper Press, Inc., 1990.

McGoldrick, M., Pearce, J. K., and Giordano, J. *Ethnicity and Family Therapy.* New York: Guilford Press, 1982.

Morris, D., Collett, P., Marsh, P., and O'Shaughnessy, M. *Gestures: Their Origins and Distribution.* New York: Stein and Day, 1979.

Novak, Michael. *The Rise of the Unmeltable Ethnics: Politics and Culture in the Seventies.* New York: Macmillan Publishing, 1971.

Papajohn, John and Spiegel, John. *Transactions in Families.* San Francisco: Jossey-Bass Publishers, 1975.

Petsonk, Judith and Remsen, Jim. *The Intermarriage Handbook.* New York: Morrow, 1988.

Pinderhughes, Elaine. *Understanding Race, Ethnicity, & Power.* New York: The Free Press, 1989.

Schneider, Susan Weidman. *Intermarriage: The Challenge of Living with Differences Between Christians & Jews.* New York: The Free Press, 1989.

Simon, Rita. *Adoption, Race & Identity: From Infancy Through Adolescence.* Westport Connecticut: Praeger Publishers, 1992.

Spickard, Paul R. *Mixed Blood: Intermarriage and Ethnic Identity in Twentieth-Century America.* Madison, WI: University of Wisconsin Press, 1989.

Sung, Betty Lee. *Chinese American Intermarriage.* New York: Center for Migration Studies, 1990.

Takaki, Ronald. *A Different Mirror: A History of Multicultural America.* Boston: Little Brown & Co., 1993.

Terkel, Studs. *Race: How Blacks and Whites Think and Feel About the American Obsession.* New York: The New Press, 1992.

Thernstrom, Stephen, ed. *Harvard Encyclopedia of American Ethnic Groups.* Cambridge: Harvard University Press, 1980.

Wattenberg, Ben J. *The First Universal Nation.* New York: The Free Press, 1991.

West, Cornel. *Race Matters.* Boston: Beacon Press, 1993.

White, Steve and Ruth. *Free Indeed: the Autobiography of an Interracial Couple.* Gardena, CA: A Place for Us Ministry, 1989.

Zborowski, Marc. *People in Pain.* San Francisco: Jossey-Bass Publishers, 1969.

INDEX

adolescents:
  identity development in, 240–41
  letting them grow up to choose their own
    paths, 293–96
  searching for solid sense of identity in,
    248–49, 252–54, 256, 259–61
adoptions and adoptees, 244, 246, 258–63
affairs, 209–13
African-Americans:
  author's roots and, 16, 18
  and awareness of social contexts of
    relationships, 35–36, 38–39
  and children of mixed marriages, *see*
    mulattos and clarifying cultural and
    religious identities, 110, 120
  and creating family identities, 166, 170–76
  cultural dimensions of, 81–82
  and dealing with parents, family, friends, and
    foes, 187–93, 195–204, 208, 214, 221–22
  and exercises dealing with opposition to
    relationships, 221–22
  and helping children develop solid identities,
    265, 276–79, 282–83, 286, 292
  and identifying culturally and religious based
    issues, 26, 33, 35–36, 38–39
  and motivations in selecting partners, 45–46,
    48–52, 54
  prejudice and, 195–204, 286, 292
  in radically changing world, 8, 10
  transformation of identities of, 14
  and typical problems resulting from cultural
    differences, 4–5
Alba, Richard, 11
Allen, Woody, 58
ambivalence, normalization of, 276–79
ambivalent identification, 50
American Jewish Committee, 6
American Psychiatric Association, 10–11
Americans, cultural dimensions of, 89–92,
  101–3
Annie Hall, 58
anti-Semitism, 20, 195–97, 287
  and classification of races, 300
  and creating family identities, 172
  and identifying culturally and religious based
    issues, 36
  and transformation of identities, 12

Argentinian-Americans, 30–32
Armenians and Armenian-Americans:
  and clarifying cultural and religious
    identities, 108
  cultural dimensions of, 81, 94–104
  and dealing with parents, family, friends, and
    foes, 193
  genocide of, 23, 81, 94–95
  intermarriages between Turks and, 23–24
Asian-Americans, 7, 195, 282
  and awareness of social contexts of
    relationships, 38
  and clarifying cultural and religious
    identities, 110, 112–13
  and creating family identities, 163–66
  and identifying culturally and religious based
    issues, 33, 38
  and motivations in selecting partners, 48–49,
    51, 54
  transformation of identities of, 14
Association of MultiEthnic Americans
  (AMEA), 246, 298–99

Baha'i, 47, 246
balanced family-identity solution, 150
Balinese, 56–57, 18–19
baptisms, 143–44
Baptists, 243
  and creating family identities, 153–59, 175–76
  transformation of identities of, 13
bar mitzvahs, 248
Bazile, Leon M., 36
Bellah, Robert, 54
Berzon, J. R., 229–30
Bilbo, Ted, III, 187–88
blacks:
  and helping children develop solid identities,
    272–75
  see also specific black ethnic groups
Boll, Eleanor, 230
Bossard, James, 230
Bowen, ReVonda, 222
Brazilian-Americans, 279–81
Britons and British-Americans:
  cultural dimensions of, 89, 93
  and helping children develop solid identities,
    279–81

RISE JUSTMAN COHEN

JOEL CROHN, Ph.D., is a psychologist in private practice in San Rafael and Berkeley, California. He has conducted a major research project on interfaith marriage for the American Jewish Committee, and has lectured nationally for professional and lay audiences on marriage and intermarriage for over a decade. He is a past president of the Marin County Psychological Association and is on the faculty of the Asian Family Institute in San Francisco.

For more information, Dr. Crohn can be contacted at Jcrohn@aol.com or at (415) 456-1166.